Street.
25.0 27.0 27.0 27.0 27.0 27.0 27.0 27.0 27.0 27.0 27.0 25.0 25.0
98.9
C 50 49 48 47 46 45 44 43 42 41 40 39
25.0 27.0 27.0 27.0 27.0 27.0 27.0 27.0 27.0 27.0 27.0 25.0 25.0
100.0
320.0
Street.
R K
184.0
50.0
Carriage way & foot walk
184.0
38 37 36 35 34 33 32
$26.3\frac{3}{7}$
125.0
75.0
184.0
50.0
Third Avenue
Street.
320.0
26.8 27.0 27.0 27.0 27.0 27.0 27.0 27.0 27.0 27.0 27.0 25.0 25.0
100.0
F 20 21 22 23 24 25 26 27 28 29 30 31
92.0
26.8 27.0 27.0 27.0 27.0 27.0 27.0 27.0 27.0 27.0 27.0 25.0 25.0
B. Ruggles in the City
Lots.
Decr 1st 1831
Edwin Smith City Surveyor
Street.

D1209591

GRAMERCY PARK

An Illustrated History of a New York Neighborhood

Gramercy Park, looking west.

GRAMERCY PARK

An Illustrated History of a New York Neighborhood

by Stephen Garmey

Foreword by Paul Goldberger

Contemporary Photographs by Philip Howard

Balsam Press, Inc.
Rutledge Books

Picture Credits and Acknowledgements

Courtesy of Avery Architectural and Fine Arts Library, Columbia University: Plates 54, 59, 84, 85; Courtesy of City College Archives, New York City: Plates 76, 77, 89, 116; Courtesy of Columbia University: Plate 15; Courtesy of The Cooper-Hewitt Museum, The Smithsonian Institution's National Museum of Design: Plates 130, 132, 136, 148; Courtesy of Metropolitan Life Insurance Co: Plate 230; Courtesy of the Print Archives of The Museum of The City of New York: Plates 31, 32, 45, 52, 100, 188, 193, 220; Courtesy of The New-York Historical Society, New York City: Plates 6, 7, 9, 21, 43, 60, 78, 98, 103, 104, 108, 109, 110, 119, 124, 125, 129, 131, 133, 134, 137, 162, 170, 173, 185, 186, 187, 190, 200, 228; Courtesy of The New York Public Library, Astor, Lenox and Tilden Foundations: Rare Books and Manuscripts Division; Samuel B. Ruggles Papers: Plates 25, 27, 30; U.S. History, Local History & Geneology Division: Plates 39, 51, 91, 114, 216, 221; Courtesy of *The New Yorker Magazine Inc.* and Saul Steinberg, drawing by Steinberg, © 1983: Plate 225; Courtesy of The Players: Plates 154, 155; Courtesy of Manlio Abele: Plate 64; Courtesy of Louis Colaianni: Plate 158; Courtesy of Helen Haskell for use of a photograph by Douglas Haskell: Plate 102; Courtesy of Philip Howard: jacket photographs, frontispiece, Plates 26, 36, 56, 57, 58,111, 123, 149, 153, 174, 203, 206, 207, 214, 218, 224; Courtesy of Jean Pike: Plate 68; Courtesy of Sakas Brothers: Plate 217. Thanks are due to Debora Musikar for restoring certain photographs.

Acknowledgement is made for use of material from the following sources: *Boyhood in Gramercy Park* by Henry Noble MacCracken, © 1949, by permission of Maisry MacCracken; *The Diary of George Templeton Strong* edited by Alan Nevins and Milton Halsey Thomas, © 1952, by permission of Macmillan & Co.; *Gramercy Park, Memories of a New York Girlhood* by Gladys Brooks, © 1958 by Gladys Brooks by permission of McIntosh and Otis, Inc.; "A Reporter At Large, No. 9 Lexington Avenue" by Geoffrey T. Hellman from *The New Yorker Magazine*, © 1938, 1966, *The New Yorker Magazine, Inc.*, by permission of *The New Yorker Magazine, Inc.*

Copyright © 1984 by Stephen Garmey
All rights reserved. No part of this work may be reproduced or transmitted in any form or by any means without written permission.

Library of Congress Cataloging in Publication Data
Garmey, Stephen, 1933–
Gramercy Park, an illustrated history of a New York neighborhood.

Includes index.
1. Gramercy Park (New York, N.Y.)—History. 2. Gramercy Park (New York, N.Y.)—Buildings. 3. Gramercy Park (New York, N.Y.)—Description. 4. Architecture—New York (N.Y.) 5. New York (N.Y.)—History. 6. New York (N.Y.)—Description. 7. New York, (N.Y.)—Buildings. I. Title.
F128.68.G77G37 1984 974.7'1 84-11070
ISBN 0-917439-00-7

Designed by Allan Mogel
Edited by Barbara Krohn
Distributed by Kampmann & Company
Nine East Fortieth Street
New York, New York 10016

Contents

Chronology of Gramercy Park Land Acquisition

1651 Peter Stuyvesant buys the land from the West India Company.
1674 Judith Stuyvesant, the director general's widow, deeds four acres of this land to Francisco Bastiaense, a freed slave. On his death, the property reverts to the Stuyvesant family.
1746 James Delancey, the lieutenant governor of New York in the 1750's, buys the Stuyvesant land north of present Twentieth Street.
1747 Delancey sells the property to his brother-in-law John Watts, who develops it into Rose Hill Farm.
1761 James Duane buys the four acres that had once belonged to Francisco Bastiaense from Peter Stuyvesant's grandson Gerardus.

1763 Duane buys ten adjoining acres of Rose Hill Farm and establishes Gramercy Farm. No picture of his house, known as Gramercy Seat, exists, but it was no doubt similar to Petersfield, the contemporary neighboring farmhouse of Petrus Stuyvesant.

1776–83 Gramercy Farm is occupied by the British, including Major General Daniel Jones and the commander of the British fleet, Admiral Digby.
1786 James Duane adds a final six acres of Rose Hill to complete Gramercy Farm.
1797 Duane's five children inherit the farm.
1810–26 Sarah Duane Featherstonhaugh mortgages her share of the farm to Jane Renwick, the grandmother of the architect, James Renwick.
1830 Jane Renwick is forced to foreclose and becomes the fifth private owner of Gramercy Park land.
1831 Samuel B. Ruggles acquires Gramercy Farm and establishes the Park.

Preface and Acknowledgments

The visitor to Gramercy Park often finds it hard to believe he is still in New York City and only a short distance from midtown. Lexington Avenue makes its way down Murray Hill, past the Indian food markets and unnoticed old houses like the one near Twenty-eighth Street whose plaque announces that, here, on September 20, 1881, at 2:15 A.M., Chester Alan Arthur became President because James Garfield had been assassinated. It continues past the huge armory at Twenty-sixth Street where Marcel Duchamp's celebrated nude descended her staircase in 1914 and revealed the European revolution in modern art, and on past elegant old stables now converted into parking garages. Suddenly, the avenue ends abruptly in a small green park.

Actually, it begins, for it was here that the founder of that little square first conceived of Lexington Avenue, bought land for it in 1831 and, New Englander that he was, named it for the Battle of Lexington, the first engagement of the American Revolution. His name was Samuel B. Ruggles, and he acted not a moment too soon, for the area was rapidly being built up and, before long, no such avenue could have been put through. The city fathers had approved a grid plan for the city's streets, quite lacking in parks and open spaces. Without the foresight of Ruggles and a few others, there would be even less open space now in New York than there is.

Today the Park seems almost a mirage—like a London square of a hundred years ago—with graceful trees, shady lawns, cast-iron gates, and flagstone sidewalks. The fine brick houses on the west side are almost as beautiful as when they were built in the 1840's. Calvert Vaux's stately National Arts Club on the south side, and beyond it, Stanford White's The Players and the Stuyvesant Fish house, all face the square with the same quiet authority they have always had.

Over the years, such celebrated people as Peter Cooper, William Steinway, Edwin Booth, and Hart Crane have chosen to live here. One Park resident, Samuel J. Tilden, was elected President by the people of the United States, if not by the electoral college; and Cyrus Field planned the laying of the Atlantic cable at his house in Gramercy Park. Herman Melville, Henry James, Winslow Homer and Edith Wharton lived in the vicinity of the Park, and *The Pirates of Penzance* was completed here; Stephen Crane finished *The Red Badge of Courage* in a room he shared on Twenty-third Street. The Hotel Kenmore, which was later built at the same address, had as its manager Nathanael West, and William Sidney Porter, known as O. Henry, used to live on Irving Place and drink at Healy's Cafe, now Pete's Tavern. Theodore Roosevelt played in the Park as a child, and so did John F. Kennedy during the time his parents lived at the Gramercy Park Hotel. Lyonel Feininger lived the final eighteen years of his life on Twenty-second Street, a block or two from the Park, and there created his great series of Manhattan paintings.

As recently as 1830, however, the Park did not exist. The area was still farmland. How it came to be, how its architecture came to be built, and who lived here during its golden era at the turn of the century and afterward, is a fascinating story, to be unfolded in the chapters that follow. It is an essentially New York story of how very dissimilar people in the face of often considerable civic opposition became a genuine neighborhood. The Park today, with its rich conflict of architecture and rare tall trees, persists in live, uneasy tension with its surrounding city, expressing the true vitality of that city.

Many people have helped and encouraged me in this project. In particular, I want to express my gratitude to Douglas Donald who first suggested the idea of the book to me, and to the other directors of the Gramercy Neighborhood Associates for their indispensable help and support. I would also like to thank the Trustees of Gramercy Park, and especially their chairwoman, Constance Gibson, and secretary, Jane Walburn, for their generosity in making available to me their marvelous historical records.

Among the others who have provided me with essential information, I would like especially to mention Irene Abdusheli, Dr. Manlio Abele, Lily Auchincloss, Rabbi Irving Block, Professor Barbara Dunlap, Anne Eristoff, Helen Gavales, Frederick Gorree, Helen Haskell, Karen Hitzig, Olive Huber, Alden James, Marguerite Jossel, Herbert Mitchell, Tonio Palmer, Janet Parks, the Reverend Thomas Pike, Willson Powell, Louis Rachow, Stephen Senigo, Lorraine Sherwood, Peter White and Nancy Zuger.

I want to thank my editor, Barbara Krohn, for her care and patience in seeing the book from manuscript to publication; Philip Howard whose precise photographer's eye has revealed the Park in fresh ways to me; Eugene Weise for his indefatigable enthusiasm about forgotten history; and my dear friend, Adolf K. Placzek, whose learned zest for architecture has always been my inspiration. Finally, I want to thank my wife Jane, my sternest critic, with whom it has been a delight to live in Gramercy Park.

Stephen Garmey
New York, 1984

Samuel B. Ruggles
and Mary R. Ruggles
his wife
to
Charles Augustus Davis
and others, Trustees.

Deed.
of Gramercy Park
Decr. 17. 1831

Foreword

It is not right that there should be but one Gramercy Park in New York; the idea of it is too reasonable, too completely sensible in terms of all that urban living should be, not to have been repeated up and down Manhattan and all across the denser sections of the other four boroughs. What better way could there be to ameliorate the crowding of urban life than by setting aside squares, lining them with houses, and then letting the square in the middle serve as a private park for those on the periphery?

"Private park" is an odd term, highly elitist in its tone—it seems to call to mind the English squares to which Gramercy Park is often compared, and has associations of exclusion. All true; Gramercy Park is not open to us all. But it is just as easy to think of it not as a private park but as a common yard—as an open space shared by all the members of the community that surrounds it, who put aside their various differences and separate identities and become, in this sense at least, members of a kind of commune. Gramercy Park is communal property more than it is private property—not public in the conventional sense, but hardly private in the conventional sense, either.

That makes it all the more rare in this tense and crowded city. Is there anywhere else in New York with so exquisite a balance of the public and the private, so wondrous a mix of these two realms that the city seems, so often, to make a practice of keeping apart? For most New Yorkers, indoor space is private and outdoor space is public; those few exceptions, like terraces and little gardens behind townhouses, are usually too small to have any kind of public function. One thinks of the great common gardens uniting the townhouses of Turtle Bay Gardens, or the smaller but equally appealing inner garden in one block between East Sixty-fifth and East Sixty-sixth streets; Gramercy Park represents something more civilized than either of these, for its joys are visible to us all. We may not be able to go into the Park, but we can see it as we walk by, and linger beside it, and thus its presence is of true public benefit. It is outdoor space, at once public and private.

Every outdoor urban space is a kind of room, a room without a ceiling, but a room all the same. Gramercy Park is particularly roomlike, perhaps because the gates give it a sense of enclosure that goes beyond that of a normal New York square, but also, I think, because the buildings that line the Park make such fine walls. The north side rises high and in considerable unity, a collection of buildings that are particularly characteristic of the New York apartment style of the early decades of this century. Happily, this high wall is on the north side of the Park and blocks not sunlight but only the sense of connection to the busy blocks of midtown.

The Park's finest architecture is on the west, south, and east—the great row of nineteenth-century townhouses on the west, the opulent club brownstones on the south, the dignified but unusually welcoming apartment house at No. 34 on the east. And what is not up to these buildings in sheer quality is still rich in association—the mansard-roofed mansion at No. 19, once the Stuyvesant Fish house and long the residence of Benjamin Sonnenberg, where for nearly fifty years all of New York seemed to gather, coming to the Park at once to escape the city and, at least socially, to delve all the more deeply into it; or the inviting apartment house at No. 24, where classical details make an unusually felicitious facade, behind which the spirit of Richard Watson Gilder, who commissioned the building, long held sway.

As architecture, these buildings represent an eclectic mix that is particularly characteristic of New York, and stand as a reminder that however much Gramercy Park as an idea may call to mind London, and however much the developer Samuel Ruggles may have been motivated by an idealism that seems out of place in Manhattan, the essential New York-ness of the place still prevails. It is a mix of styles and periods and building types—and I have not even mentioned the old Friends Meeting House that is now the Brotherhood Synagogue, or Calvary Church, or the new buildings that bring a hint of postwar reality to the edges of the Park.

That reality is always there, however, still; it is not true that Gramercy Park is the place in New York where time stops. New York allows no Williamsburgs, and should not. But it is where time becomes a little more manageable, a little less threatening—and so, too, does the city itself become easier. To those lucky enough to have this as their vantage point, the noises recede, the sky appears, the sun washes over all in wonderful play with the shade of trees, so different from the shadow of skyscrapers. The buildings join together to create a complex and coherent, though not entirely harmonious, whole. The chaos and confusion of the city do not disappear from Gramercy Park—they are held at bay, and that, in the end, is much more as it should be.

For years, this special place has cried out for proper documentation. There is not a guidebook to New York that does not make some flattering reference to Gramercy Park, but no one in our time has told the Park's full story—the history of Samuel Ruggles's idea and of the Park's becoming; the building of the first houses; the growth and change on all four sides of the Park over the years. Stephen Garmey, as an architect, architectural historian, and connoisseur—not to mention a resident of the Park as associate rector of the parish of Calvary-St. George's—is ideally suited to this task. *Gramercy Park: An Illustrated History of a New York Neighborhood* is a pleasure to read and, thanks to the splendid array of photographs from all of the Park's periods, a pleasure to look at. It celebrates not only the Park itself—this book also, because it is written with an understanding of all that the Park implies, does honor to New York and to the very idea of urban living.

PAUL GOLDBERGER
New York City, June 1984

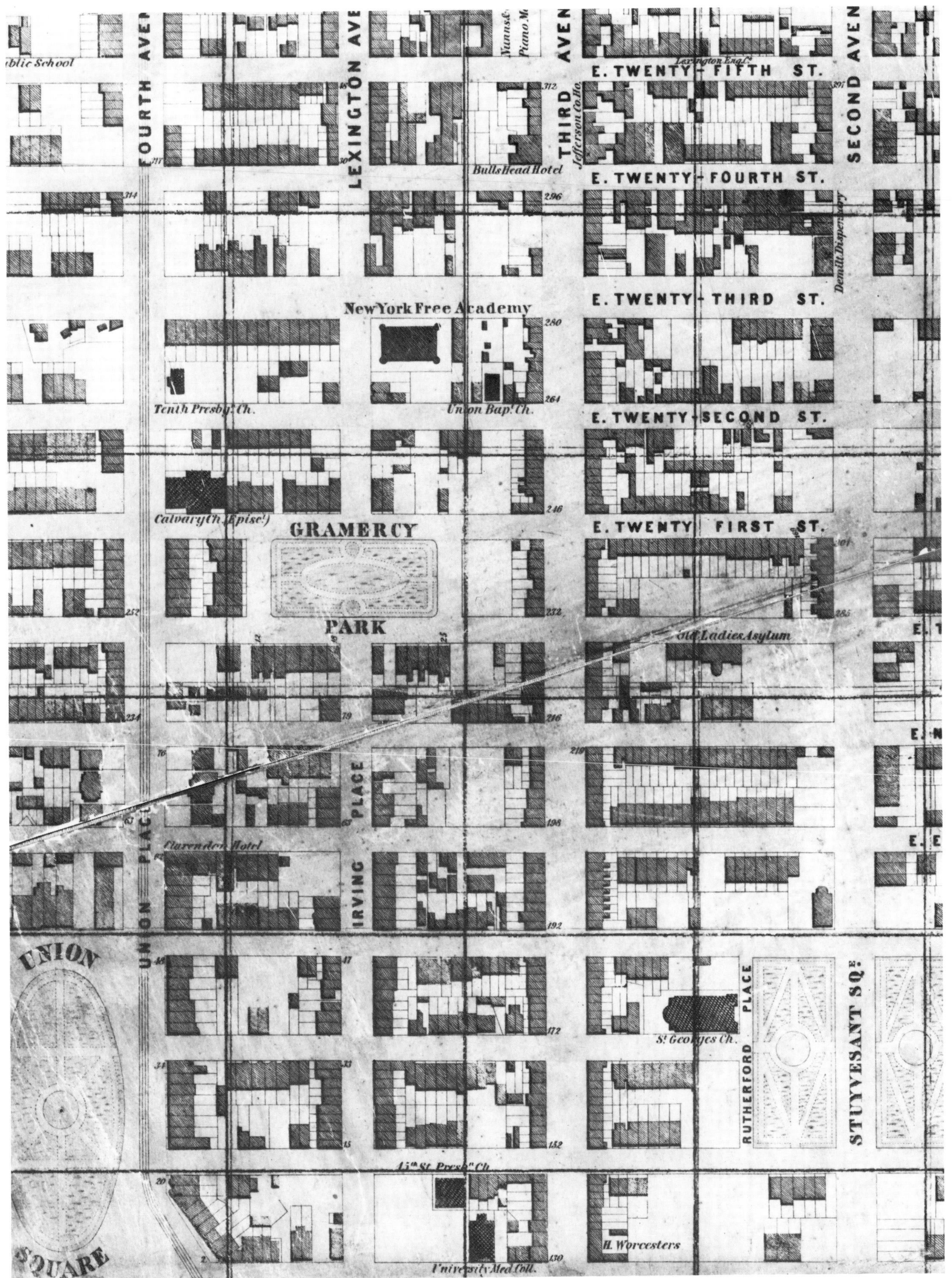

Detail from New York City map published by M. Dripps in 1851.

Plate 1 *Ratzer Map, 1767. Gramercy Farm is identified by the name of its owner, James Duane, and lies just south of where the road to Kingsbridge branches off from The Bowry* [sic] *Lane.*

1

Earliest Beginnings and Illustrious Owners

The land that became Gramercy Park was once part of a large tract which Peter Stuyvesant bought on March 12, 1651, along with its "dwelling house, barns, woods, six cows, two horses, and two young Negroes" from the Dutch West India Company. It extended roughly from what is today Third Street on the south to Thirtieth Street on the north, and from the East River to Fourth Avenue and Broadway. Near the northwest corner of this land was "a certain place or riseing [*sic*] hillock called Crommessie," according to a conveyance dated "the ninth year of his Sacred Majesty, King William the Third, Annoque Dom. 1697." The name of the property derived from two Dutch words: *krom,* meaning "crooked," and *messje,* "small knife," and was suggested by the contours of a brook or *vly,* that skirted the hill to the northeast. It used to be thought that *Gramercy* came from the French words *grand merci,* or "many thanks," but early references to the area as Crommessie were so frequent that little doubt remains that Gramercy is simply that Dutch word anglicized.

What happened to the brook? Where is the hillock today? What was the early look of that landscape? The answers to these questions can be pieced together from clues in the history of New York City.

In the mid-seventeenth century, the dense woods and salt marshes of this part of Manhattan island were still occupied by Indians and only beginning to be farmed by the Dutch. Parcels of land of up to twenty acres were regularly granted to freed slaves to farm, not so much out of charity, perhaps, as to guarantee a buffer zone against Indian attack. One such farm, between what is today Park Avenue South and Broadway from Nineteenth to Twenty-first streets, was deeded by Peter Stuyvesant's widow, Judith, on September 24, 1674, to Francisco Bastiaense, a former slave.

An interesting glimpse into one of the domestic issues of the day is given in this deed. Stray animals were the bane of New Amsterdam (or New Orange, as the city was called in 1674, when it had been retaken by the Dutch). Judith Stuyvesant was not about to add to this problem, so she put a proviso into the deed that its new owner be obliged to keep his fences in good repair. His animals, at least, were not going to wander. On Bastiaense's death, however, the little farm reverted to the Stuyvesant family.

In 1746, most of the Stuyvesant land north of what is today Twentieth Street was sold to James Delancey. The new owner was one of the most influential men in New York and was to become lieutenant governor in the 1750's and later chief justice of the Provincial Supreme Court. Delancey's main estate, the largest private holding in the city, was in the area of the street now named for him, a mile or so to the south. He bought his new parcel of land apparently on speculation, for he sold it the very next year to his brother-in-law, John Watts, a member, and later president, of the governor's council. Watts developed the land north of Twenty-first Street, or Love Lane as it was called in the eighteenth century, into the large farm known as Rose Hill.

The four acres once owned by Francisco Bastiaense were sold in 1761 by Peter Stuyvesant's grand-

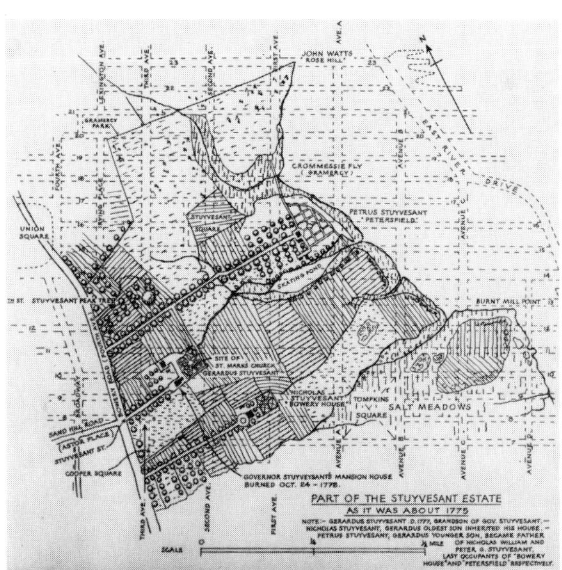

Plate 2

Plate 3

Plate 4

son, Gerardus, to another illustrious New Yorker, James Duane. Then a twenty-eight-year-old lawyer just coming into prominence in the city, Duane was to become New York's first mayor after the Revolution and, in 1789, the first judge President Washington appointed to the United States District Court in the city. The land was in need of improvement, for Duane wrote to his father-in-law, Robert Livingston, the proprietor of Livingston Manor on the Hudson:

> If you can lay up some bran for me to be sent by the first trip the sloop makes, it will much oblige me. There never was I believe so dear a year for provender, and I must keep a number of horses or expect no good of my farm, as the land is very poor. I have got a good stock of dung this winter, so that I have a prospect of reaping the fruits of my expenses very soon.[1]

Apparently the remedy worked and the farm thrived, because on December 28, 1763, Duane bought an adjoining ten acres from John Watts, including the land that would one day become Gramercy Park. It was there, sometime in the next three years, that he built the country residence that, anglicizing Crommessie, he called Gramercy Seat. We know this because the house and gardens of his farm are shown on a map drawn in 1767 by Bernard Ratzer, cartographer to His Majesty's 60th Royal American Regiment. They appear in the vicinity of what is today Gramercy Park West. In the 1840's, the well dug for the house came to light during excavation for the houses on Gramercy Park West. Also, part of the stone wall that formed the southern boundary of Duane's property still lies buried beneath the surface of Twentieth Street about 150 feet east of Third Avenue.

Duane was elected to the first Continental Congress in 1774, and during the Revolutionary War, he was an active patriot. Like John Jay, he was for resistance but did not believe in going to extremes. Very much an anglophile, in fact, according to the National Cyclopaedia of American Biography, an "anglomaniac," in 1775, he advocated a settlement with England that would have affirmed British supremacy. He opposed the Declaration of Independence until the very last, and attempted to delay it as long as possible in the hope that an agreement might be reached. His twentieth-century biographer, Edward P. Alexander, has called him a "revolutionary conservative."

Duane moved his family out of New York in June 1776. They were away for the duration of the war, most of which time he spent working with the Continental Congress. When the war was over and Washington made his great reentry into New York in November 1783, Duane was part of his entourage,

Plate 5

Plate 2 *Map of the Stuyvesant land in the late eighteenth century.*
Plate 3 *Petersfield, the brick farmhouse built before 1765 and painted yellow. The home of Petrus Stuyvesant, the great grandson of the director general, it was located just east of First Avenue between Fifteenth and Sixteenth streets; demolished in 1832.*
Plate 4 *Petersfield, looking from the entrance on the Bouwerie to the house. Gramercy Farm, immediately to the north, must have looked much the same in the eighteenth century. Rendering by E. P. Chrystie, 1951.*
Plate 5 *James Duane, mayor of New York, 1784–89, who established Gramercy Farm.*

Plate 6 *Map of James Duane's land, November 5, 1763, measured in acres, rods, and perches (1 chain = 100 links = 66 feet). The parcel to the west is that which once belonged to Francisco Bastiaense.*

Plate 6

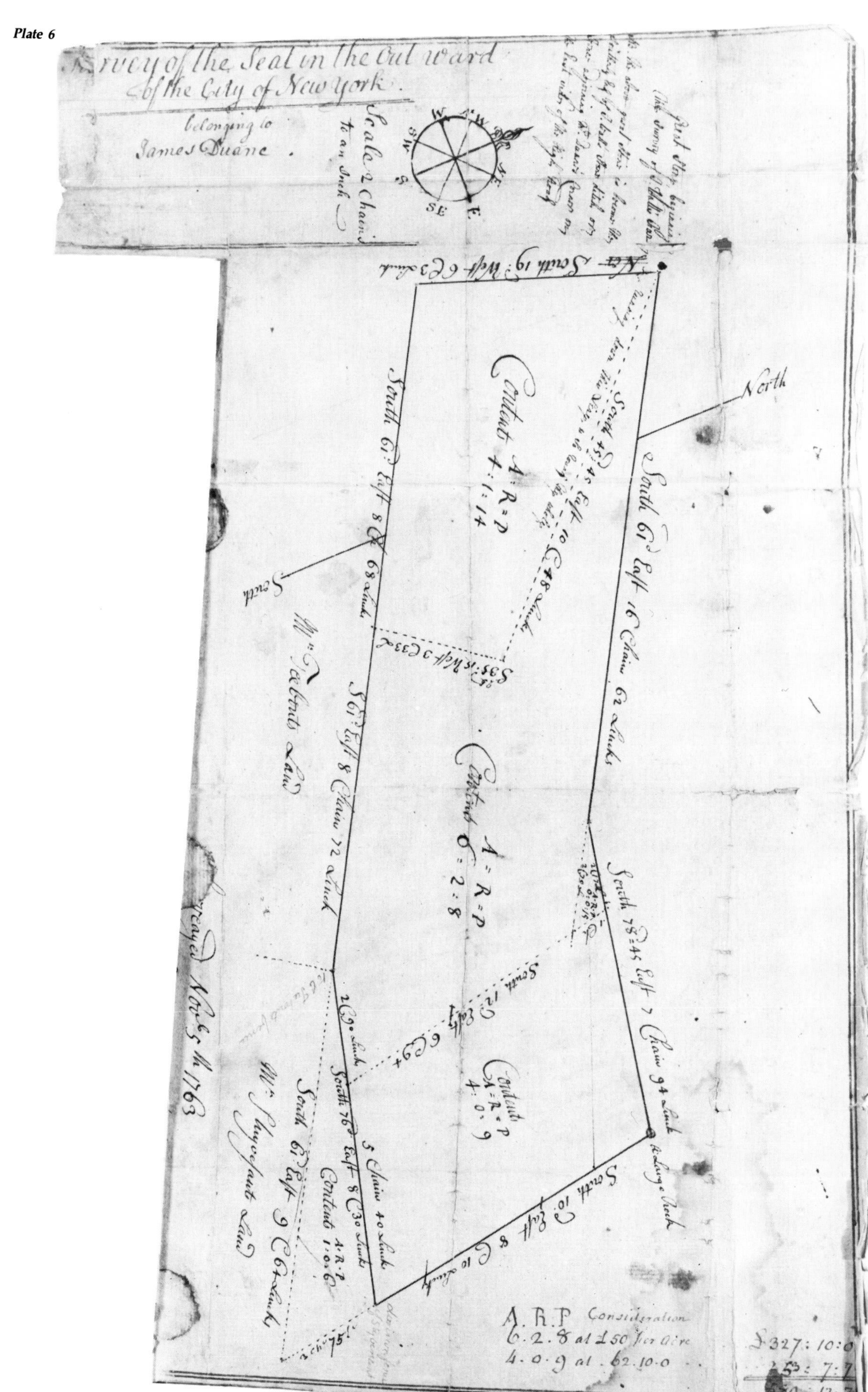

Plate 7 *Map of the six acres James Duane bought from John Watts, Jr., in 1786 to complete Gramercy Farm. The "small cedar tree newly trimmed" at the southwest corner was at what is today No. 241 East Twenty-first Street, and "Mr. Cruger's barn" was at the present corner of Third Avenue and Twenty-third Street.*

Plate 7

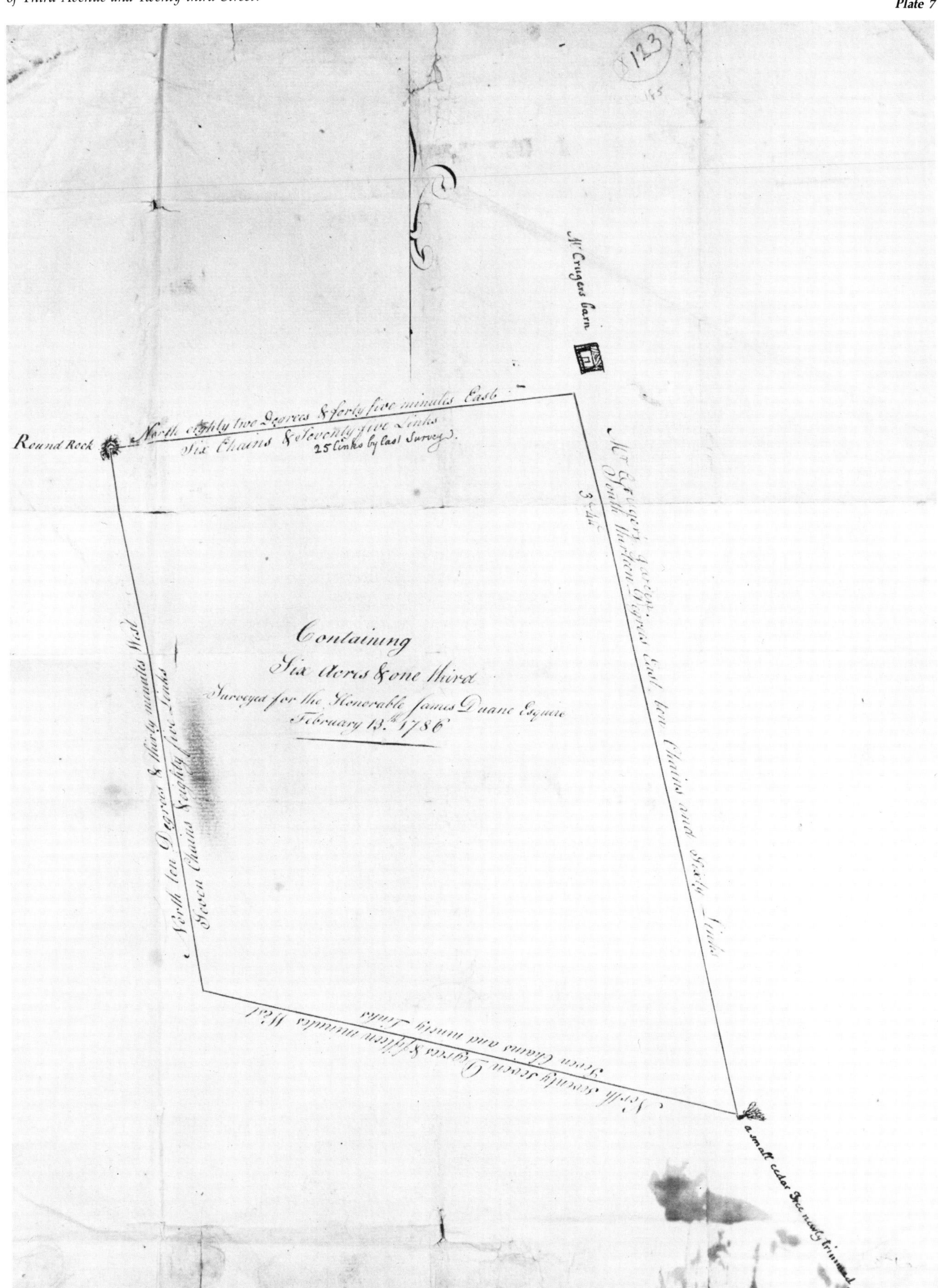

dressed no doubt in the then-fashionable "cord de roy" riding britches balanced by a blue coat. Washington's procession approached the city down Bouwerie Road (now Broadway south of Twenty-third Street); they passed directly by the entrance to Gramercy Farm, and one can imagine Duane's eagerness, having been away seven and a half years, to see the house again. In September, he had written to his wife, "The time is swiftly approaching when there will be no occasion for seperation [*sic*] and when we shall sit down in domestic Comfort—with God's blessing—after all the Trials and Storms which have drawn us into Exile and torn us from each other."[2]

Plate 8

And in another letter written to her on December 4, Duane describes the actual arrival:

> Tuesday, the 25th of November, accompanied by the General, we made a triumphant entry into the City amidst the joyful acclamations of the citizens who set no bounds to their expressions of satisfaction on this memorable event. We were preceded by a body of our Troops who made a fine appearance. On their coming within sight of the several posts, the British Guards moved off without Form or Ceremony. . . . I found our Farm in tolerable order: but no Improvements worth mentioning except part of the ground has been well manured. The houses in town are in a wretched condition.[3]

During the Revolutionary War, the major houses of New York and the surrounding farms were occupied by British troops, who often did considerable damage. Gramercy Seat, however, was fortunate to have been the temporary residence of two eminent English soldiers, Major General Daniel Jones and Admiral Robert Digby. Jones had succeeded General Clinton as commander of the British Army in New York in 1778; he was a gentleman soldier who, on May 30 of that year, issued the gratifying order that "commanding officers [were] to be answerable that no fences Near their Camps are Damaged, Nor Gardens and Cultivated Grounds trod down or injured." Admiral Digby arrived in New York in September 1781, as commander in chief of the British fleet, and made a number of improvements to Gramercy Farm during his occupation of the property.

In July 1783, Judge Duane's brother-in-law had written to reassure him that his

> small farm on York Island [was] in very good order owing to its being in the possession of Admiral Digby. Tho he has not resided there this summer, still his people remain the quiet possessors. Mr. John Watts has offered to use his influence to take possession of it . . . for as soon as the admiral leaves the place, some other person will take possession of it unless Mr. Watts interferes and procures an order from the commandant for it. . . . I make no doubt but what Digby on his leaving America will deliver up the quiet possession to Mr. Watts. . . . It is vain for me to give you a description of New York in its present state. All is confution [*sic*]. Horror and fear.[4]

On December 22, Duane again wrote to his wife, who still had not returned to the city, and this letter provides our most detailed description of Gramercy Farm.

> The garden is laid out in good taste and I believe not a tree has been wilfully destroyed; tho' we shall

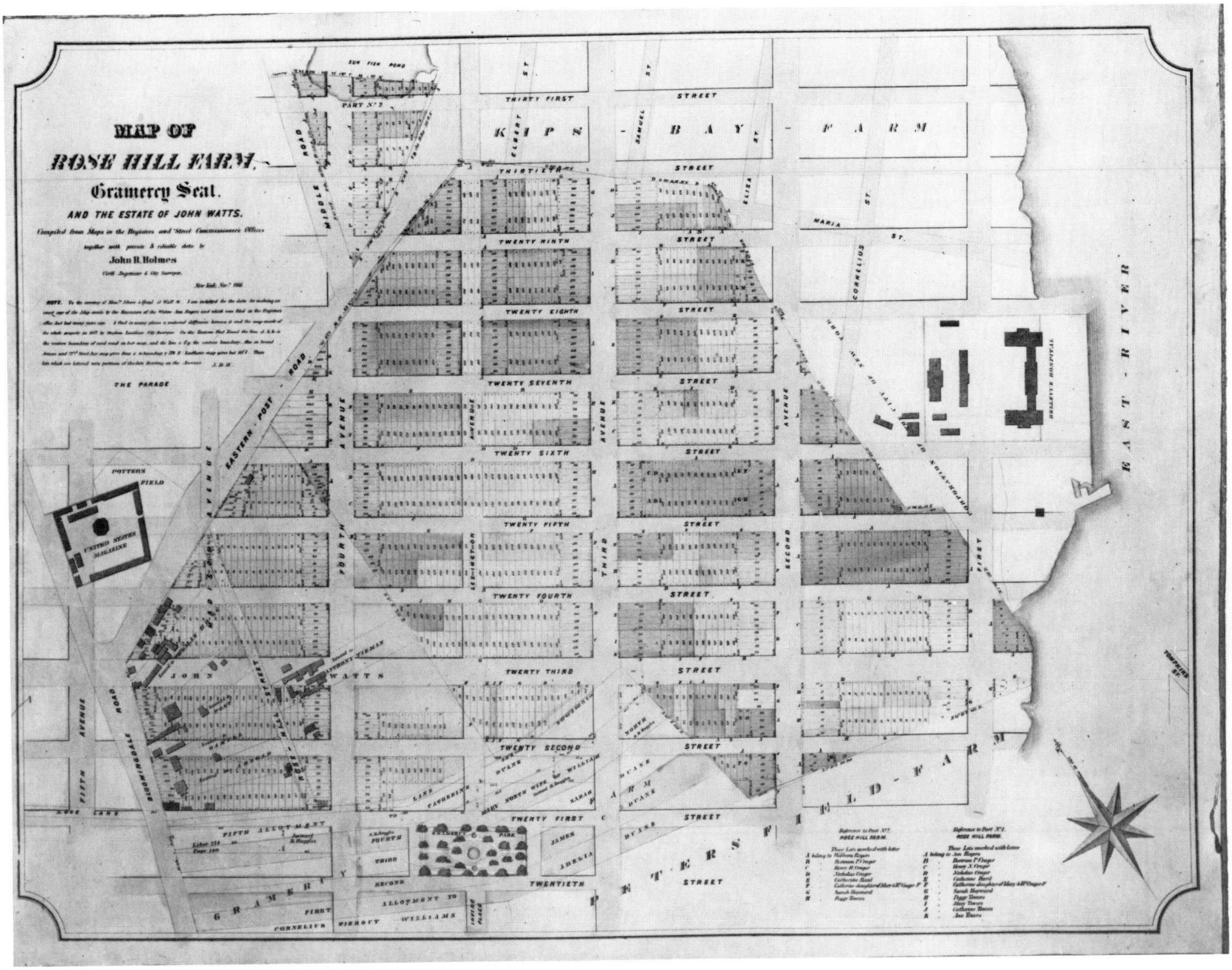

Plate 9

Plate 10

Plate 8 *Map of Manhattan farms in the eighteenth century, prepared for* Valentine's Manual, *1852, by Edward De Witt. Rose Hill Farm (Nos. 65–66) lies east of Broadway, just south of where the old Post Road branched off to the northeast. Gramercy Farm borders it on the south. (No. 64).*

Plate 9 *Map drawn in 1866 by John B. Holmes, "Civil Ingenieur* [sic] *and City Surveyor," of Rose Hill Farm, [the estate of John Watts, Jr., and Gramercy Farm], showing buildings in the area, c. 1820, and streets as they were later laid out.*

Plate 10 *View north from Love Lane and Bloomingdale Road (Twenty-second Street and Broadway), c. 1820. Buck's Horn Tavern can be seen at lower right. Rendering by E. P. Chrystie, 1951.*

miss the large walnut and the almond tree which died. There is no addition to the dwelling house; but the cellar has been improved at a considerable expense by alteration within, and by a cistern at the door which receives the water in wet seasons from whence it is conveyed by a pump to a drain across the farm terminating near the poultry house in a duck pond. The same drain communicates with the pump at the kitchen door; and as it passes under the ground it keeps the whole clean and dry. There is an addition of two rooms to the kitchen and a piazza to the front of the whole and stoves made within for cooking. There is also a summer house of lattice work on the hill behind the house. The garden is enclosed in a rail fence all around, but it is much contracted. Upon the whole it is a delightful place, and wants nothing but a good house in the center, where it was originally designed, to be a seat fit for any Republican. I believe I shall let the part which Beeker had, and reserve the house, garden and half the kitchen as formerly, that we may use it if we please, or part with it to a friend in the summer if it is too troublesome. Beeker (I mean our old tenant) wishes to have a new lease as formerly. He thinks it is the most profitable place on the Island and assures me that the grounds are highly enriched.[5]

The reference to the hill behind the house with its lattice summer house is worth noting as it is the only known eighteenth-century description of Crommessie Hill. In the New York *Mercury* of March 4, 1782, there appeared an advertisement for the sale of a "beautiful villa, situated on the Bowery Rd., about two miles and a half from this city," including twenty-two acres of "luxurious meadow and arable land." It has been suggested that this was in fact Gramercy Farm, but during the Revolution the farm consisted of only fourteen acres, not twenty-two, and it seems unlikely that in 1782, with the end of the war almost in sight and Admiral Digby in possession of the house, Duane would have been offering it for sale.

John Watts, Sr., was apparently even more of an anglophile than his neighbor, for he had been declared "'ipso facto' convicted and attainted of the offense of voluntarily adhering to the King of Great Britain, and all his estate . . . thereby forfeited and vested in the people of this State." The land was later released by the Commissioners of Forfeiture to Watts's sons, and it was from them, in 1786, that James Duane, at the time mayor of New York, bought the remaining six acres that gave Gramercy Farm its final shape.

When he retired in April 1794, Duane moved to Schenectady County, where he had huge holdings, including the town of Duanesburg. He was offered three thousand pounds for Gramercy Farm when he left, but refused to accept it. At his death on February 1, 1797, he left the property to his wife and on her death, to their five children. In 1803, they divided the farm into five equal allotments, each with an equal frontage on the Bouwerie Road. Since there was no mention of the house in this division, it is likely that it was no longer in existence by this time. It was, in any case, definitely gone by 1819, because it did not appear on a map of farms that John Randel made that year.

Plate 11 *House, c. 1800, on Twenty-third Street near Fourth Avenue, once the home of Daniel Tiemann, mayor of New York. This view was made after 1853, when Fourth Avenue Presbyterian Church, visible behind the house, was built.*

Duane's heirs continued to own their shares of Gramercy Farm well into the nineteenth century. Sarah Duane Featherstonhaugh, however, who owned the section that contained most of what would become Gramercy Park, twice had to mortgage her allotment. She "granted, bargained, sold, aliened, released, enfeaffed, conveyed and confirmed" it (as mortgages were then described) to Jane Renwick, receiving $7,500 from her in 1810 and another $3,500 in 1826. Mrs. Renwick, the grandmother of the architect James Renwick, Jr., had emigrated to New York with her English husband in 1794 from Scotland, where as a girl she had been celebrated as the inspiration for Robert Burns's poem "The Blue-eyed Lassie" (see Appendix B). The poet had visited her father's Dumfries parsonage and written the poem on the flyleaf of the family Bible. Widowed in 1808, Mrs. Renwick had continued to live in New York, and was a friend of Washington Irving's.

Sarah Featherstonhaugh died in 1828, and when her husband failed to make payments on the two mortgages, Mrs. Renwick was forced to foreclose in

1830, becoming the fifth in the succession of private owners of Gramercy Park land. (Each of her predecessors—Stuyvesant, Delancey, Watts, and Duane—has a New York City street given his name,[6] and her name has also been honored in this way: Renwick Street was named for her son, James Renwick, Sr., the illustrious engineer and Columbia College professor.) She owned the land, however, for less than a year. It was from her that Samuel B. Ruggles bought it for his park in 1831.

Notes

[1] James Duane to Robert Livingston, February 26, 1763, Roosevelt Library, Hyde Park, New York.

[2] Edward P. Alexander, *A Revolutionary Conservative, James Duane* (New York: Columbia University Press, 1938), p. 155.

[3] James Duane to his wife, December 4, 1783; transcript in possession of The New York Historical Society, New York.

[4] Henry Livingstone to James Duane, July 16, 1783; The New York Historical Society, New York.

[5] James Duane to his wife, December 22, 1783; transcript in possession of The New York Historical Society, New York.

[6] Watts Street, however, is named for John Watts, Jr.

Plate 12

Plate 13

Plate 12 *Buck's Horn Tavern, Bouwerie Road, was located in the path of present-day Twenty-second Street. It and the bowling alley behind it also appear in Plate 9.*

Plate 13 *The "Gates weeping willow," called after the Gates family whose farmhouse appears at Twenty-fourth Street near Second Avenue. The tree has been described as being on Third Avenue near Twenty-second Street, which would mean it was a tree on Gramercy Farm.*

Plate 14

Plate 14 *St. John's Park in 1867, showing St. John's Chapel (1803–07), during the destruction of the park for the building of Cornelius Vanderbilt's Hudson River Railroad freight house.*
Plate 15 *Samuel B. Ruggles as a young man. Portrait by Henry Inman.*

2

Samuel B. Ruggles Plans His Park

Samuel Bulkley Ruggles, who would become the founder of Gramercy Park, was born in 1800 in New Milford, Connecticut, but grew up in Poughkeepsie, New York. His father was a prominent New Milford lawyer and twice a member of the Connecticut Assembly, but he had moved his law practice to Poughkeepsie around 1804. Samuel entered Yale in the sophomore class at the age of twelve in order to, as he later put it, "learn a little more federalism from President Dwight."[1] In September 1814, he was graduated from the college, the youngest in his class, and went to study law under his father. He was licensed to practice law in the Court of Common Pleas in 1821, and the next year qualified for the Court of Chancery. In 1821, or at the beginning of 1822, he moved to New York, married Mary Rosalie Rathbone, and set up his own law practice.

The city was expanding rapidly northward at the time, following a grid plan worked out by the street commissioners between 1807 and 1811. The commissioners' intention had been to protect the new areas of the city from the whims of individual proprietors, so that the streets would be orderly and not opened and closed at will. They acknowledged in their report that they had deliberated

> whether they should confine themselves to rectilinear . . . streets, or . . . whether to adopt some of those supposed improvements, by circles, ovals, and stars, which certainly embellish a plan. . . . They could not but bear in mind [however] that . . . straight-sided, and right-angled houses are the most cheap to build and the most convenient to live in. . . . It may, to

Plate 15

> many, be a matter of surprise that so few vacant spaces have been left, and those so small, for the benefit of fresh air and consequent preservation of health. Certainly, if the City of New York were destined to stand on the side of a small stream, such as the Seine or the Thames, a great number of ample places might be needful; but those large arms of the sea which embrace Manhattan Island, render its situation . . . particularly felicitous.[2]

Many New Yorkers did indeed see the grid as an implacable straitjacket violating the terrain. When later street commissioners, including James Renwick, Sr., father of the architect, were charged in 1823 with implementing the grid as far as Thirty-fourth Street, they complained in their report that the plan had an "entire absence of public squares, essential to the general health."[3]

Surveyors working for the commissioners had run into considerable opposition in their preparations for the new arbitrary streets and avenues, which were to disregard completely the contours of the island. It is recorded that "on one occasion, while drawing the line of an avenue directly through the kitchen of an estimable old woman who had sold vegetables for a living . . . the surveyors were pelted with cabbages and artichokes until . . . compelled to retreat in the exact reverse of good order."[4]

When the commissioners came to deal with the area around Gramercy Farm, they found that Crommessie Vly, or Cedar Creek as it was also called, presented real problems. It was fed by several springs between what are now Fifth and Sixth avenues, from Twenty-first to Twenty-seventh streets; spread into the Rose Hill duck pond, in what is today Madison Square; and then meandered to the East River at about Eighteenth Street (Plate 18), cutting a gully with "bold and rocky" walls, almost forty feet deep in places.[5] The commissioners proposed that instead of tunneling the water under the streets of the grid, which would require enormous filling operations, a new diagonal street, sloping to the river, be created in order to carry the water over its surface. The legislative red tape necessary to make such a change, however, proved to be too time-consuming, and the brook was eventually carried, as it is today, in conduits.

The application of the grid to the undulating terrain of Gramercy and Rose Hill farms proved to be a huge task. The commissioners' detailed profiles of the area were made available to the public in 1825 and indicated precisely where the land was to be cut or filled to regulate it. Their fifty-eight sheets in four portfolios are now apparently lost, but it is known that they gave the present elevation above sea level and the corresponding required elevation for two points, fifty feet apart, on every lot in the district. Every landowner could thereby determine the alterations that needed to be made to his property. An 1832 commissioner's profile for streets below Twenty-third Street from Third Avenue to the river (Plate 19) shows the gully of Crommessie Vly, across which Third Avenue had already been built, requiring an embankment of about eighteen feet of earth. To the east was a hill about twenty-eight feet high, the crest of which had to be moved into the neighboring gully to create an even slope for the streets.

Much of the work in the area of Gramercy Park was undertaken by Samuel B. Ruggles, for in the 1820's and 1830's, he was the chief landowner and developer of the district. He had begun investing in real estate in about 1825 and had been so successful at buying and selling land that, in 1831, he had given up his active law practice to devote himself entirely to city development. No mere speculator, he concerned himself with the problems of traffic flow, standards of residential building construction, and, most importantly of all, the preservation of open spaces. Adamantly opposed to the lack of parks provided by the commissioners' plans, he was active throughout his life in correcting that deficiency. In the early 1830's, he helped develop a collection of vacant lots into Union Square and built his own house there; in 1845, he was one of those who petitioned the city to complete Madison Square. He later encouraged his son to do much of the legal work for the creation of Central Park; and at the age of seventy-eight, his memorial to the New York legislature helped block the city's seizure of Washington Square for an armory. The assembly and development of Gramercy Park was his paramount achievement.

In 1831, few New Yorkers were as aware as Ruggles was of the causes and implications of the current surge in the city's population. He recognized that it came partly as a result of the completion of the Erie Canal in 1825, which had greatly increased the demand on the goods and services of the New York market, in effect adding Ohio, Indiana, and half of Kentucky to it. Ruggles was a perceptive economist. He argued that whereas in a prevailing agrarian economy cities had been seen as parasites on the country, now

> the only legitimate business of [a] city was to *distribute* for the country—and its wealth and extent must always be commensurate with the wealth and extent of the country for which it distributes. . . . We must forthwith get more hands. . . . We really need a population of three or four hundred thousand [the population at the time was about two hundred thousand] . . . and that stalwart, well-fed race beyond the

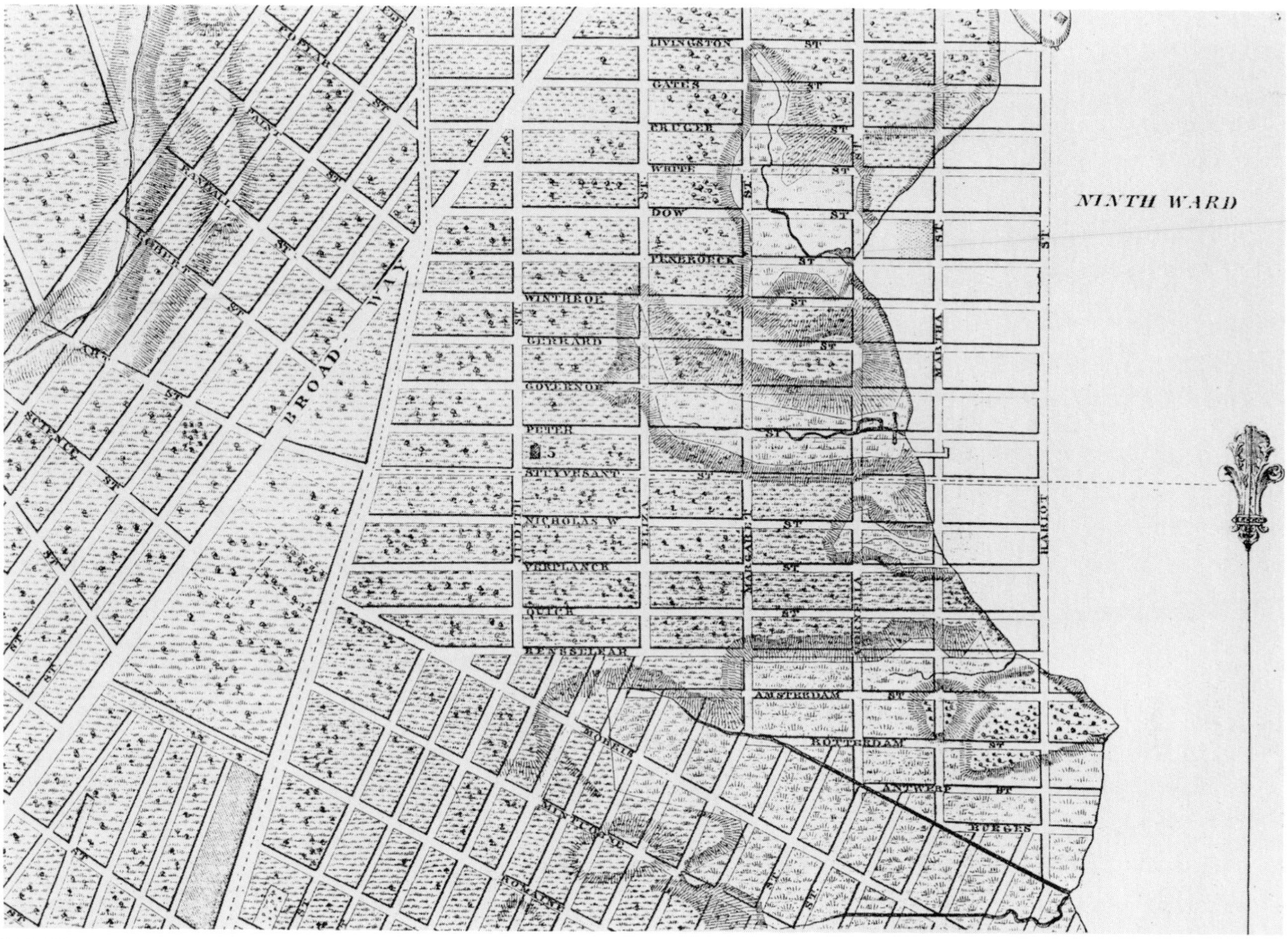

Plate 16

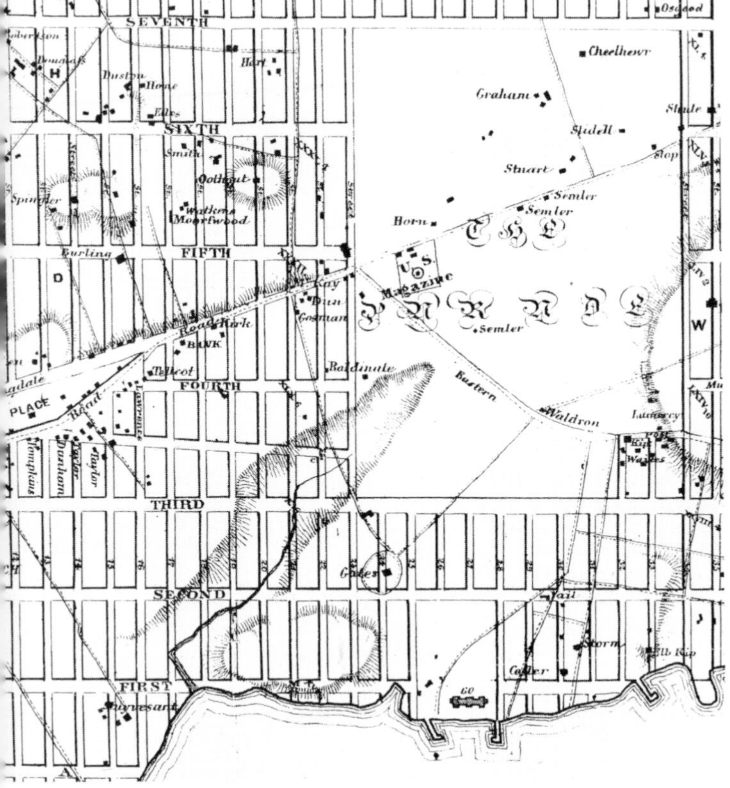

Plate 17

Plate 16 *Section of map, dated November 1803, drawn from a survey by Casimir Goerck and Joseph Mangin, city surveyors. Broadway is shown crossing the Bouwerie at roughly Fourteenth Street and continuing approximately along the route now taken by Irving Place. Streets are laid out parallel to today's Stuyvesant Street and have names of local families. Gramercy Park would lie in the vicinity of Gates Street between Eliza and Margaret streets.*

Plate 17 *Section of map, dated April 3, 1807, drawn by William Bridges for the street commissioners. The house shown east of Fourth Avenue, north of Twenty-first Street, may be Gramercy Seat, incorrectly placed a block north of its actual location, as is the northern boundary of Gramercy Farm.*

Plate 18 *Section of topographical map drawn in 1865 by Egbert L. Viele, showing the original contours of Crommessie Vly. Pre-regulation elevations are given at the corners of the superimposed grid of streets.*
Plate 19 *Street commissioners profile, 1832, showing the original lay of the land east of Third Avenue and the proposed street levels. The route of the sewer line carrying Crommessie Vly water is shown following Twenty-second Street, Second Avenue, and Eighteenth Street.*
Plate 20 *Map of Gramercy Farm, 1831, drawn for Samuel B. Ruggles.*

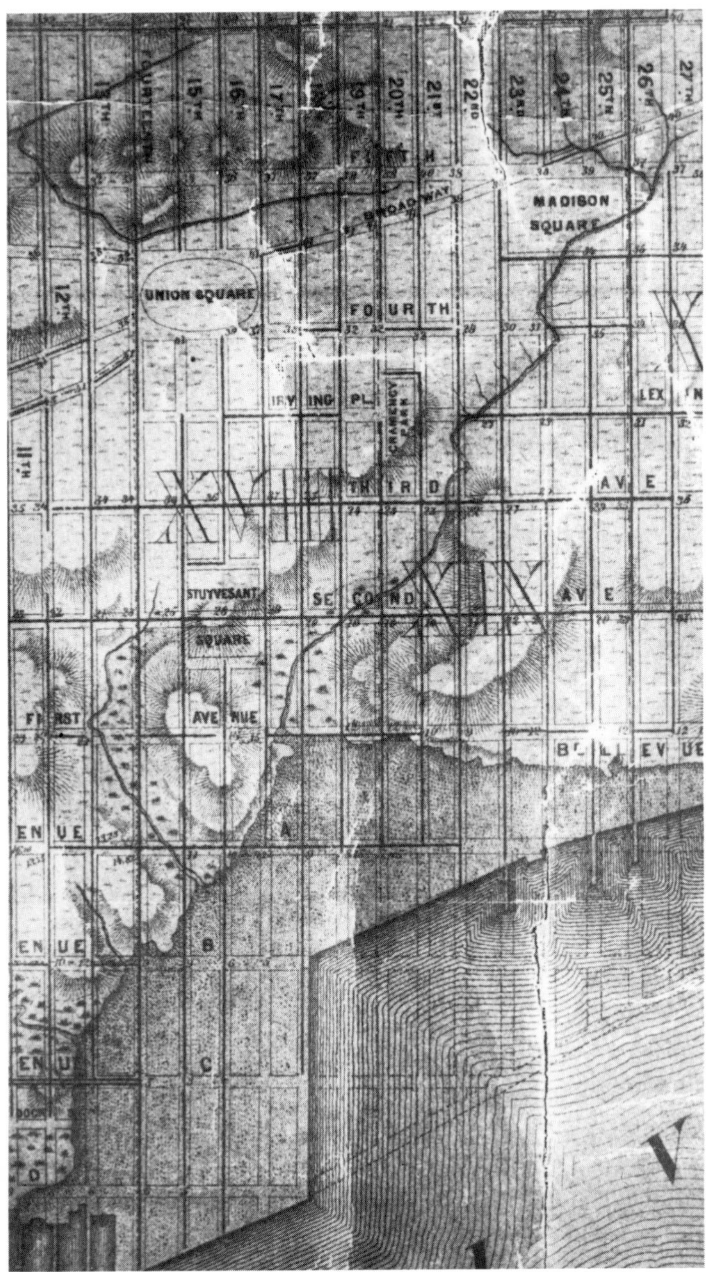

Plate 18

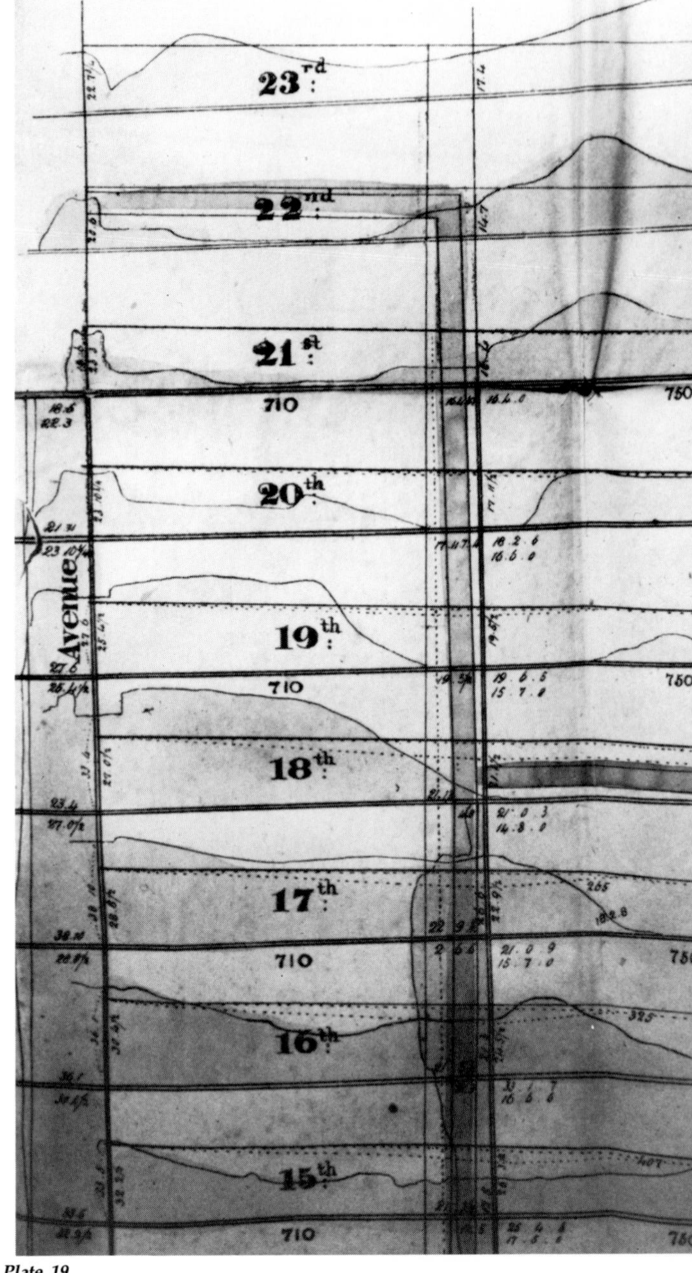

Plate 19

Plate 20

> Alleghenies—they are a locomotive race: we must make a railroad for them, and let them come to us often and cheap.[6]

The value of taxable real estate in Manhattan, he pointed out, had grown from $52 million in 1825 to $95 million in 1831.

> It is now marching onward, and cannot stop. Within five years after the railroad from Albany shall reach Lake Erie, the real estate upon this little rocky island will be taxed at 250 millions of dollars. Now it really behooves us to look around and contrive how to find money enough to build our city. Our population cannot increase less rapidly than 15,000 annually. . . . The money [to build its houses] we must borrow. . . . And why should not the city be built with borrowed money? Why should not the lender of capital . . . assist enterprising builders in improving the city?[7]

Borrow Ruggles did, from banks and from individuals, for he began his real-estate ventures with very little capital. He invested in land north of Fourteenth Street where, he realized, the burgeoning population would undoubtedly live. By 1833, he had purchased land enough for over five hundred building lots, although most of it was heavily mortgaged. Twenty-two acres of this land (less that which had become city streets) had been Gramercy Farm, four-fifths of it still owned in 1831, the year he bought it, by the heirs of James Duane. The record of this complex purchase was carefully documented, and its chronology shows how quickly Ruggles was able to operate. The following is the list of his transactions during nine months of 1831:

February 8	Deposited $5,000 on Allotment Three of Gramercy Farm with Jane Renwick.
February 9	Deposited $1,000 on Allotment Four with William North.
February 23	Traded land with Adelia Duane Pell, and for an additional $1,000 received the section of Allotment One that he needed for the park.
March 10	Sold an interest in Allotments Three and Four to his friends Robert Weeks and Seixas Nathan for $10,000.
March 10	Deposited another $6,000 on Allotment Four.
March 10	Mortgaged Allotment Four.
March 15	Deposited $1,000 on Allotment Two with James C. Duane.
March 24	Paid another $18,000 on Allotment Two.
March 30	Sold land from Allotment One to William H. Harison.
April 20	Paid Mrs. Renwick the remaining $14,625 on Allotment Three.
April 30	Paid another $15,000 on Allotment Four.
May 3	Traded land with Catherine L. Duane to acquire the parts of Allotment Five needed for the park.
May 16	Bought from Peter G. Stuyvesant, for $4,500, land required on the south side of the park.
May 25	Bought a strip of Allotment One from William H. Harison for $1.
May 31	Gained releases on part of Allotment One.
June 1	Sold an interest in Allotment Two to Weeks and Nathan for $5,000.
June 15	Traded more land with Catherine L. Duane for $3,000.
July 16	Gained further releases on Allotment One.
September 29	Bought at public auction, for $28,000, the remaining parts of Allotment One.
October 3	Gained further releases on Allotments One and Two.
October 12	Bought land from Stuyvesant for $6,500.
October 26	Bought more land from Catherine L. Duane for $4,500.
November 10	Bought more land from Stuyvesant for $5,100.

Ruggles was a shrewd businessman, and in these twenty-three transactions, over nine months' time, he had pieced together all the land required for Gramercy Park and its surrounding lots. The process was complicated by the fact that the northern boundary of Gramercy Farm had followed the irregular line of Love Lane, an eighteenth-century local road. When Twentieth and Twenty-first streets were put through, they made oblique angles with the old boundary, creating awkward triangles of land. The adjustment of property lines to make them conform to the new streets was accomplished by trading land with neighbors.

Having not yet seen London, Ruggles was probably most influenced in the actual arrangement of his park by St. John's Park, also known as Hudson

Square, in lower Manhattan, between Varick, Beach, Hudson, and Laight streets. It had been laid out in 1803 by Trinity Church, but its houses were only begun in the late 1820's; Trinity, having offered ninety-nine-year leases with a requirement that quality row houses be built on the sixty-four lots, had found few takers. In 1827, the church sold the lots and deeded the square to the owners. A cast-iron fence was built in 1828, and the locked park was laid out with gravel paths and two hundred ornamental trees, shrubs, and flower beds. St. John's Park lasted only until 1866, however, when it was bought by Cornelius Vanderbilt for one million dollars, the owner of each house receiving thirteen thousand dollars for his share of the park. But in the early 1830's, the substantial brick houses rising around it undoubtedly inspired Ruggles as he formulated his plans for Gramercy Park.

St. John's Park had been modeled on eighteenth-century London squares, and this was perhaps one reason why patriotic New Yorkers had refused to build there for twenty-five years. But by 1831, people were quick to cite the new London squares as a precedent for Gramercy Park. When Ruggles petitioned the city on November 21, 1831, for tax-exempt status for his park, the committee chosen to present a report on his petition wrote on December 5:

> The want of a sufficient number of open and public squares in this extensive and densely populated metropolis, is a cause of frequent and just complaint, inasmuch as they would greatly tend to embellish and ornament the city. . . . It is really to be

Plate 21

Plate 22

Plate 21 *View south from what is today Broadway and and Eighteenth Street to the union of Bouwerie Lane and Broadway, for which Union Square was named, 1820. Late nineteenth-century rendering.*

Plate 22 *Union Square, 1849, drawn by James Smillie. Renwick's Church of the Puritans is at the left, and Calvary Church is in the distance.*

lamented that the whole of that part of this island south of 14th Street, which contains a population amounting to 191,059 souls, has only five open squares of any extent, viz. the Battery, Bowling Green, the Park [City Hall], Washington Parade Ground, and Hudson Square, the latter of which is private property and liable at any time to be built upon by the owners of the lots fronting thereon.

As this is the first time that any question relative to open or public squares has ever come before this Board, the Committee will be excused, if they digress a little from the immediate subject under consideration, and exhibit some facts, which will clearly show that the Common Council ought speedily to adopt measures, not only to lay out more public squares, but also to facilitate enterprising individuals in laying out private squares, whenever it can be done without prejudice to the public interest.

With regard to the particular square proposed to be laid out by the petitioner, . . . he intends to lay out said block in an open square 520 feet long from east to west, and extending north from 20th to 21st street, if the Corporation will facilitate him in that undertaking.

There can be no doubt but that the proposed square will greatly ornament that part of the city, when a dense population shall extend as far north as 21st street. The lots fronting on the square are about 27 feet wide, and the petitioner intends to prevent the purchasers of those lots from erecting any other buildings thereon than private dwelling houses. He also proposes to enclose the square with an ornamental iron fence, maintain the same at his own expense, and keep it forever unoccupied by buildings so as to admit the free circulation of air. The square, in the opinion of your Committee, will be judiciously located, being on the property which was a part of the country seat of the late Judge Duane, about 750 feet north of the termination of Union Place; in a central position, on high and salubrious ground, between the 3rd and 4th Avenues, which will be the two great outlets of the middle part of the city.

The dimensions of the proposed square are sufficiently extensive to justify the Common Council in affording the petitioner any reasonable facilities not injurious to the public interest. When compared with squares in this and other cities, its size will warrant the expectation that it will be an elegant improvement. In length it will be 520 feet. . . .

The report then confirmed Ruggles's prediction that the city would "be densely populated as far north as the proposed square within a moderately short period of time," that the square would soon "be surrounded by substantial and valuable buildings . . . and that the taxable value of lots fronting on squares [was] at least double what it would be, if those squares had not been opened." If the taxes on the sixty-six lots surrounding Gramercy Park were increased, then even though the forty-two lots of the Park itself were exempted, the income on the area would be greater than it would be were the Park not there. The committee therefore concluded that from "a financial point of view . . . it was highly expedient to encourage the opening of squares, particularly when done solely at individual expense." They expressed their opinion that public squares may be laid out in the northern sections of the city, "before land shall arrive at so high a price that it cannot be obtained for public purposes, without materially affecting our finances."[8]

On December 30, the Board of Assistant Aldermen resolved itself into a committee of the whole to deal with the report. Its resolution stated that if the aldermen concurred, the counsel of the Corporation should prepare the draft of a law to the effect that whenever the proprietor(s) of lands in the city of New York "shall at his or their sole expense lay out such lands in an open square and shall . . . bind himself or themselves to keep such square open and unoccupied by buildings, the lands composing such square shall be exempted from taxation and assessment provided the Corporation consent." On February 13, 1832, the law committee of the Board of Aldermen made a report as an amendment to Ruggles's petition exempting the land from taxation so long as it was kept solely as an ornamental square. The board concurred.[9]

In the meantime, on December 17, 1831, Ruggles had deeded the forty-two lots of his Park to five Trustees, and was ready to proceed with its actual construction.

Notes

[1] Samuel B. Ruggles to Francis Wayland, September 1, 1866, Ruggles Papers, Manuscript Division, New York Public Library, New York.

[2] Street Commissioners Report, April 1, 1811, New York Historical Society, New York.

[3] Street Commissioners Report, November 7, 1825, New York Historical Society, New York.

[4] Martha Lamb, *History of the City of New York* (New York: A.S.Barnes, 1880), vol. 3, p. 572.

[5] Street Commissioners Report, November 7, 1825, New York Historical Society, New York.

[6] Samuel B. Ruggles to N. P. Tallmadge, January 23, 1832, Ruggles Papers, Manuscript Division, New York Public Library, New York.

[7] Ibid.

[8] *Documents of Board of Assistants*, vol. 1, no. 37 (New York: Printed by order of the Common Council, 1838), pp. 125–133.

[9] Minutes of the Board of Assistant Aldermen, *Proceedings of the Board of Assistants*, 1831-1832 (New York: Municipal Reference and Research Center).

Plate 23 *View south from what is today Broadway and Eighteenth Street, showing excavation required to level Union Square.*

3

Preparing the Ground

The Trustees to whom Samuel B. Ruggles deeded the land for the Park were Charles Augustus Davis, a merchant; Robert D. Weeks and Thomas R. Mercein, "gentlemen"; his own brother, Philo T. Ruggles, a lawyer; and Thomas L. Wells, also a lawyer. The Deed, signed on December 17, 1831, states that Ruggles and his wife would

> devote and appropriate the said forty-two lots of land to the formation and establishment of an ornamental private Square or Park, with carriage ways and foot walks at the south-eastern and north-western ends thereof, for the use, benefit and enjoyment of the owners and occupants of 66 surrounding lots of land . . . with a view to enhance the value thereof. . . . Now therefore . . . in consideration of the sum of Ten Dollars . . . [they] do grant, bargain, sell and convey . . . all those certain 42 lots of land lying and being in the now Twelfth Ward of the City of New York, being part of the Gramercy Farm of the Honorable James Duane, deceased.

Twentieth and Twenty-first streets had been opened, regulated (that is, graded), and subtracted from the acreage of Gramercy Farm before the land was bought by Ruggles. The cost of opening and regulating had been assessed to the Duane heirs; Mrs. Renwick, as mortgagee of Allotment Three, had paid $340 for opening Twentieth Street, and $89 for opening and $3,585 for regulating Twenty-first Street. The regulation of the Park itself and the sixty-six surrounding lots was, at the time of the original Deed, yet to be accomplished.

Ruggles was very clear in this Deed as to what could or could not be built around the Park. No one was ever to

> erect within 40 feet of the front of any . . . of the said lots . . . any other buildings save brick or stone dwelling houses of at least three stories in height, and . . . [never] erect . . . any livery stable, slaughter house, smith shop, forge, furnace, steam engine, brass foundry, nail or other iron factory, or any manufactory of gunpowder, glue, varnish, vitriol, ink or turpentine, or for the tanning, dressing or preparing skins, hides or leather, or any brewery, distillery, public museum, theatre, circus, place for the exhibition of animals, or any other trade or business dangerous or offensive to the neighbouring [*sic*] inhabitants.

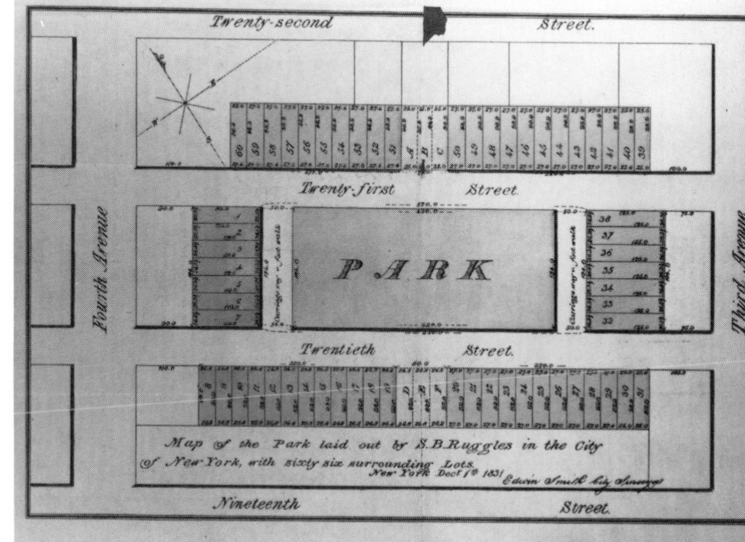

Plate 24 *Gramercy Park, 1831, drawn by Edwin Smith, city surveyor. Lots A–F gave way to Irving Place and Lexington Avenue.*

The Trustees agreed that by May 1, 1833, they would

> surround and enclose by means of an iron fence with stone coping and ornamental gates a portion of the . . . land, as an ornamental Park or Square, and by January 1, 1834, . . . lay out . . . ornamental grounds and walks, and plant and place therein trees, shrubbery and appropriate decorations, the cost of all which including the said fence . . . not [to] exceed $12,000, . . . and . . . preserve, maintain and keep . . . the said grounds, plantations and decorations in proper order and preservation, the annual cost of which . . . [after January 1, 1834] shall not exceed $600.

Residents of the Park were to have "free ingress and egress" subject to rules and regulations agreed to by two-thirds of the lot owners. And once three of the Trustees had died, left New York, or resigned, three others were to be elected by a majority of the lot owners.

The Deed was recorded on December 20, 1831, at three-thirty in the afternoon. Early in 1832, Ruggles began to prepare the land. It was an enormous task; the terrain, as described in a street committee report of January 28, 1833, was "exceedingly uneven, requiring excavation and embankment of upwards of a million loads of earth," to conform it to the required level.

> This great and valuable work, [is being] prosecuted [by Ruggles] with characteristic and unremitting activity, so that the whole will probably be completed within the present year; thus levelling, regulating, and rendering available for use in our rapidly increasing population, a broad central section of this city, extending from 15th to 27th Street.[1]

A load of earth was then calculated as being nine cubic feet and cost anywhere from five cents to nine cents to move by horse cart. A million loads, therefore, would have cost over fifty thousand dollars, no small sum in 1832. The precise amount of earth that had to be moved to create Gramercy Park itself is not known. According to the abstract of Ruggles's title (now in The New York Historical Society), "the whole of the land forming 'the riseing hillock of Crommessie' [had] recently been excavated to a depth of 17 feet below the natural surface." As can be seen from the Viele Topographical Map (Plate 18), which is as accurate a depiction of Crommessie Vly as exists, the land fell away fairly sharply at the northeast corner of the Park. (The forty-foot rocky banks of the stream described by James Renwick, Sr., and his fellow commissioners lay somewhere along this stream.) The higher ground of Crommessie Hill to the southwest was, therefore, moved here, to bring the park lots to the required level, roughly that of the previously built Third Avenue embankment. (Third Avenue had been opened in 1814, leveled, and, because it was outside the city's "lamp district," equipped in 1830 with fourteen lamps between Fourteenth and Twenty-eighth streets. It was much used as a trotting course.)

Two glimpses of the process of earth moving undertaken by Ruggles in the neighborhood of, but not right on, the Park have survived (among the Ruggles papers deposited at the New York Public Library), and help to develop a picture of the actual construction of Gramercy Park. At the southwest corner of Twenty-first Street and Second Avenue, lots Ruggles owned that fell on the northern slope of the gully of Crommessie Vly required filling. His records show that the corner lot required 1,525 loads of earth costing $83.57; the next to the south of it, 2,959 loads at $127.07; and so on down the block, each lot requiring a different amount of fill. We can reasonably deduce a similar requirement for the corresponding slope of the gully at the southwest corner of Twenty-first Street and Third Avenue.

The other detailed record that has survived is for the regulation of Twenty-sixth Street between the Post Road and Third Avenue, which Ruggles undertook with his contractor, George A. Furst, in 1837.

July 3	carts and labor	$ 47.06
July 17	carts and labor	145.78
	misc. fees	5.75
	filling	153.04
	blacksmith bill	10.00
	dockage for stone	17.25
August 1	salaries and carts	295.31
	8 brooms	.66
	paver	6.18
August 4	2,303 loads of fill @ $.06 each	138.18
August 14	laborers	170.56
September 11	filling	40.05
September 21	1,325 ft. curb @ $.50 per ft.	692.50
	1,420 ft. gutter @ $.40 per ft.	568.00
	Total	$2,290.29
	less	24.94
		from sale of earth

For this work, Ruggles was allowed by the city to assess adjacent property owners $3,615.09, and he realized a profit of $1,350.74, which he shared with Furst: $540.30, or 40 percent to himself, and $810.44, or 60 percent to Furst.[2]

The most revealing record of the creation of the Park, however, is found in an exchange of letters between Ruggles and Furst. They date from July 1832,

1832?

July 12.

wrote to Furd to direct Smith & Pettigrew to pave 20th Street, as if the new street stopped at 20th Street. so that the curb would be in one unbroken line on S. side of the Park — according to this diagram.

Park

side walk

20th Street

side walk

new street

side walk.

Because it would visibly shew the Corpn. that it would be most expedient not to open the new street through the Park — at least not for the present. —

also to cause the temporary wooden fence to be put up 2 feet south of line of Park — to be three boards high —

To enquire if Brund had got his money of the Rail Road Co. — & to make out his account for the balance — as it would absolve me from any implied responsibility. —

~~To see if the [illegible]~~

S.B.

Plate 25 *Memorandum in Samuel B. Ruggles's hand concerning construction of Gramercy Park.*

and would not exist had there not been an outbreak of cholera in New York that summer, for the duration of which Ruggles had moved his family up the Hudson to Newburgh, and therefore had to give instructions to his contractor by letter. The work of leveling the northwest corner of the Park was in progress, and Ruggles's neighbor north of Twenty-first Street, John Watts, was at work cutting and filling his land. Ruggles wrote on July 7 to Furst:

> Please draw me a rough diagram showing how near the edge of the eave [of the fill] has approached to Watts' line . . . the northern end of the drain terminating on Mr. Watts' line is a point from which you can easily measure in a northerly course to report how far the filling has passed north of it, and how far the eave is now east of Watts' line.
>
> I will thank you to ascertain when . . . the work of digging the land for Watts [is finished]—the moment that is done I wish the residue of Miss Duane's land [James Duane's daughter from whom Ruggles had bought the northern strip of her father's farm] to be cleared. . . . If Mr. Quin [a workman] will himself agree *without delay or shuffling* to dig it off, it is well to *see that he does it*. If he refuses or delays at all—then get Brunt [a workman] to dig it off without delay. Brunt may deposit the earth in Twenty-first Street east of Third Avenue—allowing for the same not more than 5 cents per load, previously [ascertaining] . . . the amount of earth now on it. But if Quin finds you are in earnest, he will consent to take the dirt away and dump it with the rest of his filling. Thus take the trouble of contracting with Brunt and the expense of having the earth measured. . . . Please let me know in your next letter what progress Quin makes in digging off and clearing the Park of stone and filling it with mould [earth]. I wish him distinctly to understand that he must not delay. He wished to wait for rain in order to plough the Park with a little more ease to himself but I cannot agree to wait for that. The Steam Boat Novelty which leaves New York in the morning at 7 o'clock A.M. generally arrives here at about 2 o'clock P.M. so that you can come up and see me and return the same day whenever a . . . conference shall be necessary. . . .[3]

Furst wrote on July 11:

> Since yesterday afternoon we have had here without intermission a cold heavy rain so that nothing could have been done out of doors. . . . People in the street are dressed like December with overcoats and cloaks. . . . The report today is . . . 50 deaths [from cholera]. People continue to leave the City.[4]

The next day, July 12, Ruggles wrote a memorandum to himself (Plate 25) that gives another precise record of the progress the Park was making:

> [I] wrote to Furst to direct Smith and Pettigrew to pave 20th street as if the new street [Irving Place was as yet unnamed] stopped at 20th Street, so that the curb would be in one unbroken line on S. side of the Park . . . because it would visibly shew the [City] that it would be expedient not to open the new street through the Park—at least not for the present. [It was not yet absolutely clear that Gramercy Park was safe from bisection.] Also to cause the temporary wooden fence to be put up 2 feet south of the line of Park and to be three boards high.[5]

These accounts give a picture of how Ruggles went about the actual construction of the Park. A year before, he had been furiously buying up land, selling, mortgaging, trading it, piecing together what was needed for the project. Now, with equal energy and impatience, he was overseeing all the necessary work to prepare that land to become the Park he had envisioned. We do not know exactly when the iron fence that surrounds the Park was erected, or how much it cost. In all likelihood it replaced the 1832 wooden fence not long thereafter and was paid for by Ruggles himself, as there is no record of the Trustees or lot owners sharing in its cost. The street committee report of January 28, 1833, states that he was, at that time, surrounding a Park "with an elegant iron

Plate 26 *Gramercy Park; west gate.*

fence." And in a confirmatory Deed drawn up on December 24, 1833, where the Trustees' 1831 agreement is repeated—to "surround and enclose [a part of the Park] by means of an iron fence . . . and plant and place therein trees, shrubbery and appropriate decorations, the first cost of all which including the said fence shall not exceed $12,000"—the words *all* and *including the said fence* have been dropped. Perhaps this was because the fence had already been erected. When the Trustees, at their December 30, 1844, meeting, itemized the work that had been done in the Park back to 1838, what it had cost, and how the money had been raised, the only iron work mentioned was that for two gates installed by S. B. Althouse for $465. The minutes state:

> Mr. Althouse's bill, if free from error and overcharge, would show that a fence around the Park made after the patern [*sic*] of these gates would—*after allowing for the fence already there*—cost $55,800—it is recommended that Mr. Norman White who contracted for this work with Mr. Althouse—be authorized to adjust and settle this bill.

The implication here of the "would . . . cost" is that the $55,800 fence had not been approved. There is no further mention, however, of such approval, of raising this money, or of the construction of a new fence in the minutes of any meeting thereafter, although these minutes always accounted precisely for every penny spent. This would seem to be confirmation that "the fence already there" in 1844 was the fence that is there today. Beautiful as it is, it could not have cost $55,800, for the similar iron fence erected in 1828 for St. John's Park cost $25,000, and the longer and more ornate Stuyvesant Square fence of 1848 only $20,000.

The gates that Althouse did supply, presumably for the east and west sides of the Park, are described in great detail in the minutes:

May 8, 1844

4 wrot iron Columns	3,132 lbs. @ 10¢	$313.20
Lead	57 lbs. @ 5¢	2.85
2 gates	867 lbs.	—
less for Upt Bars	170 lbs. 697 lbs. @ 10¢	69.70
2 brass heels	9 lbs. @ 35¢	3.50
2 locks with 4 keys & putting on		18.00
Braces, Rests and bolts	167 lbs. @ 10¢	16.70
James Harriots & Co. Bill Stone work		36.00
Painting		6.00
		$465.60

The confirmatory Deed of December 24, 1833, just referred to, was drawn up because "doubts had been entertained concerning the validity" of the first Deed. In the intervening two years, most of the sixty lots around the Park had been sold, and it was thought advisable to redefine the terms of the gift and to clarify the rights of the new owners.

By this time, in response to Ruggles's suggestion, the New York state legislature had allowed the opening of Irving Place, named by Ruggles for Washington Irving. (The *AIA Guide to New York City* points out however, that the theory that Irving had ever lived on the street "is but wishful thinking.") The 1833 Deed stated that the "piece or parcel of land" designated for the new street ran "through the centre [*sic*] of the . . . Park, or nearly so."

Ruggles was living at 705 Broadway in 1833, but he moved into a house at 36 Bond Street, then a distinctly fashionable address, the next year. That same year, he was among those involved in the construction of the Erie Railroad, and also presented the New York Board of Aldermen with a plan to make Union Place (later Square) into a civic center. Though nothing came of this plan, the area was regulated and graded in 1834. Much of the cost of this was assessed to land that Ruggles owned between there and Gramercy Park, particularly along Fourth Avenue, which had been opened north of Seventeenth Street in 1833. He soon undertook, with George Furst, the building of curbs and sidewalks on the newly opened streets and by November 1, 1837, had assigned to his contractor over seventy thousand dollars to pay for these improvements. In 1836, he petitioned the street committee to name the new street, which ran "through his own lands" north of Gramercy Park, Lexington Avenue, after the first engagement of the Revolutionary War. President Charles King of Columbia College noted in 1852 that he had selected this name "with the just pride of a New England man."[6]

The commissioners' plan had not included the new avenue; having assumed that most traffic in Manhattan would be river to river, the commissioners had laid down many more streets than avenues per mile. Had not Ruggles and others sensed this deficiency when they did, and bought up land for extra avenues when this was still possible, midtown congestion today would be even worse than it is. And if Ruggles had not modestly named his new avenue Lexington rather than after himself, people would today be riding the Ruggles Avenue line of the IRT.

In 1832, Ruggles had leased all the lots on Fourth Avenue, or Union Place, between Fifteenth and just north of Nineteenth streets for thirty years, with the privilege to renew for another fifty years. In his petition to the city to open Fourth Avenue north of Seventeenth Street, which was approved January 28, 1833, he had stated the need for ready access to his property, as he would be erecting "expensive and ornamental" houses there during the following summer. Fourth Avenue was, in fact, already partially open as a result of the construction of railroad tracks.

Ruggles later landscaped the block fronts on both sides of Fourth Avenue between Eighteenth and Nineteenth streets with ornamental gardens in front of set-back, two- and three-story houses (Plate 31), which can just be glimpsed in the 1869 photograph in Plate 28. They were described by George De Forest Barton, who grew up in the neighborhood, as "the most attractive blocks in the city."[7]

Ruggles sold most of his leases, but on three lots between Fifteenth and Sixteenth streets on the east side of Union Place, he built substantial four-story houses in 1838 and 1839. One of these, at No. 24 Union Place, two doors north of Fifteenth Street, he built for himself, though the house was owned by his father-in-law, John Rathbone. Ruggles lived there

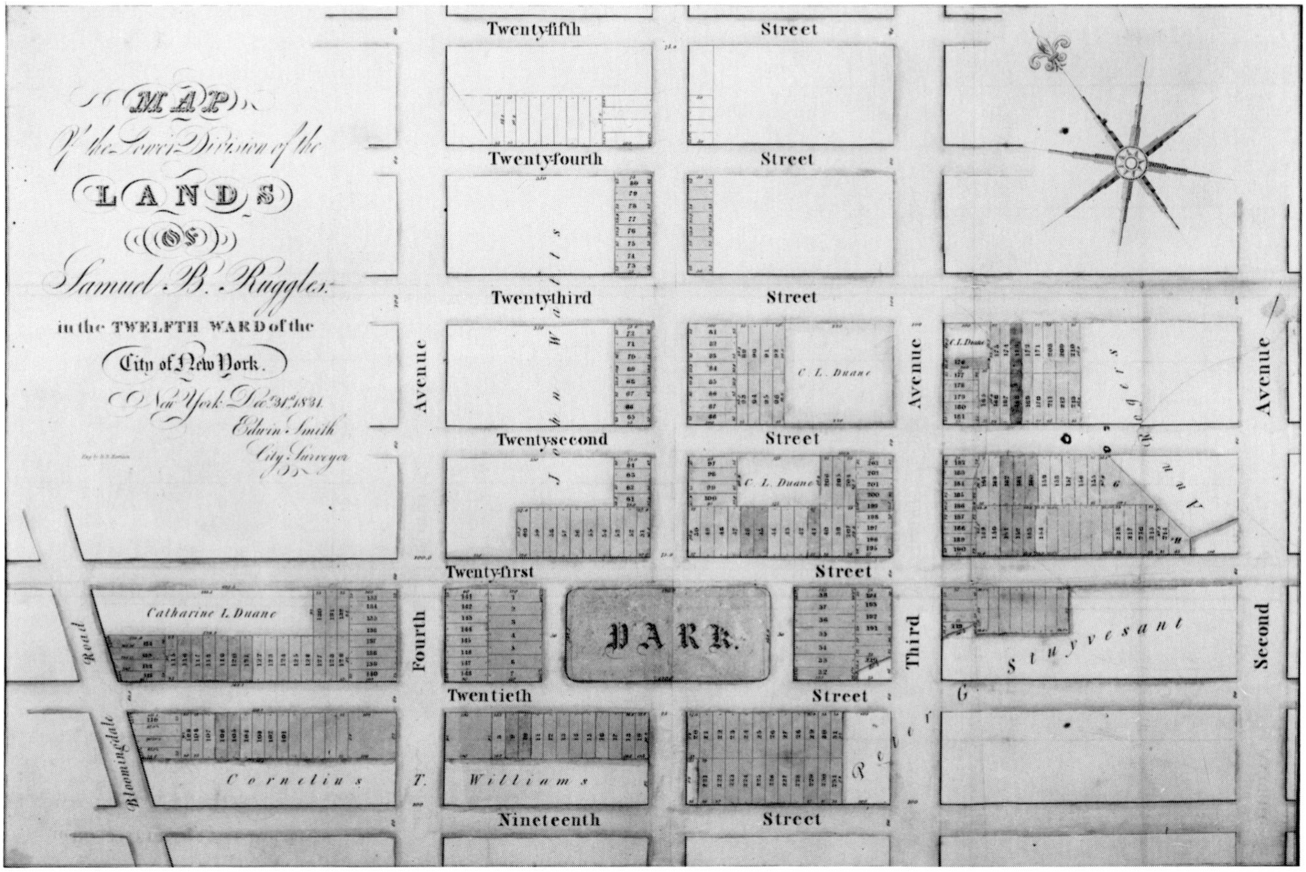

Plate 27

Plate 27 *Map of Samuel B. Ruggles's lands at the end of 1831, drawn by Edwin Smith, city surveyor.*
Plate 28 *View south on Fourth Avenue to Union Place, 1869, from the roof of the Twenty-third Street YMCA. Towers of Fourth Avenue Presbyterian Church are in the foreground; beyond them, the towers of Calvary Church and the dome of All Souls Church can be seen. Ruggles's landscaping of the block between Eighteenth and Nineteenth streets is visible, with the Clarendon Hotel beyond it.*
Plate 29 *Union Place, 1878.*
Plate 30 *Sketch of four of Ruggles's lots on Union Place, preliminary to the building of his own house at No. 24 (14 on this sketch).*
Plate 31 *East side of Union Place at Eighteenth Street, c. 1870, showing Ruggles's set-back houses at the left and the Clarendon Hotel.*

Plate 28

Plate 29

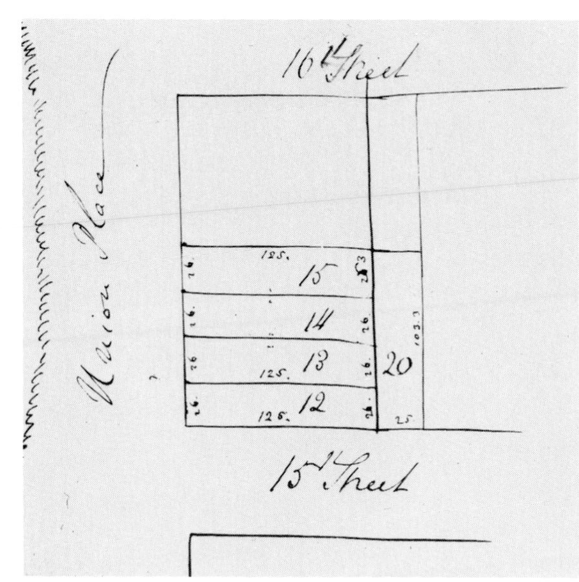

Plate 30

Plate 31

Plate 32

Plate 33

with his wife and family for the rest of his life. He became a trustee of Columbia College, a member of the New York State Assembly, and an intimate friend of John Jacob Astor and Peter Cooper. He was also a patron of the opera and the theater, a staunch Episcopalian, and a longtime vestryman of Calvary Church at Twenty-first Street. In addition, over the years he had amassed a library with many books in French and Italian. At either side of a sideboard in his house, he kept two silver pitchers (Plate 35), which had been presented to him by Robert Weeks and Seixas Nathan in gratitude of his establishment of Gramercy Park as a permanent gift to the city. The pitchers can be seen today at The New York Historical Society.

Ruggles's house was demolished not long after his death in 1881. A photograph of it (Plate 33) was taken around 1880 and shows it already flanked by two of the ever-encroaching commercial buildings that had by then almost completely surrounded the Square.

Plate 34

Plate 35

Notes

[1] *Documents of the Board of Assistants*, vol. 2, no. 47 (New York: Printed by order of the Common Council 1838), p. 290.

[2] Billing Record, Ruggles Papers, Manuscript Division, New York Public Library, New York.

[3] Samuel B. Ruggles to George A. Furst, July 7, 1832, Ruggles Papers, Manuscript Division, New York Public Library, New York.

[4] George A. Furst to Samuel B. Ruggles, July 11, 1832, Ruggles Papers, Manuscript Division, New York Public Library, New York.

[5] Memorandum, July 12, 1832, Ruggles Papers, Manuscript Division, New York Public Library, New York.

[6] D. G. Brinton Thompson, *Ruggles of New York* (New York: Columbia University Press, 1946), p. 59.

[7] *Valentine's Manual of Old New York*, edited by Henry Collins Brown, no. 7, New Series, New York, 1923, p. 202.

Plate 36

Plate 32 *No. 70 Union Place, the Doremus house, on the east side of the street, between Eighteenth and Nineteenth streets.*
Plate 33 *No. 24 Union Place, the home of Samuel B. Ruggles. Photograph (1880) shows the house flanked by newer commercial buildings.*
Plate 34 *Samuel B. Ruggles. Daguerreotype taken in middle age.*
Plate 35 *Silver pitchers presented to Samuel B. Ruggles by two of the original Park Trustees, Robert Weeks and Seixas Nathan.*
Plate 36 *Samuel B. Ruggles monument in Gramercy Park; presented by his grandson John Ruggles Strong in 1919. Medallion by Edmond T. Quinn, copied from one taken from life; Tennessee marble shaft designed by Charles I. Berg.*

Plate 37

Plate 37 *Gramercy Park, looking southwest, 1984.*
Plate 38 *Detail from New York City map published in London in 1840. Shading indicates area built up by this date. Black line along Fourth Avenue is the New York and Harlem Railroad. Lexington Avenue was not yet named and is labeled Irving Place.*

4

Planting the Park

Little progress was made on Gramercy Park during the middle 1830's, perhaps because Ruggles was so occupied with other projects, or because of the severe depression New York underwent in 1837. The date by which the Trustees had agreed to complete the ornamental grounds and walks came and went; the Park, in fact, became known as "Sam Ruggles's vacant lot." It was still quite adventurously out of town.

In the spring of 1838, however, the Trustees engaged a gardener to begin the planting of the Park. His name was James Virtue, and the agreement with him, the "bill of trees" as one of the Trustees, Charles Augustus Davis, referred to it, has happily survived. Davis had it written into the minutes of a later meeting held on December 30, 1844, because he thought it would "be of interest in future years." It is, in fact, a document of such precision and detail that it offers intimate contact with the activity in the Park that spring, and deserves to be given here in its entirety.

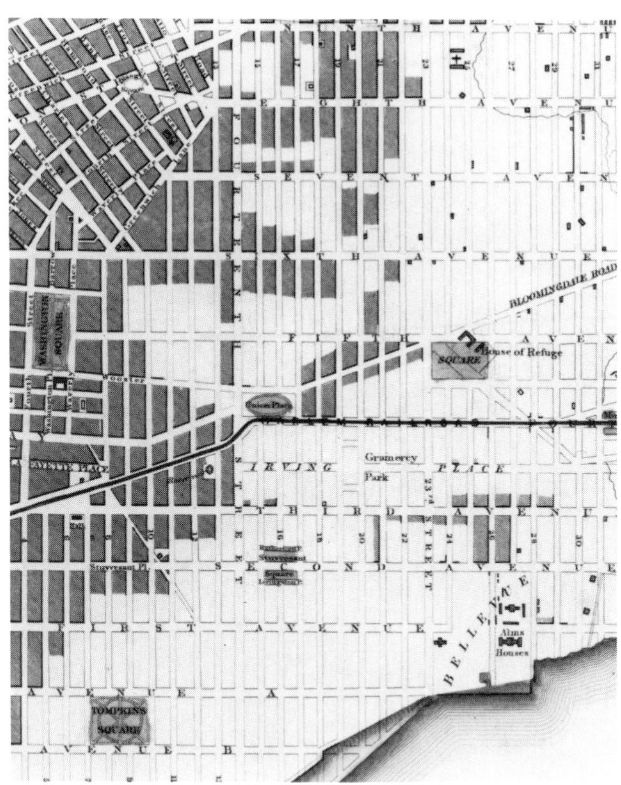

Plate 38

> It is hereby agreed between Chas. A. Davis and James Virtue, that the said James Virtue is to obtain and perperly [*sic*] plant out in Gramercy Square, 1st, one thousand healthy plants called 'Privit or Prim' being considered a quantity sufficient to surround the said Park inside its fence, and to plant the same in a suitable manner so that their growth shall be secured.
>
> 2nd, that the said James Virtue is to procure and plant out about one hundred Trees in said Park consisting of *Horse Chesnuts* [*sic*], *Willows, lindens, Helianthus* [*sic*], *Maples, Catalpas* and other ornamental Trees, assorted and judiciously planted to accord as near as practicable with a plan now handed to said James Virtue by the said Charles A. Davis and bearing the name of the latter written on the face thereof—showing the arrangement of the walks, etc. [This has not survived.]
>
> 3rd, that the said James Virtue is to arrange such of the walks and borders according to said plan in said Park, as may be found necessary for the present year—it not being intended to complete and finish *said walks* this present year.

And the said Charles A. Davis hereby agrees to pay to the said James Virtue the fair and just cost of said shrubs and Trees with reasonable expenses in transporting same, and also to pay him for his labor whilst engaged in work on the said Park, at the rate of One Dollar and seventy-five cents per day—and that all claims made by the said James Virtue under this agreement shall be made on the said Charles A. Davis at the close of each and every month—and in the event or case of any disagreement growing out of what may be deemed excessive charge or in the event of any complaint by the said Charles A. Davis as to the workmanship or the character of the Trees or shrubs furnished by the said James Virtue—the same shall be submitted to reference by disinterested persons, the said Chas. A. Davis and the said James Virtue selecting one competent person each, and they, if necessary, selecting a third, and their decision, or a majority of the same, shall be considered binding—it being understood that this precaution is taken in consequence of the said C. A. Davis not being familiar with the nature and character of the work required.

New York 30 March 1838

Bills of James Virtue

Gramercy Park

[The prices of most of the trees and shrubs are given in shillings perhaps because they were ordered from England.]

Trees

10 Ailanthus		at 7/(Shillings)	$ 8.75
8 Horsechestnut		14/	14.--
4 Sugar Maple	$2		8.--
3 Sugar Maple		6/	21.25
5 W'ng Willows		8/	5.--
2 Larch	$2		4.--
4 Mountain Ash		10/	5.--
2 Beech	$2		4.--
2 Elms	$2		4.--
5 Elms		6/	3.75
2 Tulip Trees	$2		4.--
3 Bird Cherry		7/	2.62-1/2
10 English Ash		8/	10.--
9 English Lindens		10/	11.25
8 English Lindens		6/	6.--
2 Poplars Tickmahick		14/	3.50
14 Sycamore		7/	12.25
8 Catalpas		14/	14.--
5 Butonbals		6/	3.75
2 Scarlet Maple		8/	2.--
13 English Walnut		8/	13.--
2 Paper Mulberries		5/	1.25
			$142.37-1/2

Plate 39

Received, New-York, June 4th 1842 from Saml B Ruggles, in behalf of Chas A Davis & others trustees Six Hundred & seven 89/100 Dollars, being the amount deposited with the Street Commissioner to redeem the following described Property, which was sold at the Corporation Sale on the sixth day of October 1841 viz:

1840

Grammercy Park Lot situate in 21st Street south side between 3d Avenue and 4th Avenue assessed to Grammercy Park for laying Sidewalks in 21st Street

confirmed October 6th 1837 and numbered 49.
on Map of the Assessment

Sold for $ 487.46
Interest, $ 119.43
Advertising 1.00
$ 607.89

John Ewen
Street Commissioner
per Edward Ewen

Shrubs

60 Sprial Vrutex	1/3	$9.31-1/4
7 Laburnums	2/6	2.18-3/4
26 Dbl. Altheas	2/6	8.12-1/2
25 Snowballs	3/	9.37-1/2
22 Snowballs	2/	5.50
25 Lilacs	3/6	10/93-3/4
15 Lilacs	1/6	2.81-1/4
12 Syringas	2/	3.--
24 Syringas	1/3	3.75
11 Corchorus Japonica	1/3	1.68-3/4
12 Dogwood	2/	3.00
9 Dogwood	1/6	1.68-3/4
7 upright Honey Suckle	3/	2.62-1/2
31 Frieze Tree	2/	7.75
5 Judas Tree	3/	1.87-1/2
2 King Willow	2/	.50
5 Nine Barkd. Spirea	2/6	1.56-1/4
9 Magnolia Trepeteta	2/	2.25
26 Snowberries	1/6	4.87-1/2
24 Ribes Aurea	2/	6.--
13 Spindle Tree	2/6	4.06-1/4
6 Red Indian Currant	2/	1.50
8 Hypencuns	1/9	1.75
2 Viburnum	3/	.75
6 Symphon Racimosa	2/	1.50
2 Persian Lilacs	3/	.75
1000 Privets for Hedge $5. per hundred		50.--
		$149.12-1/2

For Labour Men's time

	Day's Work	at 14 shillings = $1.75
April 2	1	
3	1/2	.87-1/2
4	4	7.--
5	4	7.--
6	4	7.--
7	3	5.25
9	3	5.25
10	3	5.25
11	2-1/2	4.37-1/2
12	4	7.--
13	4	7.--
14	4	7.--
15	4	7.--
17	4	7.--
18	4	7.--
19	5	7.75
20	5-1/2	7.87-1/2
21	5-1/2	7.87-1/2
23	2	3.50
25	1	1.75
		$115.50

Rec'd of Chas A. Davis Four Hundred and fourteen Dollars in full for the annex'd Bill and hereby agree to replace by work any tree or trees which shall be found to prove incapable of taking root, and to adjust such as may prove badly planted. New York 10 May 1838 $414

In August 1839, there was another bill from Virtue for work done from March 13 to 18:

To work pruning and planting in Gramercy Park 6 days @ 14/ per day.		$10.50
April 28–May 8 Digging and cleaning 12-1/2 days		21.87-1/2
Trees	4 Catalpas at 8/	4.--
	2 Horse Chesnut 10/	2.50
	2 Willows 6/	1.50
	2 Basswood 8/	2.00
	1 White Mulberry	1.00
	1 Elm	1.00
	2 Mountain Ash 7/	1.75
	2 Abel 10/	2.50
	2 Ailanthus 10/	2.50
	6 Sugar Maple 7/	5.25
Shrubs	4 Snowballs 2/	1.00
	15 Persian Lilacs 2/	3.75
	8 Double Altheas 2/6	2.50
	11 Berberasses 2/	3.00
	12 Relese & Spireas	2.75
July 26–29 To 3-1/2 days work cleaning		6.12-1/2
		$ 75.50

James Virtue 14 Desbroses St. [*sic*] or at Thorburns, or at Hogges or at Smiths Seed Store 388 Broadway.

Plate 40

Plate 39 *City receipt, June 4, 1842, for Samuel B. Ruggles's payment of the assessment for the laying of sidewalk on the north side of the Park.*
Plate 40 *Madison Avenue, looking northwest from Fifty-fifth Street, c. 1870, showing the Northwest Reformed Dutch Church under construction and "Marble Row" at the far left.*

By the summer of 1839, the Park was thus elaborately planted with fifty different kinds of trees and shrubs. Another gardener, William Laird, was hired, and, over the next few years, there were bills for grass cutting, filling, graveling of walks (begun on November 5, 1840, for $152.65, though the bill wasn't paid for two years and $20 was added in interest), digging sewers, city assessment for the paving of Twenty-first Street in June 1842 (Plate 39), repaving Gramercy Park West (324 yards at 10¢ = $32.40), curbs and gutters, and 52 feet of flagging from curb to gate ($5.20). Money had been collected from lot owners by both Ruggles and Charles Davis, who had themselves laid out the money for much of this work; each lot was assessed at ten dollars a year for seven years as of 1838. In that year, there were twenty-three individual owners, and Ruggles himself still owned five lots on the north side; by 1844, he had sold these increasing the number of owners to twenty-eight.

In 1844, new Trustees had to be elected, for of the original Trustees Thomas Mercein had died and Philo Ruggles and Thomas Wells had resigned. They were replaced by Norman White, who owned lots 1, 2, 4, 5, 6, and 9; James W. Gerard, the owner of parts of 17 and 18; and William Samuel Johnson, who owned 20 and 21. When the newly constituted board first met on November 15, 1844, a committee was appointed to draw up by-laws, and a financial committee to examine the somewhat disorganized state of bills and assessments, paid and unpaid.

A city map of 1840 (Plate 38) designating the areas so far built up shows that some construction had taken place north of Union Square on both sides of Broadway, and on the west side of Third Avenue there were a few buildings north of Twenty-first Street, increasing in density between Twenty-fifth and Twenty-seventh streets. Otherwise, the district was open land. The streets and avenues had, by this time, been leveled, but their artificial grid had left gaping interstices, and the few eighteenth- or early-nineteenth-century houses that had survived had little relationship to the streets unless they had been realigned.

There is virtually no photographic documentation of the city this early. To gain a picture of what the area around Gramercy Park must have looked like, we must turn to later photographs taken farther north. The process of laying down the grid of streets as they moved slowly up the island was much the same thirty years later. The basic scene in a photograph taken thirty years later and thirty-five blocks farther north (Plate 40) is probably not dissimilar from that at, for instance, Third Avenue and Twentieth Street in 1840. Gramercy Park probably appeared like an oasis in a wilderness of devastation, its fifty varieties of little ornamental trees and shrubs progressing

Plate 41 *The 1866 water nymph fountain by an anonymous artist shown in operation, water issuing from the top and from both lower tiers. It stood twenty-one feet high, seven feet taller than the statue of Edwin Booth (Plate 149). The Japanese lantern (Plate 148) to the right belonged to Stanford White. Houses on Twenty-first Street can be seen beyond the fence, the window to the left of the fountain being in the bowed front of George Templeton Strong's house at No. 113.*

nicely behind their cast-iron fence, but flagrantly exposed, without the surrounding buildings that were meant to protect them. The first house on the Park was built only in 1843.

The Dripps Map of 1850 (Plate 42) shows the layout of gravel walks in the Park itself: a large elipse and a path around the perimeter with two circular arrangements at the north and south gates. By this time, a fountain had also been constructed, but it is not shown. The minutes of the November 15, 1844, Trustees' meeting record that it had been resolved that it was "expedient that a Jet d'Eau [later referred to as a 'Jit a Eau' and then as 'jet de Eau'] be erected." Charles Davis was asked to look into the matter.

If there was confusion as to the Fountain's spelling, there was greater confusion as to its design and how it would be paid for. At the March 5, 1845, meeting of the Trustees, a report was presented stating that the city, subject to the mayor's signature, had approved the use of the newly arrived Croton water for this fountain. As to its design, there had been an interview with a certain "Mr. Catherwood, an artist of acknowledged taste, and who lived two years in Rome and is familiar with its Fountains, who will cheerfully aid the Committee and plan and superintend the erection of the Fountain, for a reasonable compensation." The committee believed it would be necessary "to raise Three Thousand Dollars, which will be sufficient to erect the Basin, the necessary pipes, and upper Basins or cups to receive the water, which falls from one into the other; leaving the additional ornamental Statuary around the Fountain for future appropriation and erection." The money was to come from voluntary contributions in the "hope that no one will object to subscribe the necessary sum, as the Fountain will be a great ornament to the Park and a striking feature to that part of the City, and will add . . . when erected and in operation $500 to the value of every lot for sale."

The proposal, delightfully naive in its enthusiasm, was "to carry out as near as may be the Plan of one of the Fountains erected in front of St. Peter's Church in Rome, which are acknowledged to be the most beautiful in Europe." One "great advantage of this plan of Fountain [would] be that it is very effective at a moderate expenditure of water, much less than the quantity used by any of the Public Fountains yet put up in this City."

The mayor signed the permission; Mr. Coffin, the president of the Board of Water Commissioners, approved a four-inch jet, with the occasional use of other five-inch jets; the annual cost of the water was set at twenty dollars. The Novelty Iron Works provided the lowest bid to "take the key of the Park, make the Basin, furnish all the Pipes and Stopcocks, do all the Excavation, make the Fountain, erect and paint it and return the key with the Fountain complete, the larger plan for $5,300, the lesser one for $4,800." At the December 16 meeting, it was resolved to appeal to lot owners for fifty dollars each and so raise three thousand dollars because "a tasteful fountain cannot be built for less than" that. But at the following meeting, on April 9, 1846, it was decided that "it [was] inexpedient, as yet, to erect a fountain in the Park," and the proposal was tabled.

At their next meeting on March 24, 1847, the Trustees resolved "that for the preservation and due Culture of the Grass, Shrubbery and Flowers of the Park, two Hydrants, one at each end of the elipse, are needed, and that in making such hydrants, it is expedient to construct an ornamental *Jet d'eau* in the center of the Elipse." The Park gardener, Alexander Wilson, was reappointed at two hundred dollars for his eight-month term, and instructed to purchase a hundred dollars worth of sand to improve the walks of the Park. On April 3, plans for a "drip Fountain" were presented and approved, and its construction authorized "at an expense not exceeding $1,500" to be collected from the lot owners.

The work was begun late that fall and completed in the spring of 1848. The sculpture that surmounted the fountain is unfortunately nowhere described. That it did, in fact, exist, however, is proven by the resolution at a Trustees' meeting on April 28, 1866, "to sell the old fountain statue without delay, and pay in the proceeds . . . [which turned out to be $40.98] toward the expense of a new statue," which was to cost no more than $150. This was the water nymph by an anonymous artist which remained in place until 1918, when it was moved to the east side of the Park.

Plate 42 *Detail from New York City map published by M. Dripps in 1851, showing the extent to which Gramercy Park area was built up at that time. The east side of the Park was still an open marble yard. The first Calvary Church building had been sold to Tenth Presbyterian Church.*

Plate 43 *Gramercy Park West, looking north toward Nos. 103–109 East Twenty-first Street, September 1905. Visible are Calvary Church rectory and the houses built for Philip Kearny, Olivia Templeton, and George Washington Strong. Shutters are closed because people were still out of town for the summer.*

5

George Templeton Strong and His "Palazzo"

Of the earliest houses built around Gramercy Park, the one for which the fullest contemporary description survives belonged to George Templeton Strong. Born in 1820, Strong grew up in downtown New York in his family's house at No. 108 Greenwich Street near the corner of Rector, and as a child he played in Battery Park and got to know all the docks along West Street. His father, George Washington Strong, was a prominent lawyer who walked to his office every morning on Pine or, later, Wall Street, and who so enjoyed the *Iliad* or the New Testament in Greek that he had to limit the amount of reading he could allow himself on weekdays, and only on Sunday indulge in it as he pleased. He considered his son's education to be so important that, having sent him to Columbia Grammar School, he boasted of spending every evening with him from six to ten o'clock while he studied. The boy went on to Columbia College, where he also distinguished himself as a brilliant student, and at eighteen, he entered his father's law office, becoming, as time went on, a specialist in realty and probate cases. At fifteen, he had begun a diary that he kept all his life and in which he described everything that happened in some detail and often with sharp wit—four million words in all. It is in this diary that we have one of the best surviving records of life on Gramercy Park in its early years.[1]

Strong first mentions the Park in 1845 in an entry he wrote after taking a walk up Fifth Avenue on the evening of June 15. Musing about where he might want to live, he recorded that around his family's house on Greenwich Street "the metropolis is beginning to pass all toleration, and I think we shall be forced to become emigrants before we're much older. I'm thinking more and more of buying [in Gramercy Park] . . . . There's a nice lot on the corner of Twentieth Street and the anonymous little street that bounds Gramercy Park on the west whereon I've fixed my regards." But so, unknown to Strong, had its owner, Charles Augustus Davis, who would be building his own house on that lot the next year. The following evening, Strong went back and wrote that "Gramercy Park looks like a comfortable place—must make further inquiries touching real estate in that vicinage."

On those June evenings in 1845 he would have seen only two completed houses on Gramercy Park, Nos. 5 and 6, which had been built two years before. Nos. 14 through 20 were under construction and would be finished that year; No. 22 had been begun and would be finished the following year. But aside from these nine houses, all the other fifty-one lots around the Park were still vacant. If Strong did make any inquiries, nothing came of them, and it was not until almost two years later, on May 23, 1847, that he made any further mention of the matter. By this time, he could describe Greenwich Street as "a street of emigrant boarding houses and dirty drinking shops . . . not a pleasant place to live. So I shall not be greatly surprised if an emigration to the north is effected at last. I'm going to take the first step tomorrow morning by pricing some lots on Gramercy Park." But again there was nothing further confided to his diary.

That April he had gone to a soiree at No. 24 Union Place and met Samuel Ruggles's daughter, Ellen. He saw her again the following winter, and in the spring of 1848, he fell in love with her. From then on things moved quickly. A wedding was announced and, by the end of April, Strong's father had, himself, decided to buy lots 55 through 58 on the north side of Gramercy Park and build three houses on them—one for himself; one for his sister-in-law, Olivia Templeton, who had lived next door on Greenwich Street; and the third as a wedding present to his son and future daughter-in-law. In 1833, this land had been sold by Ruggles to one of the original Trustees, Thomas L. Wells. George Washington Strong, however, bought the four lots from Ruggles, who apparently had bought them back from the Wells family so that he could convey them directly to Strong.

In his diary on July 26, 1848, Strong wrote that "the house-building plans have undergone a series of mutations." He described how originally they had planned to build three wide houses on the four lots. But then both his aunt and his father decided they didn't want anything so grand. As Strong puts it, his father "became refractory" and "struck" for a house of ordinary width. They ended up building two houses twenty-seven and a half feet wide, and one at thirty-five feet with a twenty foot garden next to it.

On April 28, he wrote that excavation was to have begun for the houses

> [on] Wednesday night [April 26] at 23 minutes past seven P.M. Hibernia [Irish workmen, presumably] came to the rescue yesterday morning; twenty "sons of toil" with prehensile paws supplied them by nature with evident reference to the handling of the spade and the wielding of the pickaxe and congenital hollows on the shoulder wonderfully adapted to make the carrying of the hod a luxury instead of a labor commenced the task yesterday morning.
>
> What the object may be of putting us into a forty-foot house and how soon such an establishment is going to reduce us to an insolvent state, and whether it is or is not absurd in me to acquiesce in this lamb-like way I've not yet clearly settled in my mind.

The wedding took place in Grace Church on May 15, and on July 26, he was able to write that the new houses were well under construction:

> Mr. Ruggles very kindly gives us a stone front and a kind of architectural bay window for Ellen's boudoir or snuggery on the west side. The house will cost a clear $25,000., of which fact I don't think my father has yet a full realizing sense. As to furnishing, I've called in a little $2000 investment which will do something, and for the balance I trust to economy of income during the coming year, and those comprehensive words "somehow or other."
>
> Going into so large a house and starting on so grand a scale is not in accordance with my "private judgment." But they tell me I'm safe and I hope it will be so. . . .

Plate 44 *Map of Gramercy Park area. Shaded building is the George Templeton Strong house.*
Plate 45 *No. 113 East Twenty-first Street (formerly No. 74); house built by George Templeton Strong. Photograph, 1919.*

> In all my happiness there's but one drawback—a sad kind of indefinite foreboding that it is too great to last, a feeling that in this world people cannot expect more than a short interval of contentment and prosperity and perfect happiness like what I'm now enjoying.

He reported further on its progress on September 10:

> [the] Gramercy Park houses [were] prospering. . . . How I shall furnish the *Schloss am Square* [his name for his new house] when it's finished, without borrowing, is an inscrutable problem about which I think it prudent not to trouble my head at present.

But on September 30, he still had misgivings about the costs:

> The Twenty-First Street Palazzo coming on fast. In the name of the Sphinx, *what* will I do with it when it's finished and possession delivered? Carpets and mirrors and Louis Quatorze chairs and Buhl tables and ormolu gimcracks cost money, and unless I happen to pick up a large roll of $100 bank notes in the street and fail in discovering the loser, or find myself unexpectedly remembered with a bouncing legacy in the will of some one of my numerous clients who may have been struck with an admiring appreciation of my talents, virtues, and accomplishments, or commit a brilliant and successful bank robbery, or am somehow favored with some sort of unprecedented good luck, I don't see but that I'm likely to find the question of ways and means complicated and embarrassing.

In October, he and his wife moved into a house owned by Samuel Ruggles at No. 54 Union Place, between Seventeenth and Eighteenth streets, until their house was ready. Throughout the next year, he recorded his feelings and the slow but steady construction of his new little castle:

> [*February 19, 1849*] Commenced on Friday the melancholy business of taking down the books from my shelves in Greenwich Street and boxing them up for removal to the basement of No. 54, where they are to remain till the Twenty-first Street house is ready for them. It's mournful work pulling them down from the places where I've been so happy in putting them and from which they've looked down on me through so many long desolate winter evenings, the shelves where I've watched them accumulating and multiplying so long. As yet I've made but little impression on the job before me, but after the first ten minutes of removal there was a great gap left that will never be filled up again. I believe my sense of local attachment must be very strong, for it made me feel quite disconsolate to look at the breach I had made.

> [*March 1*] First day of Spring. . . . Operations recommenced on the Twenty-first Street Palazzo and the stairs now going up.

> [*March 16*] Prosecuted the book-packing job yesterday afternoon and got my thirteenth box packed full. I shall send up the first division of the library before long. . . . Meantime I'm nervous about them and apprehensive, not of moth and rust, but of rats and damp, and I shall feel fidgety and uneasy till they are fairly disinterred and ranked on their new shelves.
>
> I look in at the Palazzo Strong almost daily now, and my heart is rejoiced by the sight of some daily progress—small but consolatory as far as it goes. The stairs is now up and rampant; the "white finish" is establishing itself in the third story, certain bold creations of carpenter work that look like window frames are accumulated in the parlor, and the aspect of affairs is much more encouraging and hopeful than it was during the long winter period of entire inactivity. I wish the house was finished. I wish the furniture was bought. I wish the furniture was paid for.

> [*March 21*] Conferences with Harriot and Henry [the contractors] touching doors, stained glass, "cornishes," centerpieces, and "enrichments." Heaven be praised that I'm in the hands of honest people, for my stupendous ignorance and my capability of being imposed on would be tempting and irresistible facilities to a knavish builder. As it is, I sometimes think that that house will hurry me into an early grave. It is not particularly pleasant to be running up big bills for oneself to pay but it's ten times worse to be running them up in this way; and though I know that my father won't breathe a syllable of dissatisfaction at any of these expenditures, yet it's bitterly annoying to feel that I'm incurring them for him, and I sometimes seem to feel my hair turning gray as I meditate on plumbers' bills, extra finish, and dealings with workers in marble.

Plate 46 *George Templeton Strong. Photograph made from an 1857 daguerreotype.*

[*March 22*] My malediction on marble mantels! How much more simple, how far less expensive, how inexpressibly superior in dignity, comfort, cheerfulness, and artistic effect was the fire in the middle of the floor and the hole in the middle of the ceiling wherewith our respectable Anglo-Saxon ancestors warmed the wall of the grange and the Refectorium of the Mynchery! Why should we shrink from the smoke which so many illustrious Ethelwalds and Etherlberts, not to speak of their more illustrious Norman invaders—DeVeres and Taillefers and Courterrais—not only tolerated but snuffed up with enjoyment. . . .

[*March 30*] Palazzo is advancing rapidly; arches run in the hall, cornices commencing in front parlors and second story . . .

[*April 30*] Comfortless, desolate, and uninhabitable is the aspect of the house, everything out of order, every place cumbered with the precious rubbish that has been painfully carried up from 108.

[*May 4*] Front stoop finished, everything advancing with tolerable rapidity. . . .

[*May 25*] Most reckless expenditure of plaster in the hall; a grand frieze runs around it like that of the Parthenon depicting a sort of procession of *Testaceous Mollusca*. I shall name it the "Battle of the Bivalves."

[*June 6*] . . . They're going on fast in Twenty-first Street, laying marble in the hall, got up Ellen's pretty boudoir window, mantels in the second story. . . .

[*June 13*] Palazzo gets on but slowly. N.B. If I had foreseen the annoyance that house was to give me, I'd never have had it built . . . endless additions and alterations over and above the contract. . . . Some of these, by the by, have been put in by Messrs. Harriot and Henry contrary to my positive directions, but the parties interfering did so out of good nature and inability to keep from devising and improving and arranging. However, it must be stopped. . . .

[*June 15*] That prodigious Twenty-first Street house staring me in the face, and saying from every one of its drawing rooms and boudoirs: "We shall have to be furnished next fall. . . . "

Ruskin is right—no man's happiness was ever promoted by the splendors of rosewood and brocatelle and ormolu and tapestry carpets; they'll never give pleasure to their possessor or to those who come and see them, except as a perfect suit of tattooing gives pleasure to a Sandwich Islander. The tyranny of custom makes the one agreeable to us in spite of the expense, and the other agreeable to the scarified savage in spite of the pain of his acquisition.

[*July 31*] In the *Schloss* the doors are hung in the third story and basement, library advancing, and door trimmings in progress in parlors. Henry [the contractor] concedes that it may be a *little* later than September 1 before it's quite finished.

Plate 47 *The Strong houses, with spires of Calvary Church in the distance, as they appeared in the 1850's. Rendering by E. P. Chrystie, 1951.*

[*August 3*] Got into the *Schloss* last night by the back window, by help of a stepladder, and inspected its progress. . . .

[*September 21*] The Palazzo comes on fast. Furniture will soon begin to appear and the wilderness and the solitary places will blossom like the rose, with gilt gas fixtures, furnaces, and yellow brocatelle. One carpet indeed has already defined its position, in the third story, and tomorrow the furnaces are to be fired up and the gas turned on. My books, that is the part of them that reposed in the little Fourth Avenue basement, are looking lovely from behind their plate glass, and nothing remains to be done in that department but to provide for the quartos that are stowed away at my father's. Certainly the Palazzo is handsome, well arranged and well built; there's not a house in the city I'd prefer to live in. . . .

[*September 28*] No. 54 was abandoned last night. We were to have slept in the Palazzo, but the house had a raw, uninhabited, unwholesome shade of chilliness in its atmosphere, so I turned Ellen out of it, took tea at home for the last time, slept at my father's and breakfasted there this morning—board and lodging gratis and no additional charge for mosquitoes, of which vermin I killed four under the net this morning. . . . The Palazzo is beginning to look as if it might be habitable and comfortable at no remote period. The organ is going up in the third parlor. Dining room carpeted, second story all finished and filled with furniture, a mighty maze and quite without plan, a chaos of chairs and tables. Certain females called Smack have got through with their appointed task—that of making covers for parlor furniture—and the parlors will be carpeted next week.

[*October 1*] Spent the afternoon in putting up and getting rid of the last arrearages of my library. Took our first meal in the new house that evening: a very satisfactory tea with Mr. & Mrs. Ruggles, my father and mother. . . . Slept there that night. [The house, it appears, cost $30,427.94, which had been advanced by George Washington Strong to be deducted from inheritance without interest.]

[*October 28*] We are beginning to look more like a habitation for Christian men and women now, and less like a deserted garret or the ruins of Palmyra or any other type of unfurnished desolation and loneliness . . . the three parlors . . . in uncarpeted nakedness. Yesterday, however, the work of organizing chaos began and carpets are now down, and furniture partly in its place. The music room is furnished and the dining room likewise. . . . The vast 'middle room' . . . is as sparsely settled (with chairs and sofas) as the Great West.

[*October 30*] "Scratchcoated" throughout and coming on reasonably fast. It looks spacious, scrumptious and imposing. . . .

[*December 31*] Sit down to write this evening in dress coat and state breeches—not as of old to announce that I've got to go to a party, but to certify to incredulous generations yet to come that I'm going to have one!!!

. . . Doubtless it will be very nice, provided the ice cream don't make default or the boned turkey forget to come or all the champagne prove bad, or some other contretemps happen. . . .

Quarter to eight: the tocsin of the street door bell will soon begin to sound the alarm. Very strange that I never used to appreciate or realize the awful state of mind in which people have been who have received me on various occasions at parties big and little, not withstanding their beaming countenances and nonchalant demeanor. . . .

After the completion of the house, Strong mentions Gramercy Park itself only infrequently in his diary. There are, however, glimpses, such as that for February 17, 1851, when the news arrived that the steam sailing ship *Atlantic,* which had been in dangerous seas, was safe.

A herd of highly excited newsboys communicated [the news] to Gramercy Square at about 11:30 P.M. [I] tumbled out of bed, and downstairs in an ethereal costume, and got an extra. I did not get the rheumatism, though the winds of heaven visited my legs roughly as I bellowed for a paper at the front door. . . .

And on February 27, 1852, he wrote that "Charles Augustus Davis wants to toady [Washington] Irving by getting the name of Gramercy Park changed to Irving Place and sticking a statue of Irving, or [Peter] Cooper—I don't know which—in the centre [*sic*] of it." Needless to say, nothing came of this.

The diary remains, however, the longest, most intimate chronicle of day-to-day life behind any Gramercy Park windows, and continued on through the quarter century that Strong lived there. He describes playing Mozart symphonies, four-handed, on

Plate 48 *Gramercy Park, northwest quadrant, c. 1916, presided over by N. LeBrun and Sons' superb Metropolitan Life Tower of 1909.*

a February evening; reading the latest installments of Charles Dickens's *Bleak House* as they came out; and a Christmas Eve—which, in 1853, was an "appropriate bitter frosty night" and "lively Ellie receiving and sending out presents, and enthusiastic over the black lace I got her. Sophie [a nursemaid] has dressed up a little table with all Johnny's [the Strongs' first child] presents . . . and candles and Christmas greens, and

Plate 49 *Nos. 113–121 East Twenty-first Street, 1919.*
Plate 50 *Nos. 103–109 East Twenty-first Street being demolished, 1927.*
Plate 51 *Nos. 113–115 East Twenty-first Street, 1928, the year they were demolished. No. 60 Gramercy Park is just being completed.*

Plate 49

Plate 50

Plate 51

everybody that came into the house has been trotted up to the nursery to see." Each entry, no matter what the subject, infuses with lasting freshness these moments in long-gone days in a house now itself gone. As he wrote in his diary for April 2, 1850, about the Fourth Avenue house he had lived in while his own was being built:

> I never pass . . . [it] and look up at those windows . . . without thinking how much every commonplace abode in this city has to tell of the tragedy and comedy of life that has passed within it. . . . How serious a thing is any row of monotonous twenty-five foot brick fronts, if one considers what each of them has witnessed. . . . A house gains a kind of domestic consecration from [its] goings on. . . . Births and deaths and marriages and all the events of social life, pleasant meetings, nice visits, sorrowful partings, household troubles escaped or endured—of such things is made up the Life, as it were, of every Dwelling Place of Men—and a new house that has had no time to be the theatre of human action and sorrow and joy, and has no *past* to be remembered or imagined by those who sojourn in it, is like a western prairie, or an unexplored tropical forest when thought of in connection with the richly storied towns and cities of the Old World where generation has followed generation. . . .

Note

[1] Alan Nevins and M.H. Thomas, eds., *The Diary of George Templeton Strong*, 4 vols. (New York: Macmillan & Co., 1952).

Plate 52 *Nos. 3 and 4 Gramercy Park, 1936. Photograph by Berenice Abbott.*

6

Major Architects Begin Building

When George Templeton Strong paid his first visit to Gramercy Park in June 1845, only two houses were standing on the west side of the Park, and none at all on the entire north side. When he returned in May 1847, some definite changes had taken place. The lot he had admired at the corner of Twentieth Street and the Park was the site of a handsome house designed by one of the most famous architects of his day, Alexander Jackson Davis. And almost next door to the lots on the north side, which he himself was to build on the next year, was a large church that had just been built by his old friend James Renwick, Jr. Davis and Renwick were the first of the four nationally known architects who were to work directly on the Park, the others being Calvert Vaux and Stanford White.

Though he lived most of his life in New York City, Alexander Jackson Davis (1803–92) was not primarily an urban architect, but a designer of Gothic Revival country villas. His best work is boldly geometrical, characterized by steep gables and decorative bracketing, and for his grander commissions he provided marvelously picturesque houses that look like castles, churches, or temples. Lyndhurst at Tarrytown, New York, his most famous surviving house, was built from 1838 to 1842 in the Gothic style, and in 1846, he had just finished a crenellated suburban castle at Fifth Avenue and Thirty-seventh Street for W. Coventry H. Waddell. He also had tried his hand at extensive rows of houses such as London Terrace on Twenty-third Street, which ran the full distance between Ninth and Tenth avenues and was also completed in 1846.

In 1842, Davis made a sketch of a symmetrical group of houses for the entire west side of Gramercy Park (Plate 54). The identical flanking houses in the sketch, the severity of which is softened only by cast-iron porches, are very like the 1834 Brevoort house on Fifth Avenue attributed to Davis and Ithiel Town. The centerpiece of the scheme is more ornate, its roofline decorated with balustrades stepping down on either side. Davis also drew its extended cast-iron veranda in greater detail on the sketch. While the project was never realized, ornamental verandas like these were ultimately used on four of the houses that were built on Gramercy Park West—Nos. 5 and 6 in 1843, and the beautiful symmetrical pair of No. 3 and No. 4 in 1847 (Plate 52).

Iron railings, fences, and balconies were not uncommon in New York during this period. Firms such as Daniel Badger's Architectural Ironworks or J.B. and W.W. Cornell (Plate 55) produced them in great quantity. At No. 3 and No. 4 Gramercy Park, almost the complete repertoire of Greek Revival design is displayed: anthemion (stylized honeysuckle), vines, frets (Greek keys), rosettes, wheels (the classical symbol of eternity), and floral arrangements of many kinds. Classical motifs were popular in this country not least because they reminded newly independent Americans of the Greek roots of their democracy. Now, in the new medium of cast iron, by which intricate designs could be endlessly and economically repeated, the world of classical ornament, previously restricted to prohibitively expensive carved wood or stone, was suddenly available to any prosperous citizen. Soon it blossomed around doorways and windows all over New York, replacing the former Federal severity.

Nowhere except perhaps in New Orleans did it

Plate 53

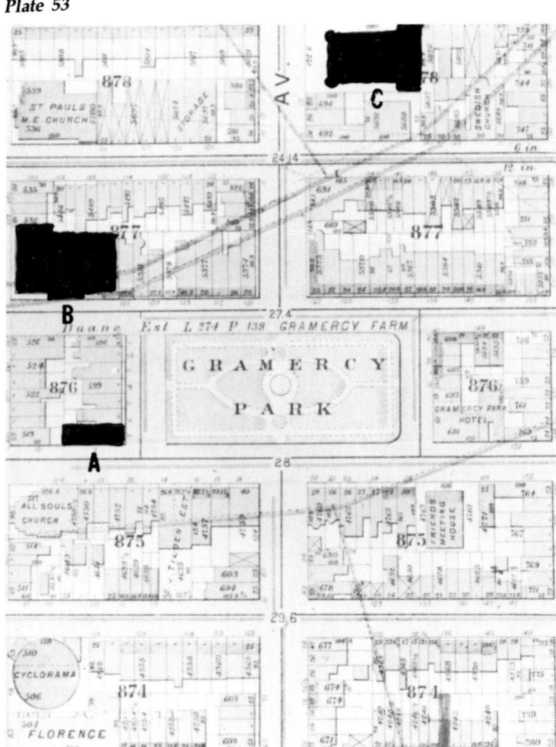

Plate 53 *Map of Gramercy Park area. Shaded buildings are a) Charles A. Davis house; b) Calvary Church and rectory; and c) Free Academy.*
Plate 54 *Sketch of a proposal by Alexander Jackson Davis for the west side of Gramercy Park, February 1842.*

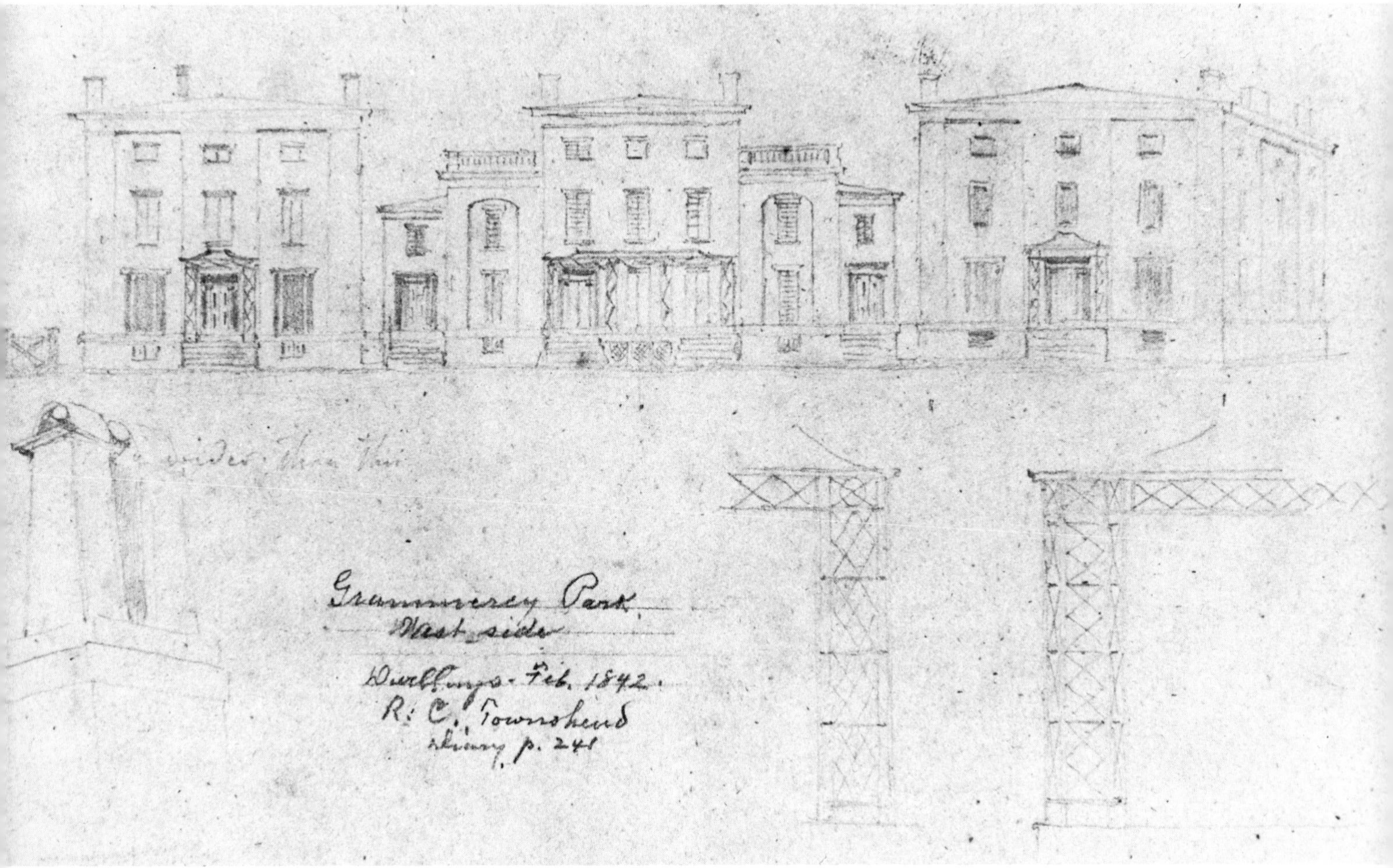

Plate 54

Plate 55

Plate 56

appear in such stunning profusion as at Gramercy Park West; however, its richness increased when "mayor's lamps" were placed in front of No. 4, the house bought in 1847 by James Harper, a former mayor of New York. This custom of special lamps dated from the days when mayors wanted to be available in case of nighttime emergency.

Davis's major work in Gramercy Park, however, was the house he designed for Charles Augustus Davis (no relation) at No. 7 (Plate 58). Charles Augustus Davis had been one of the original Trustees of the Park, and had bought all the lots on the west side from Ruggles before 1833. The house built for him was not the one in the architect's 1842 sketch, for by the time Alexander Jackson Davis received the commission, the row houses immediately next door had already been built, limiting his freedom with the project.

An elevation of the new house drawn by the architect in 1846 survives and agrees in many of its details with the actual house as it appeared in a photograph taken in 1905, seven years before it was demolished (Plate 59). The house lacked the prominent skylights and balcony that had relieved its severity in the original elevation, and had two-story bay windows. However, the arrangement of windows, the cornice, and the cut-stone trim were there in 1905 exactly as drawn in the original elevation.

Several of the mason's bids, all dated in the spring of 1846, also survive for the house. One, from

Plate 55 *Display advertisement, Cornell Iron Works, c. 1859.*
Plate 56 *No. 4 Gramercy Park; ironwork on balustrade.*

James Herriot for $8,373, agrees to dig the cellar; pave it with round stone; provide bluestone rubble-work walls, two floors of exterior walls using Philadelphia pressed brick (Calahah brick at the rear); and supply "deafening" on three floors (the use of pugging, or bricks and mortar, between floors for sound-proofing), cut stone for the exterior trim, and plastered lath for the entrance hall and parlors. Another, dated April 6, from the firm of Latson and Stewart, Third Avenue at Twenty-second Street, reads charmingly, "We repose to bild [*sic*] your house."

In May 1846, at the same time that Alexander Jackson Davis was watching construction begin on his Gramercy Park house, James Renwick, Jr., could have

Plate 57

Plate 58

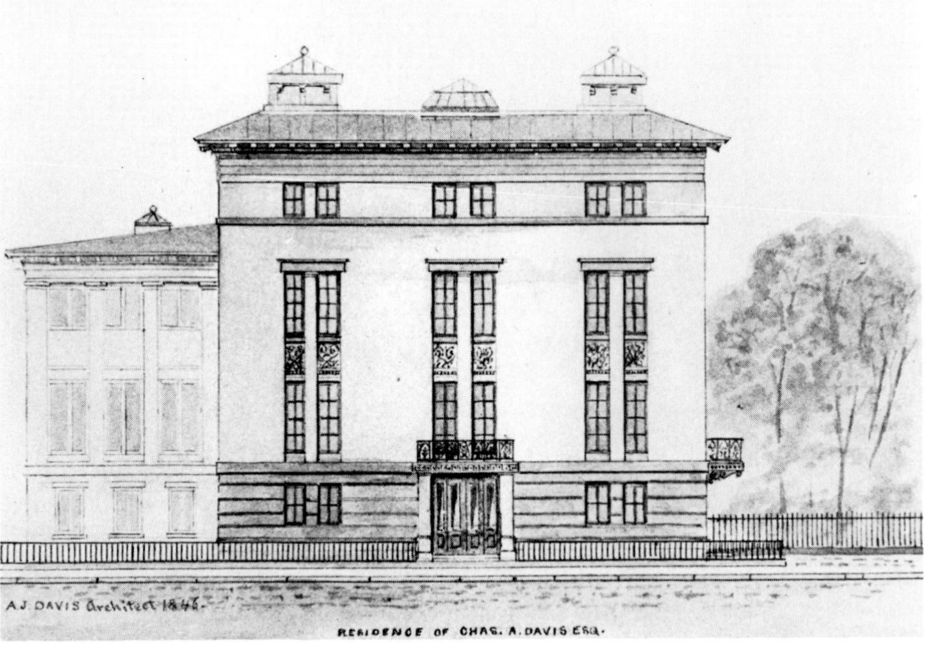

Plate 59

Plate 60

been found just around the corner watching the excavation for Calvary Church. Just two houses, No. 5 and No. 6 Gramercy Park West, stood between the two construction sites, though Nos. 3 and 4 also had just been begun. It had been only fourteen years since the land had been leveled and, at this end of the Park, seventeen feet of earth removed, and there was probably scarcely a tree in sight except in the Park itself and around its immediate perimeter. The scene must have looked not unlike that in Plate 65, for all the houses being built in the neighborhood were, of course, to be row houses, but often built in groups of two or three.

At the corner of Fourth Avenue and Twenty-second Street, however, was the original building of Calvary Church, a small frame structure surrounded by eighteen little trees. It had been moved there in 1841 from its original site, farther up Fourth Avenue (or Rail Road as it was also called) at Thirtieth Street, which had turned out to be too far out in the "country." The list of contributors who had paid for the move was headed by Samuel B. Ruggles, who had put himself down for a hundred dollars, one fourth of the cost. The contractor had agreed to "carry and convey" the church down Rail Road, and promised that it would be "delivered and deposited" within twenty-five days in "as good plight and condition" as before. He did not specify by what means it would be moved; he may have used the new tracks of the New York and Harlem Railroad, which ran down the middle of Fourth Avenue. Four years after the church was moved, however, the little building had proved to be too small, and it had been decided to build again one block south at Twenty-first Street on land that had also formerly been part of Rose Hill Farm.

Early in 1845, James Renwick, Jr., was asked to

Plate 57 *No. 4 Gramercy Park; mayor's lamp.*
Plate 58 *No. 4 Gramercy Park; entrance.*
Plate 59 *No. 7 Gramercy Park; elevation of proposed house for Charles A. Davis. Drawn by Alexander Jackson Davis, 1846.*

Plate 60 *Gramercy Park West, September 1905. House by A.J. Davis in foreground. Note, iron verandas at Nos. 5 and 6 were similar to those which have survived at Nos. 3 and 4.*

Plate 61

Plate 62

Plate 63

Plate 61 Detail from an engraving by James Smillie (Plate 22), c. 1849, of the vicinity of Union Square, showing Calvary Church.
Plate 62 No. 1 Gramercy Park, c. 1900.
Plate 63 Calvary Church, 1893; the Church Missions House to the north under construction.
Plate 64 Calvary Church as it looked between 1854, when the houses north of the church were built, and 1860, when its spires were removed. Rendering by Manlio Abele, 1984.
Plate 65 Row houses on West 133rd Street near Lenox Avenue, 1882.

Plate 64

Plate 65

submit plans for the new church. He was then twenty-six and his marvelous first building, Grace Church, was already under construction at Broadway and Tenth Street. By March 7, the outline of his scheme had been marked out on the ground, and on December 8, his projected church, to be built in the white marble he had used at Grace Church, was approved. The following February, the plans were altered, substituting "brown stone of a light color" for the original marble. The change apparently was not made because brown stone was less expensive; one of the mason's bids states that to build in marble would actually cost less. But brown stone may have been selected because its use had been admired at Richard Upjohn's neighboring Church of the Holy Communion, just finished in 1845 and located at Twentieth Street and Sixth Avenue; another mason's estimate specifies that he would use stone similar to that which Upjohn had used.

Grace Church had demonstrated Renwick's early fascination with the Gothic style, which he learned from books and from his erudite father, a professor of engineering at Columbia and a person of great learning who not only kept all the latest European books on architecture on hand and available to his son, but had first-hand impressions and sketches made on a walking trip on the Continent with Washington Irving to share with him. Calvary Church, in contrast to Grace, showed the young architect beginning to experiment and depart from the strict canons of Gothic. A five-windowed skylight appeared at the peak of the apse, the pronounced gables of the west front and transepts were not maintained by the roof, and a severe, almost Romanesque eave cut off the upward thrust of the buttresses. The two identical spires were not in keeping with the basically Early English Gothic of the rest of the church, nor was the five-sided apse at the east end (Plate 68). The church was an eclectic mixture of English and continental elements. George Templeton Strong, who had been at Columbia with Renwick but had no love for him, pronounced the new church "a miracle of ugliness." He had also observed that the "pipe-cleaner columns" of Grace Church might "suggest profitable meditation on the instability of things temporal."

The idea of twin spires, as yet a new one to the Gothic Revival, may have come to Renwick from an influential 1821 engraving by the art historian Sulpice Boisseree of the proposed west end of Cologne Cathedral. The engraving would have very likely been in

Plate 66

Renwick's father's library; indeed, the cathedral itself, when finished, was to have a major impact on Renwick's masterpiece, St. Patrick's Cathedral.[1]

The Calvary spires were, in fact, the direct ancestors of those at St. Patrick's. They did not grow integrally out of their towers, however, nor straight from the ground, as they do at St. Patrick's; in fact, there never really were proper towers at Calvary: its octagonal towers sprang from gables that gave them little or no preparation. They were like an elegant continental afterthought added onto an English church; this is probably one reason Renwick removed the spires in September 1860, when they had already become unstable, and left only the octagonal bases (themselves removed in 1929). Whether or not he had learned from his mistakes at Calvary, Renwick did not repeat them at St. Patrick's.

The only photographs of Calvary Church with its spires in place are those taken around 1857, looking up Fourth Avenue past the Union Square statue of George Washington (Plates 70 and 105). Seen from this angle, one spire disappears behind the other, the discontinuity of the ensemble cannot be seen, and the beautiful proportions of the spires themselves read effectively on the skyline. (For the carpenter's specifications for one of the spires, see Appendix C.)

Once inside the church, however, the discongruities of the exterior disappear (Plate 71). The lofty vault extends unbroken for 142 feet, its interaction with the transept vaulting beautifully accomplished. It is made of plaster reinforced with horse-

Plate 67

hair. (A bill survives for a delivery of nine casks of lime, eleven loads of sand, five casks of plaster, and five bushels of hair.) The nave columns have fluted plaster on wooden cores of nine- by nine-inch white pine (iron cluster columns had at one point been suggested, but they were not used), and the mason described them as being "run with gaged mortar and capped with handsome foliage." The interior of the church has a lightness that must have been even more remarkable before stained glass darkened the windows, and a spaciousness, enhanced by the full-height transepts, that is quite unannounced by the exterior. The rounded east end, however incorrect, gathers and effectively focuses the space.

The contract for the masonry was made with Horace Butler for $25,250, and his specifications, worked out with Renwick, survive (see Appendix D). By April 20, 1846, he had excavated for the bulk of the church to a depth of eight feet below the curb line and built the foundations.

In January 1846, Renwick had also been commissioned to draw up plans for a rectory corresponding in style with the church. Lot 60 immediately behind

Plate 68

Plate 69

Plate 70

Plate 66 *Calvary Church, Fourth Avenue entrance; detail from an engraving by Samuel A. Deare, New York, 1847.*
Plate 67 *Calvary Church, Twenty-first Street entrance and rectory; detail from an engraving by Samuel A. Deare, New York, 1847.*
Plate 68 *Calvary Church; apse.*
Plate 69 *Calvary Church in the snow. Etching by Childe Hassam, nineteenth century.*
Plate 70 *View up Fourth Avenue past Henry K. Brown's statue of George Washington, showing the spires of Calvary Church, c. 1857.*

the church, which had been sold by Ruggles to Thomas L. Wells, another of the original Trustees of the Park, was acquired, and the rectory was begun in the spring of 1848. It was a steep-gabled Gothic Revival house built in the same brown stone as the church; consisting of two stories plus an attic, it was connected to the church by a double-bayed porch and entrance opening onto a small piazza (Plate 72). The windows were slender, pointed lancets except in the gables, where they were circular.

In May, while the house was under construction, Renwick made a number of changes in the original specifications, the sketches for which survive (Plate 73). These included a curving staircase and a bay window in the library at the rear of the house. The carpenter's bill for this work is dated January 26, 1849, and specifies that a skylight was not to be made of ground but of stained glass, and windowsills were to be made of locust wood rather than chestnut.

The house was ready by early that year. A photograph of an upstairs library taken somewhat later (Plate 74) shows the room lit by skylights, which in turn were lit by skylights in the roof, a favorite device of Renwick's. (It was on the flat roof outside this library that a later rector's daughter, Emelyn Washburn, and her friend, Edith Jones [Wharton], read Dante out loud to each other.) The clerestory windows in Calvary Church were lit by similar skylights, as were the side aisles in the chapel of Renwick's Free Academy, around the corner on Lexington Avenue, which was being built the same year as the rectory.

In 1848, twenty ailanthus trees had been set out in boxes along the front and side of the church and rectory, a flagstone sidewalk had been laid, and curb and gutters set. The November 1848 estimate for an iron fence like that "at Mr. Brevoort's House on 5th Avenue" was not acted on, but when a fence was finally built in 1852, it was taller and more elaborate than Mr. Brevoort's (Brevoort being, in fact, Renwick's grandfather), with the flaming urns and ornamental brackets it still boasts today.

Renwick's next commission in the neighborhood was the Free Academy, which stood at Lexington Avenue and Twenty-third Street from 1848 until it was replaced in 1928. As a result of an attempt to make higher education available to students in the city who could not afford to go to private colleges, a free high school had been proposed and, on May 7, 1847, the state legislature had passed an act calling for a public referendum. In June, it was approved by an overwhelming vote, and the Board of Education chose Renwick to build the new academy. The land was bought by the city for twenty-five thousand dollars from John and Louise La Farge, the parents of the

Plate 71

Plate 72

artist, and ground was broken early in November 1847.

George Templeton Strong noted the following in an entry in his diary on November 7: "New 'Free Academy' to be built by Jemmy Renwick after the manner of Flemish *Hotels de Ville*. Not a bad notion, if Jemmy were capable of building anything. . . . " Renwick's design was symmetrical and Gothic Revival, this being the only style he considered appropriate for a large public building (Plate 75). Its red-brick and brown-stucco walls with red-sandstone trim rose through three floors of Gothic windows to a tall, aisled chapel (Plate 76) running the full length of the building. The chapel, furnished with cane settees, had a beautiful collar-braced roof, and the side aisles were lit by skylights—no less adventurous an experiment than that in the apse of Calvary Church. The flues of its furnace were disguised as buttresses and their chimneys became towers. As reported in the New York *Tribune*, "There is no wasted room in any part of the building and the whole is brought into use up to the very peak of the roof—and the roof itself is so constructed that its chief weight is made to rest against the inner walls with scarcely any pressure against the outer." All four corners of the building had octagonal towers that rose an additional two stories above the eave and sported pepperbox turrets. They recalled the three pointed towers of the Smithsonian Institution, which Renwick had designed the previous year and was now also under construction. The Free Academy was a dramatic building befitting the bold educational experiment it housed.

The school was opened on January 15, 1849, to 143 students who were astonished to find central hot-air heating and classrooms equipped with comfortable chairs. A four-year college course was offered, preceded by an introductory class known as sub-freshman. The first president of the new academy was Horace Webster, who had been educated at West Point and was described by an early graduate as a cross between Cato and Andrew Jackson; he ruled with an iron rod. Every student was required to be in chapel by 8:40 A.M. to hear a chapter from the Bible and listen to orations by other students, for President Webster, who lived next door, was not only a strict master but superintendent of the Sunday School at St. George's Church on Stuyvesant Square. The original course of study included the classics and modern languages, and there was opportunity for specializa-

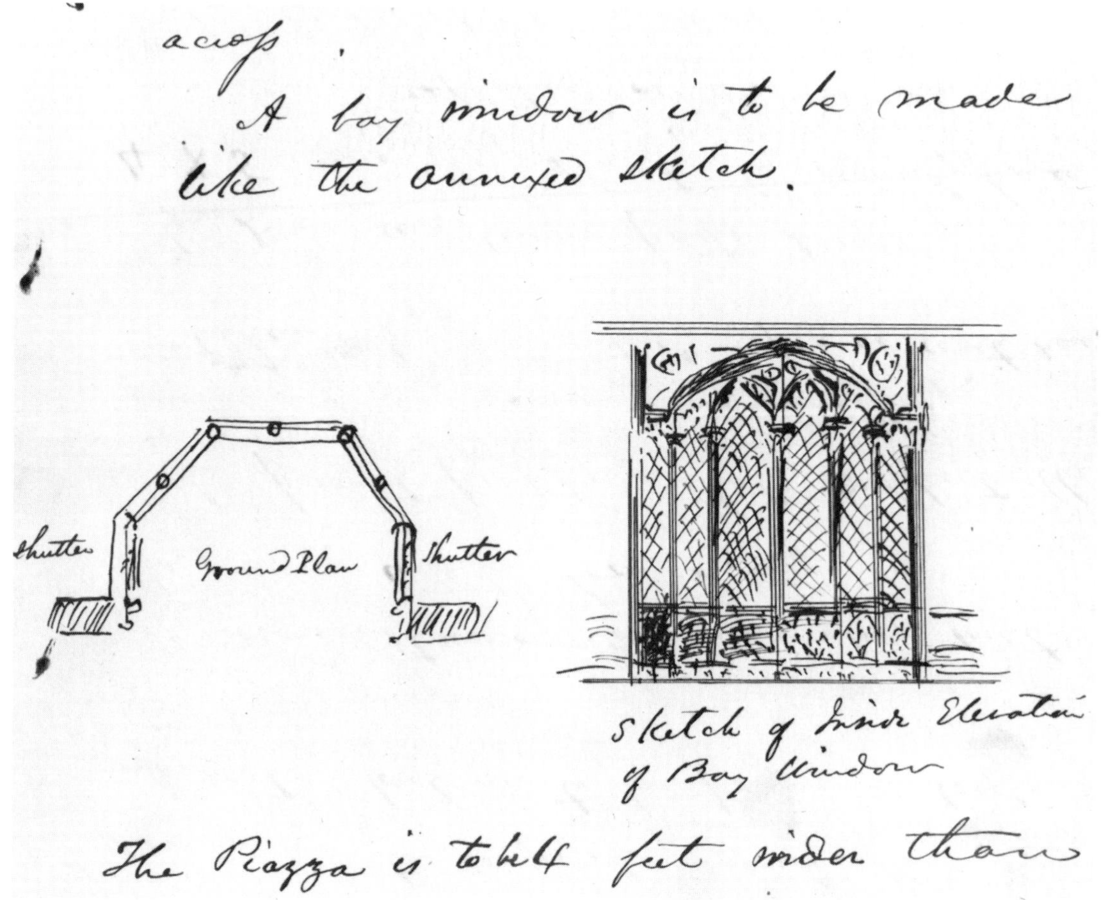

Plate 73

Plate 71 *Calvary Church, 1885.*
Plate 72 *James Renwick architecture: Calvary Church and rectory; in the distance the Free Academy. Photograph taken in 1912 during construction of the Gramercy Park Building, 257 Fourth Avenue.*
Plate 73 *Sketch by James Renwick of a proposed bay window for the rectory of Calvary Church, 1848.*

Plate 75

Plate 74 *Calvary Church Rectory; second-floor library. Photograph, c. 1885.*
Plate 75 *Free Academy, southeast corner of Lexington Avenue and Twenty-third Street. Photograph, c. 1860.*
Plate 76 *Free Academy; chapel, looking east.*
Plate 77 *Free Academy; southwest stair leading to chapel.*
Plate 78 *Clarendon Hotel, southeast corner of Fourth Avenue and Eighteenth Street. Photograph, early twentieth century, showing entrances to Eighteenth Street IRT station.*

Plate 76

Plate 77

Plate 78

tion. The academy grew rapidly in size and, in 1866, was renamed The College of the City of New York. Early in the twentieth century, the old building got to be so overcrowded that even the chapel was curtained off into classrooms; a new campus was finally built uptown on St. Nicholas Heights in 1905.

James Renwick received three further commissions in the vicinity of Gramercy Park, all on Fourth Avenue. In 1850, he built the Clarendon Hotel at Eighteenth Street for William B. Astor. It was designed in yellow brick with ornate terra-cotta window heads, brownstone trim, and cast-iron balconies (Plate 78). In 1852, William Makepeace Thackeray stayed there, and in 1871, the Grand Duke Alexis of Russia, or as George Templeton Strong called him, "our sweet young Duck of Muscovy." In his diary, Strong described the scores of people who stood outside the hotel in the rain "watching its windows . . . for a beatific vision of His Imperial Majesty" and concluded that "we are all sovereigns in America, and Alexis is a mere princeling."

In 1867, Renwick was again commissioned to build for Calvary Church, this time a small chapel at the north side of the church (Plate 63). Its single space rises deftly through open arches to a small Victorian clerestory capped by a prominent overhanging roof in multicolored slate.

Then, in 1869, he designed an imposing Beaux Arts building with a huge Second Empire mansard roof at Twenty-third Street for the YMCA. Its eclecticism was so rampant that all five floors had different Neo-Renaissance window styles. The Romanesque Fourth Avenue Presbyterian Church of 1856, next door, whose towers had once dominated the block, was now overshadowed by the YMCA's huge self-assured bulk (Plate 165).

It was, in fact, the first YMCA building in New York, and it contained the first gymnasium ever installed in a YMCA. There was even a billiard table, a gift of Mrs. J. P. Morgan, who had no idea of the association's stern disapproval of this form of recreation. The table was hidden in the basement until, in time, the prohibition softened, and it was allowed to be used at another branch.

The guiding spirit of this original Y was Robert Ross McBurney, who lived there from the day it was completed until his death in 1898, and whose office was arranged so that he could greet everyone who entered. One of his first tenants in 1869 was Louis Comfort Tiffany, who rented his first studio there.

The building lasted only until 1904. Its elaborate presence contrasted strikingly with Renwick's early plainer work two blocks south at Calvary Church, and must have made it look old-fashioned. But Renwick was always sensitive to current trends in architectural design, and once said his buildings were never intended to last much more than thirty years.

Note

[1] W. H. Pierson, Jr., *American Buildings and Their Architects* (Garden City: Anchor Books, 1980), p. 226.

Plate 79 *Peter Cooper, early 1860's. Photograph by Mathew Brady.*

7

Peter Cooper: Inventor and Friend of Inventors

In the fall of 1850, one of New York's most celebrated citizens, Peter Cooper, bought land and prepared to build himself a new house at the corner of Lexington Avenue and Twenty-second Street. Since 1826, he had lived at Fourth Avenue and Twenty-eighth Street, having moved there when it was open country. His house, in fact, had had to be positioned according to the piles of stones and iron bolts that marked where the streets would eventually go. Soon, however, the New York and Harlem Railroad was running steam engines down Fourth Avenue to Twenty-sixth Street. While steam was used only above Thirty-second Street after 1842, long trains of horse-drawn cattle cars were often left overnight on the tracks in front of the house, and the noise of the animals so disturbed the Coopers that they decided to move.

Peter Cooper had come to New York from Newburgh in 1808 at the age of seventeen to seek his fortune. He first worked for a coach maker, then in textiles and furniture, and even opened a successful grocery store at the corner of Stuyvesant Street and the Bowery. He was constantly tinkering, and, among other things, invented the first lawn mower. In 1821, he bought a glue factory at Kip's Bay, where he devised new methods of using waste products of the nearby slaughterhouses to make not only glue but isinglass, ink, household cement, neat's-foot oil, and gelatin—the first packaged gelatin produced in the United States. It was in order to be near his factory that he had moved his family to Twenty-eighth Street.

Cooper was also active in real estate in New York and in Baltimore, which in the 1820's was experiencing a building boom. He bought more land in Baltimore than could, in the end, be developed, and so he ingeniously decided to mine its iron ore, build brick kilns, and smelt his own iron. This venture depended on a proposed railroad—the Baltimore and Ohio line was beginning to lay tracks in 1829. George Stephenson's *Rocket* had proved itself in England that year, and the Delaware and Hudson Railroad imported its first engine, the *Stourbridge Lion*, from Stephenson. But the early English steam engines were too long to handle some of the sharper curves of the new American tracks, and again Peter Cooper's ingenuity came into play: he promised the president of the Baltimore and Ohio line that he would produce an engine that could negotiate these sharp curves. As he later put it, "I got up a little locomotive."[1] He found some old wheels and attached a boiler, and unable to find any iron pipes, he broke off the barrels of two muskets and used them. He produced a little engine that he first thought to call "Teapot" because it was so small, but ended up calling *Tom Thumb*. In August 1830, with Cooper at the controls and the president and directors of the B&O in an open car, *Tom Thumb* developed the great speed of 18 mph. But the next year, it lost its famous race with a horse-drawn stage because the belt slipped off its draft-fan blower and steam pressure fell. Although this was a sorely disappointing setback, Cooper's tenacity and cleverness had, in fact, helped win the larger victory of steam over horse in America. By 1834, the B&O had put seven American locomotives into use on tracks made by Cooper's ironworks.

It was, therefore, ironic that it should have been the railroad that compelled Cooper to move from

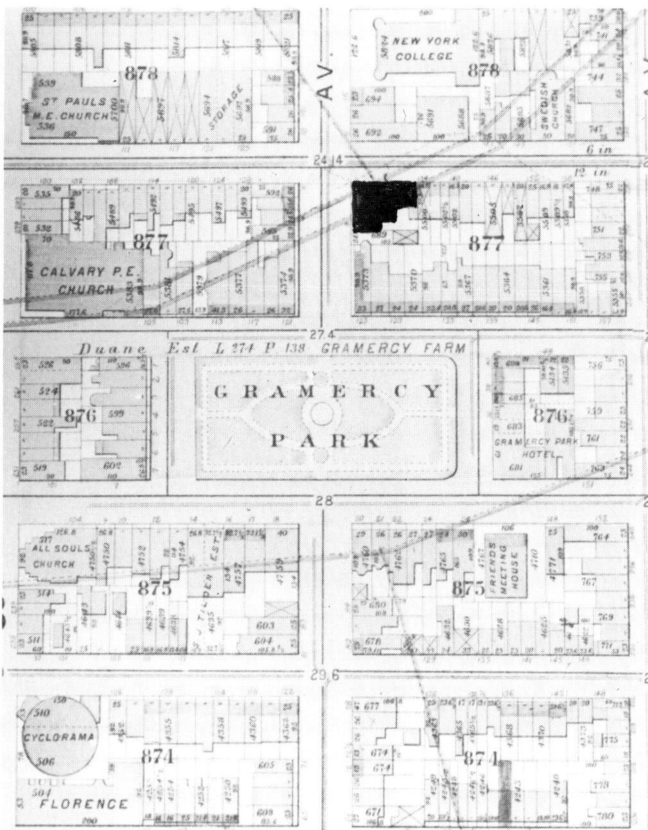

Plate 80 *Map of Gramercy Park area. Shaded building is Peter Cooper's house.*

Twenty-eighth Street down to Gramercy Park. But on September 20, 1850, he bought a plot of land 105 feet by 74 feet ¾ inches at the corner of Lexington Avenue and Twenty-second Street, from Thomas Ward. The address was No. 9 Lexington Avenue, and while it was not one of the sixty Gramercy Park lots, it was nevertheless subject to the restrictions on the Park Deed: there could be no slaughterhouse, smith shop, steam engine, iron factory, glue or ink making, etc. The list of prohibitions Ruggles had drawn up twenty years before sounds, in fact, strangely like a description of Peter Cooper's activities.

The new house, forty feet wide and fifty-six feet deep, was to be "carpenter-planned," and the specifications were prepared with some haste, for they were ready by October 4—just fourteen days after the purchase of the land. They called for a large, red-brick building with a high stoop and cast-iron window heads, a prominent cornice, and a square cupola at the center of the roof (Plates 81 and 84). The house had to be constructed on piles because its site was on land filled into what had been, twenty years before, the gully of Crommessie Vly. Behind were stables and a garden for which Cooper himself drew the plans. The garden was described as having, "in the center of a mound or circle to represent the great garden of the world, figures of our first parents, represented as looking round and listening to the voice of good saying through all that He has made, 'behold I have given you everything upon all the face of the earth.'"[2]

The house was ready by early 1852, when Peter Cooper was sixty-one years old. On entering, Cooper's study and bedroom were immediately to the right of the front door, whose bell he himself always answered. To the left were the parlor, dining room, and library; the kitchen, the servants' dining room, the room later used as the grandchildren's schoolroom, and the laundry were on the ground floor. Above the central staircase was a dome, eliptical in plan and elevation, its sash glazed with stained and enameled glass. Above the dome was a skylight at the base of the cupola, glazed with double-thickness French glass. The house was equipped with twelve bells, two being for the front door.

Little is known about Peter Cooper's wife, Sarah, except for one revealing incident related by Edward Ringwood Hewitt, the Coopers' grandson:

> [She had gone shopping one day, and had] put her hand into her dress pocket and found that her purse had been stolen. On another visit [to the same shop] it happened to her again, so she made up her mind to catch the thief in her own way. She made a strong canvas lining inside her dress, in which she sewed a canvas pocket with a strong thread. Inside the pocket she fastened pickerel fish hooks. . . . Then she stuffed the pocket with paper, and again went shopping. After a while she felt a strong tug at her dress and saw a man walking very quickly beside her. She turned and said, "I am going to the police station, and you are going with me." [The police] were obliged to dissect the hooks from the thief's hand.[3]

When Sarah Cooper died, after fifty-six years of marriage, Cooper wrote that she had been his "day star, the solace and the inspiration of his life," and it was said that even in old age "he never sat near her without holding her hand in his."[4] They had had six children, but only two had survived childhood. Cooper's description of one of his children's ordeals reveals how vulnerable people still were at this time.

> Sarah Amanda when born was a beautiful child, one of the prettiest we ever had. . . . The nurse who had charge when she was born in wintertime placed her on a pillow with her face to the bright, blazing fire. It brought on cataracts in both eyes. She became entirely blind. Dr. Mott [who later lived at No. 1 Gramercy Park] was employed to operate on her for the cataracts. When he came he brought half a dozen medical students to witness the operation. He found he had forgotten the instrument to do it with, so he made a temporary instrument to hold the eye, and when he attempted [this] it was too large and it went

> right over the eye. Then he tried to bend it more, trying three times before he could hold the eye, and ruined the eye entirely and caused the child intense suffering. . . . I was so overcome with the screams of the child that it made me almost frantic. . . . [The eye] was a different color and was terrible to look at, as well as being totally blind.[5]

Sarah Amanda died of a throat infection when she was four.

The two surviving children, Edward and Sarah Amelia, were both in their twenties but still living at home when the family moved to Gramercy Park, and the household also included two sisters of Peter Cooper. When Edward married in 1853, his father bought three lots for him across the street on Lexington Avenue; when Sarah Amelia was married to

Plate 81 *No. 9 Lexington Avenue; Peter Cooper's house.*

Abram Hewitt and moved to New Jersey, she and her husband continued to spend every winter at her parents' house.

The Hewitts later moved in all year around and occupied the northern half of the house, sharing a common dining room with the Coopers. Their son, Edward Ringwood Hewitt, who was born in 1866, has described his boyhood in the house. Among his childhood memories were those of the dams he and his brother Cooper made in the gutter when the coachman of Cyrus Field, who lived next door, washed the carriage. Above the stables, originally, there had been a conservatory with three feet of earth on its floor. Mrs. Hewitt, however, had decided to turn it into a gymnasium for Edward and his brother and a workshop for herself. Thinking the ceiling too high, a second floor had been added thirty inches above the original floor. The space between became the boys' secret hiding place. A man came regularly from the YMCA to instruct them in gymnastics, but often the boys were more interested in pranks. Peter Cooper's grandson wrote:

> One day when we had been sledding on the street, the snow melted so that the sledding was not good. However, we wanted some more coasting. So Cooper . . . suggested that we try the sled on the front stairs of [the] house, which went straight down toward the front door. We thought that it would go slowly, on carpet, but instead it ran down with lightening speed, crossed the hall, and smashed against the large panel of the front door. Fortunately, the panel burst and let us through, without our hitting anything else. We met my mother, who was just coming home, on the front steps, and nearly had a bad accident.

Sometimes, however, the boys indulged in practical jokes of a more serious nature, and the police had to be called in:

> One day, there was a big snowstorm, which provided plenty of material for snowballs. . . . [We] made one . . . perhaps thirty inches wide [on the roof of the gymnasium]. We then rolled it close to the edge of the roof on East Twenty-second Street. Below . . . as we were looking down, a drunken man came along and lurched in next to the stable doors. Cooper could not resist giving the snowball a shove. It fell squarely on the poor man. It was a wonder it did not kill him. When he dug himself out, he was sober enough to get a policeman, who came to arrest us. But, as usual, we hid under the gymnasium floor and escaped.
>
> The police finally had to put a watchman in Gramercy Park because we made so much trouble there. One of our tricks was to haul park benches up . . . to the top of the pole and then tie the rope to the topmost branch of a tree. To get the benches down, the branches had to be cut to allow the benches to fall to the ground. We thought that was wonderful. But the watchman was a busy one and so curtailed our activities that we felt that we must get rid of him in some way.
>
> A small house had been built for him to sit in at night—it was like a sentry box. After a conference, we finally hit on this scheme: we secured some giant firecrackers and a small can of gunpowder and placed both under the watchman's house one evening. When the firecrackers went off, together with the powder, the explosion rolled the house over on its side. The watchman was very frightened. He came out and ran at top speed for the gate. They never got another man to stay there. It was lucky that we did not do some serious injury to the poor man.
>
> My brother Cooper and I talked the matter over very seriously and decided that it was necessary for us to find a means of escaping from the policemen, when they started chasing us in Gramercy Park. Cooper, as usual, had an inspiration and it did not take us long to make it a reality. We sawed off some of the cast-iron bars of the high park railings near the base, with a bracket saw, then loosened the top fastening of the bars, so that one bar could swing over to the next bar. This gave us just enough room to squeeze through. Of course, nobody noticed this ingenious device, because the sawed-off bars were cut on an angle and wedged tight when replaced.
>
> The sides of Gramercy Park that were near the railings, in those days, were filled with shrubbery thick enough to hide us from those chasing us. . . . In an emergency all we had to do was to make for the shrubbery, reach one of our sawed-off bars, and slip out of the park.
>
> Of course, having taken such elaborate pains to provide ourselves with a means of escape, we then had to give ourselves something to escape from. Cooper had read in a book about a horse fiddle that made an unearthly noise. We decided to make one. Our fiddle was a wooden box about four feet long, three feet wide, and two feet deep. The corners were reinforced with strong wooden blocks, glued and screwed in place. A two-inch plank, planed smooth, about twelve feet long, was carefully rubbed with rosin. This acted as the bow. When the fiddle was to howl, two boys sat on the center of the plank to hold it down; four more boys at each end pulled it back and forth across the box. The noise was like that of a one-hundred-horsepower bull. We tried it out in the gymnasium and found that it worked fine.
>
> One dark night, at about ten-o'clock, we took this contraption out to Gramercy Park and set it up. A few minutes after it had begun to bellow we heard all the four gates of the park being opened in a hurry. We ran for the shrubbery. Cooper had thrown two giant firecrackers below the overturned box before we started to run. A lot of people were standing around wondering what had made the awful noise when

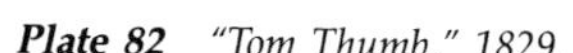
Plate 82 *"Tom Thumb," 1829.*

suddenly the giant firecrackers went off with a bang.

The police never found much of the box. And they never caught any of us. But there were shrewd guesses as to who had done the trick, so we had to keep quiet for a few days.

One of our favorite sports was to attach a fine silk thread to the lamp-post in front of our house—about seven feet from the ground—then lead it through a crack left open in the parlor window. The game was to lower the thread so that it would just touch a top hat, or derby, and knock it off. The height of skill was to snap a cigar out of a man's mouth, without letting him see the thread or allowing it to touch him. If his nose were touched it was not good, because he would always come into the house after us and we would have to hide. Whenever we saw a man start for our door we would break the thread and close the window. There was no evidence.

We were eventually caught and well punished. Another game, which I invented myself, was most successful. It is an old trick to drop red-hot pennies on the sidewalk and have passers-by pick them up—but my idea was much better. I took a five-inch spike, filed the head off, and soldered a brand-new quarter to it, with low-melting silver solder. Then, with a block of wood, I drove the spike into a crack in the sidewalk, so that the quarter was just flush with the stone.

Everyone who came by tried to pick up that shiny quarter. Of course they all broke their fingernails and most of them went on their way. A few tried to get the quarter up with their pocketknives. They always broke the blades; and they also left, usually swearing. Finally, an oldish man, with gray hair, lost the blade of his good knife in trying to get that quarter. He was a philanthropist. He went up the block, returned with a paving stone, and pounded that quarter into pulp, so that nobody would recognize it as money. This sport lasted all one Saturday afternoon. Lots of fun for a quarter. . . .

We children had noticed that our grandfather, Peter Cooper, nearly always gave to beggars if they told him the right story. Women were more likely to succeed than men. One day my sisters, Sally and Amy, dressed up as beggar-women, using the green shawls that our Irish servants wore about their heads and shoulders when they went out. They told a heart-breaking tale of woe and got even more than they expected—two dollars—for which they were heartily ashamed. . . . [6]

In addition to these delightful recollections of his boyhood, Edward Hewitt's memoirs also describe how Peter Cooper was in touch with some of the most important discoveries of the century:

When Alexander Graham Bell invented the telephone, he came to show it to my grandfather, who asked my brother Cooper and me to come into his study and see the new invention. Bell showed us how it was made and explained how it worked. When we got back to our shop, my brother said he did not see why we could not make a telephone ourselves. We set to work. I turned out the wooden earpiece, which we intended to use for both the transmitter and receiver—the carbon amplifier had not then been invented. Cooper made the coils and magnet. Then I went to Third Avenue to get a piece of black enameled iron from a tin-type photographer for the diaphragm.

When we had our two telephones completed we tried them out and found that we could talk through them. Then we had to find a place to use them. . . .

When Thomas A. Edison made the phonograph, he also brought it to Peter Cooper. Edison explained to us boys just how it worked. His original phonograph was made with a roller, on which was wound a sheet of tinfoil. The diaphragm traveled by a screw along the roller while the latter revolved. The diaphragm needle made impressions on the tinfoil; these were reproduced as sound when the roller was revolved, and the diaphragm moved by the screw in the same way.

It looked very simple. We boys could not see why we should not make one ourselves. We had the diaphragm material from our homemade telephone and could cut the screw with a die. The main trouble was with the roller, as we had no material for making it. Then I thought of the cook's rolling pin, which I promptly stole when she was in the laundry. It did not take long to rig up the whole device. We found that it would say "Hello" and a few other squeaky words. I remember going to Barnum's Circus the year before and seeing a Swiss talking machine which said a few words. There was a sign on it stating that Barnum would pay ten thousand dollars for any machine which would really talk. When he heard of Edison's phonograph, Barnum took down his sign, which we boys regarded as a mean trick on Barnum's part. . . .

Christopher Latham Stokes, who made the first typewriter, also brought it to Peter Cooper. It was a poor affair, in a square wooden box. It wrote very badly and seemed to be so complicated and expensive to make that Peter Cooper did nothing about it. The typewriter was not developed to a practical point until years later.[7]

Finally, Edward Hewitt provides us telling details of life in and around Gramercy Park during the mid-nineteenth century:

The streets about Gramercy Park were very different from those of today. Great herds of Texas longhorn steers used to be driven from the docks on the North River, up Irving Place and around Gramercy Park, to the slaughter-houses on First Avenue, beside the East River. Often, these steers got on the rampage and had to be lassoed or otherwise caught.

I remember one steer which was particularly vicious—in fact, so much so that no one could catch it. A policeman fired several times at this steer, with no result. Finally, a man in a big sombrero jumped down from the porch of the Gramercy Park Hotel [a

Plate 83 *Cover of* Puck, *May 21, 1879.*

different hotel from that of today that occupied the entire east side of the Park], and asked if the police wanted the steer out of the way. The man ran behind the steer, and, somehow, passed the beast's tail through its hind legs and gave a jerk. The steer went down on its side. The man then cut the animal's throat with a bowie knife. It was all over in an instant.[8]

New York looked very different in the seventies. The street along the side of our house on East Twenty-second Street was paved with large round cobblestones, some of them over a foot in diameter and sticking up an inch or two higher than the others. There were many mud holes in the roadway. When trucks or carriages passed over the street they made a dreadful noise with their iron tires. Telegraph poles, strung with telegraph wires which often crashed down in big storms, lined many of the streets. I remember how once all the telegraph poles as far as I could see on Lexington Avenue fell down into the street in an ice storm, with the wires badly tangling all the vehicles and the pedestrians on the sidewalks. There were many serious accidents that day.

Ashes and garbage were placed in open barrels on the sidewalk, and rag pickers, who used to pick this material over for paper and rags, often overturned the barrels into the street or onto the sidewalks. The streets were never well swept, as it was impossible to do this with the pavement of that time. My brother and I could always get all the fine, flat steel wire that we wanted for our youthful experiments from the old hoopskirts thrown away in ash-barrels.[9]

One of Peter Cooper's ambitions was to create an institution where young people could, without charge, get the education he himself had never had. He owned land at Broadway and Eighth Street, and in 1853, the cornerstone of the Cooper Union was laid. Cooper's inventiveness was evident in the design of the new building. Iron I beams of the needed size were not yet available in this country, so Cooper concocted them by bolting together railroad tracks. He also realized that he needed an elevator for Cooper Union, but, in 1853, the first practical passenger elevator was still four years away. Cooper decided that when it was produced, to be most efficient it should be round, and therefore he had a round shaft included in his building. Elevators, however, turned out to be square, and Elisha Graves Otis, their inventor, had to make up a special round one for Cooper's round shaft. The Cooper Union was finally opened in November 1859.

Peter Cooper liked to give money away. In the depression of 1873, he regularly gave fifty cents or a dollar to anyone who asked for it, and he also once gave ten thousand dollars to a struggling inventor for one of his inventions. Over the years, he put nine hundred thousand dollars into Cooper Union. However, he hated any show of wealth. He wanted his wife to have a proper carriage, but once returned one she had just purchased because he thought it entirely too fashionable. He was so respectable that when his son Edward was mayor of New York in 1879, and the press accused him of ineffectiveness, *Puck* magazine suggested his father give him a good spanking (Plate 83).

Every Sunday, Peter Cooper occupied his regular pew at All Souls Unitarian Church at the corner of Gramercy Park, though he was known to have dozed through most of the service. He wore his hair long, almost to his shoulders, and nearly always dressed in an old-fashioned black frock coat. He rode around New York in an old black buggy, looking at everything through small, thick-lensed glasses. A man with very sharp bones, he devised an air-filled cushion with a hole in the center to make sitting in hard chairs more comfortable, and persuaded his friend Charles Goodyear to manufacture it. Known as a "Peter Cooper," it became a popular item and was widely sold. One was, on formal occasions, carried for him by a member of the family should he need to sit down. He was an energetic man, and even in his nineties would take the stairs at Cooper Union when the elevator did not come fast enough. He claimed that he was freer of aches and pains on his ninety-first birthday than when he had been a boy carrying grocery baskets. He said at the end of his life, "My sun is not setting in clouds and darkness, but is going down cheerfully in a clear firmament lighted by the glory of God."[12]

Notes

[1] *Railroad Gazette,* "Peter Cooper and the First Locomotive", vol. 15, p. 225.

[2] Edward C. Mack, *Peter Cooper, Citizen of New York* (New York: Duell, Sloan and Pearce, 1949), p.180.

[3] Edward R. Hewitt, *Those Were the Days* (New York: Duell, Sloan and Pearce, 1943), pp. 47–48.

[4] Mack, op. cit., p. 53.

[5] Ibid., pp. 75–76.

[6] Hewitt, op. cit., pp. 5–9.

[7] Ibid., pp. 13–15.

[8] Ibid., p. 16.

[9] Ibid., p. 11.

[10] Mack, op. cit., p. 381.

[11] Ibid., p. 11.

[12] Mack, op. cit., p. 381.

Plate 84 *No. 9 Lexington Avenue; Stanford White had replaced the stoop with a street-level entrance for Abram Hewitt in 1885.*

8

Mayor Abram Hewitt and His Family

When Peter Cooper died in 1883, his daughter, Sarah Amelia, together with her husband, Abram Hewitt, and their six children, became the sole occupants of No. 9 Lexington Avenue. They engaged Stanford White to redecorate the house in 1885. He removed the stoop, replacing it with a ground-floor entrance and a porch with four Ionic columns, and introduced a kind of luxury Peter Cooper had always eschewed: marble stairways, Moorish ceilings, and walls of carved oak bought in England. (The Hewitts needed fourteen servants to run the house.)

Abram Hewitt had long been associated with Peter Cooper's son, Edward, in the iron business. He had amassed one of the large fortunes of his day, was elected to Congress in 1874, and served there continuously until his own election as mayor of New York in 1886. It was at this time that the mayor's lamps, which stood thereafter in front of No. 9 Lexington Avenue, were designed for the house by Stanford White. (They can be seen today in the Museum of the City of New York.)

As mayor, Hewitt attempted to rid New York of its gambling houses and prevailing vice. After a year in office, he invited the ranking police officers of the city to his house, took them into his study, and locked the door. He informed them that he had engaged a California detective agency at a cost to himself of fifty thousand dollars, and that he had enough evidence on each of them to send them to Sing Sing for life. The chief of police asked what he intended to do with the evidence. According to his son Edward, who was in the room, Hewitt replied:

> "I intend to keep it in my safe, so that whenever my orders are not executed properly these reports can be used by the District Attorney." Next day, there was the most extensive closing [of gambling houses] that New York had ever known. During my father's entire administration, he was able to control the police force with no further application of pressure. The police were always . . . agreeable to everything he wanted, and no one ever knew where he got his power. . . . [1]

Hewitt was not, however, reelected.

He died in 1903. His son, Erskine, and daughters Sarah and Eleanor (Miss Sally and Miss Nelly), never married and lived their entire lives at No. 9. When Erskine shot some pheasants his parents had kept on their estate at Ringwood, New Jersey, on the theory that if you had peacocks around you never got married, Miss Nelly and Miss Sally had had them stuffed and mounted so as to guard the house against intruding males. Miss Nelly died in 1924, and Miss Sally in 1930, and Erskine lived on in the huge house alone, with two maids and a butler, until his death in 1938. The furniture was then sold at Parke Bernet and the house was torn down to be replaced by an apartment building, but not before Geoffrey T. Hellman had

described in *The New Yorker* a visit he made to it. Such things as two Revolutionary cannon balls, George Washington's bone-handled razor and his chased-silver suspender buckles had already been sent to Parke Bernet, but the house was otherwise still intact. Hellman wrote:

> I was assisted in my tour of the house by . . . Mrs. Helen Weisschadel, a German maid who had let me in. [She] had come to the Hewitts in 1927 as seamstress to Miss Sally. When her mistress died she became parlormaid for Erskine Hewitt. [She] acted as a personal maid for his niece, Princess Viggo—a great-granddaughter of Peter Cooper, who married a cousin of the King of Denmark—when the Princess came over to divide her aunt's clothing among several museums. . . .
>
> The second floor contains the "blue library," the "green parlor," and the "red drawing room," all of which were still furnished in the appropriate colors when I saw them. Mrs. Abram Hewitt used to serve tea every afternoon in the red room. The blue library, now innocent of books, is lit by gas, but the other rooms have electricity. The dining room, on the same floor, has a Moorish ceiling. The walls are covered with elaborately carved oak with the date 1633 cut into it. An allegorical mural, which Mr. and Mrs. Abram Hewitt got from a Venetian palace on the Grand Canal, runs around most of the room just below the ceiling. It was covered with several layers of cellophane and I could only make out some dim, shadowy forms. "Mr. Hewitt wanted everything covered with cellophane, even bureaus," Mrs. Weisschadel told me, "but I talked him out of that." Behind the woodwork is strung a long series of light bulbs encircling the ceiling. They were installed by Peter Cooper Hewitt when he was a boy and, according to his brother Edward, represent the first indirect lighting in New York. "Mother thought they were too expensive, except for parties," he told me.
>
> I took a look at the pantry, a biggish room with barred windows and a safe where the silver used to be stored, and noted that the room-bell signal box still had compartments marked "Miss Sally" and "Miss Nelly." (At Ringwood, where there was no electric bell system, Miss Sally used to call for her maid by blowing a coach horn which hung on her bed.) The list of telephone numbers near the sink included Union Club, Plumber, Butcher, and Mr. Green. On my way to the music room I went back through the green and red rooms, . . . furnished in the styles of Louis XV and Louis XVI. This represented Miss Sally's taste, and her brothers used to tease her by telling her that since Louis Quincy was not related to the Boston Quincys, he shouldn't be allowed in the house. The shutters, both in the parlors and in the dining room, were closed and have been closed for something like twenty years.
>
> The music room looks out on a large courtyard where the green house used to be. The old stable, now bulging with firewood, is still there. It once housed the barouche in which Peter Cooper used to drive the mile down to Cooper Union the last twenty-five years of his life. The music room was built in the nineties and consists of part of a remodelled floor of a

Plate 85 *No. 9 Lexington Avenue; Stanford White's entrance, showing the mayor's lamps White designed for Abram Hewitt.*

small house, in back of the original mansion, which the Hewitts bought. Everything had been taken out of it when I saw it, except for a few pieces of Venetian furniture, some Greek columns, and two blue-and-white porcelain pagodas. Forty years ago this room and the adjoining ones were the scene of any number of regular and fancy-dress balls, including one to which the guests came as characters in "Alice in Wonderland" and one given in honor of Queen Liliuokalani of the Sandwich Islands. The Queen was a house guest of the Hewitts in the nineties, around the time Hawaii was annexed. Mrs. Edward Hewitt still recalls how authentic Stanford White looked when he turned up at a French Revolution party as a street rowdy, and her husband likes to mention his discovery of Mrs. Astor's diamond brooch in the gutter outside the house as a sign that no one living near Gramercy Park in those days got up before ten o'clock after a Hewitt party. A milder note of festivity was struck during this period by the ladies' orchestra founded by the Misses Hewitt. Sixteen or eighteen ladies made up the band, which met for practice in the Hewitt home. Miss Sally played first violin, Miss Nelly the viola, and Mrs. Stanford White the bass fiddle.

. . . Although the big parties practically stopped after Abram Hewitt's death in 1903, the ballroom, his son told me, wasn't built until around 1907, "about the time the girls couldn't dance any more." The room was last used in 1924, for the reception which followed the wedding of Princess Viggo. The family rounded up thirty broughams for the occasion; it was the last wedding reception in New York to which that many guests were driven up by horses. . . .

The third floor, which contains Miss Sally's and Miss Nelly's bedrooms and sitting rooms and Mr. and Mrs. Abram Hewitt's bedrooms, dressing rooms, and sitting room, was a welter of scattered chairs, sofas, fluted marble columns, clocks, linens, and ivory-handled nutpicks when I saw it. The bed was unmade in Miss Sally's room and I asked Mrs. Weisschadel about this. "Oh, that fellow hasn't made his bed," she said, referring to Francois the butler, who is using the room now in order to be within hearing range of the burglar alarm. Miss Nelly's room was full of classic landscapes and pictures of lividly active volcanoes. Mrs. Abram Hewitt's bedroom, unoccupied since her death in 1912, except when Princess Viggo used it on her stays here, was a sea of linen. Miss Hollander of the Parke-Bernet Galleries was sitting in the middle of it with a typewriter, cataloguing things.

The bed in Mayor Hewitt's room had been removed and the floor was piled high with pillows, cushions, and couch covers. Two windows in a nearby bathroom are cracked, and the family think this was done by stones thrown in the Draft Riots of 1863. There were also a couple of guest rooms on this floor and a large library, extending over most of the ballroom, which used to belong to the sisters. Miss Sally was reputed to have had the most extensive pornographic library in New York. I refrained from asking her brother about this, but he volunteered a mention of it himself. "I don't know what happened to Sally's indecent library," he said. "I never saw it. It may have gone to Cooper Union, with the rest of the books." Incidentally, Mr. Hewitt told me the guest rooms on this floor were on one occasion put to rather involuntary use. About twenty-five years ago, Mrs. Sergeant Cram, a granddaughter of Peter Cooper's son Edward, dropped in with two of her small children and their nurse. She explained to her cousins Sally and Nelly that she was going to Aiken and that she was depositing the children with them. Without waiting for a reply she went off, leaving her cousins flustered and speechless. When she came back to gather up her family several weeks later, the Hewitt sisters were so fond of their novel maternal role that it was only after considerable arguments that they gave the children back.

Mr. Hewitt said that his brother Erskine's quarters on the fourth floor were the same he had occupied as a boy. They consisted of a small bedroom, living room, and bath. There was a pile of lace in the sitting room when I was there. Except when giving his occasional dinner parties, Mr. Hewitt camped out in his little suite and rarely used the rest of the house. He would poke around everywhere Sunday mornings, however, calling the servants' attention to dust and to the necessity of having repairs made. In the days when his parents ran the house, they had a staff of fourteen and kept a repair man busy nearly full time fixing the hundreds of pieces of furniture. I inspected Mr. Hewitt's tub, an old-fashioned wooden affair lined with silvered copper. Mr. Hewitt had two glass shelves put in over the basin only a few months before he died. For the previous half-century he had kept his shaving things on the wooden rim of the bathtub.

Toward the rear of the top floor were a number of servants' rooms, and a spare room known as "the Twenty-second Street room." There was also a trunk room, with dozens of blankets, many of them horse blankets, and over thirty trunks and innumerable suitcases in it. Most of the trunks were marked "A. S. Hewitt"; an oddly shaped one was labelled "S. C. Hewitt, New York." Mrs. Weisschadel explained that this was for Miss Sally's wheelchair, which she always took with her when travelling abroad. "She was weak in the joints."[2]

The great old house which had seen so much was let to a nephew in 1938, who sold it soon thereafter. It was demolished, and one of the grand phases of Gramercy Park history came to a close.

Notes

[1] Edward R. Hewitt, *Those Were the Days* (New York: Duell, Sloan and Pearce, 1943), p. 87.

[2] Geoffrey T. Hellman, "A Reporter at Large, No. 9 Lexington Avenue," *New Yorker*, October 29, 1938, pp. 58–65.

Plate 86 *Cyrus Field, 1859.*

9

Cyrus Field and the Atlantic Cable

Next door to Peter Cooper lived Cyrus West Field. Cooper and Field were neighbors and close friends for thirty-two years, and Cooper, who was twenty-six years older, was always Field's ardent supporter, particularly in his great Atlantic cable venture. Only with Cooper's cooperation and financial support was Field able to persevere in this project and see his cable become one of the great achievements of the nineteenth century, inaugurating a new era of international communication.

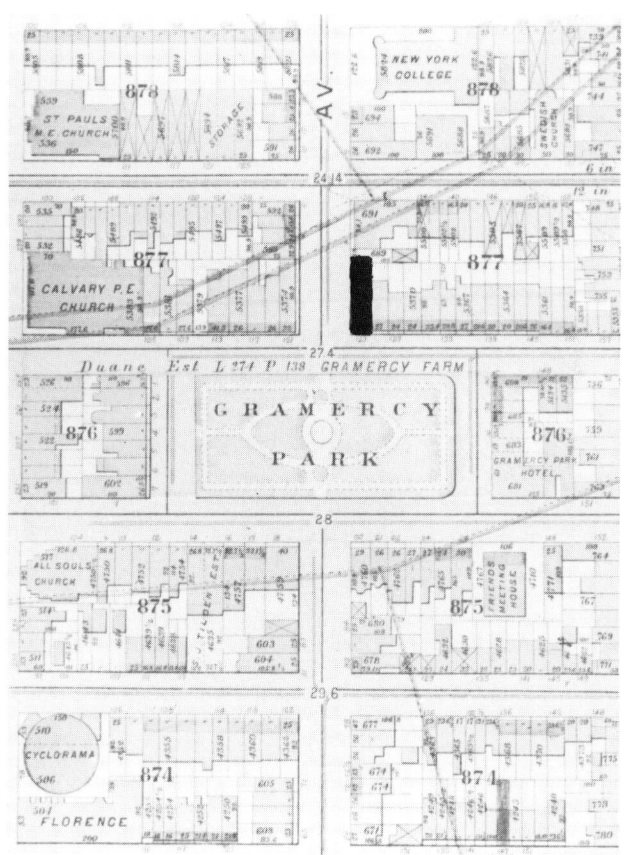

Plate 87 Map of Gramercy Park area. Shaded building is Cyrus Field's house.

Cyrus Field was born in 1819 in Stockbridge, Massachusetts, where his father was a Congregational minister. He came to New York at the age of sixteen, as Cooper had done a quarter of a century earlier, to make his own way. He got a job at A. T. Stewart's store on Broadway, as an errand boy, which required that he be at work every morning by six. Every penny that he had to borrow from his family to keep himself going was paid back to them in full. In 1840, he left the city and worked for a while as an assistant to his brother Matthew, who manufactured paper in Lee, Massachusetts. Apparently, he missed New York, however, for he decided to return and got a job with the firm of E. Root and Company as sales manager.

Hardly had he settled down and married Mary Stone of Guilford, Connecticut, than the company failed, so he went into the paper manufacturing business with his brother-in-law, Joseph Stone, and formed the firm of Cyrus W. Field and Company. In 1842, Field and his wife rented a house at No. 87 East Seventeenth Street, where they lived for ten years.

This was just east of Union Place, which Samuel B. Ruggles was busy developing at the time, but it was still country enough that the Fields could keep a cow and pasture it not far from their house.

Field worked long hours for the next ten years—as he once said, "Breakfast by lamplight, dinner and supper downtown"—and he succeeded in making a modest fortune. To express his newly improved circumstances, he bought one of the Gramercy Park lots, No. 50, at the northeast corner of Lexington Avenue, and, with his wife, drew the plans for a new house. It was to be simple on the outside; he was a New Englander and by no means wanted to announce to the public the considerable opulence that he planned for the inside.

The house was under construction by the beginning of 1851, and one day, Field took a friend, the painter Frederick Church, to show it to him. Later that spring, Church accompanied Field and his wife on a tour of the Eastern United States to see some of its famous natural wonders. Field's biographer, Samuel Carter, relates:

> At the Natural Bridge in Virginia, Field was so anxious that Church should [paint] the bridge with photographic accuracy that he climbed around the limestone cliffs collecting specimens of rock to guide [the artist] in his choice of colors. When Church disdained these props in favor of his own perception, Field pocketed the rocks to take back to New York. He aimed to check Church's finished product with his samples; if they matched, he would buy the painting. They did, and he did.[1]

When they got back to New York, having come down the Hudson by boat, the Fields found the new house ready. Cyrus's brother David Dudley Field, at the time a justice of the New York Supreme Court, had built an identical house next door, and soon the two houses were made interconnecting. A French interior designer named Baudoine was hired to do the furnishing, reportedly arousing great jealousy in George Templeton Strong, who only wished he could have afforded the same. This is said to have been the first time in New York that a professional decorator was privately engaged. Louis XIV furniture abounded, as did Italian draperies, Greek statues, marble mantels, and frescoed ceilings. There were also at least seven paintings by Frederick Church, including the celebrated "View of West Rock near New Haven." The two major requirements for the house, however, were an ample library for Field on the second floor, which looked out on Gramercy Park, and a greenhouse for his wife, another first in New York. Behind the house were the stables where the family still kept its cow, which continued to graze in the neighborhood.

Plate 88 *Nos. 123 and 125 East Twenty-first Street, the houses of Cyrus West Field and David Dudley Field.*

Field was an early riser and was in his library by seven. He began each day by making a list of what had to be done and placing it in his hat while he had breakfast. He hated to waste time; ten minutes wasted every day, he said, added up to sixty hours a year.

The Fields employed an English butler whom their children loathed because he required that, like upper-class British children, they should eat at tables separate from the rest of the family. The dining room displayed a 262-piece set of blue-and-white Minton china. Among the guests regularly entertained there were Harriet Beecher Stowe, William Cullen Bryant, and Charles Scribner. However, there was one person Mrs. Field had vowed never to entertain. She was Henriette Desportes, the French teacher at Miss Haines's Academy for Girls at Nos. 9 and 10 Gramercy Park.

Henriette Desportes had recently come from Paris, where she had been governess to the children of the Duc and Duchesse de Praslin. When the Duchesse was found murdered and the Duc accused of the

Plate 89 *Free Academy; Lexington Avenue front and president's house.*

crime, his trial became one of the most sensational of the century, followed avidly in New York as well as Paris. Henriette Desportes was implicated both as the Duc's suspected mistress and as somehow involved in the murder. When he committed suicide, she was acquitted, but suspicion hung over her and she had to leave France. It happened that the Reverend Henry Field, another of Cyrus Field's brothers, had met her in Paris and arranged for her to be offered the job at Miss Haines's school on Gramercy Park. Mrs. Cyrus Field, however, refused to have her in the house, and persisted in calling her "that murderess."

At Miss Haines's, one of Mlle. Desportes's duties was to escort thirteen little girls each morning on a walk six times around Gramercy Park, up Lexington Avenue a few blocks and back. The picture of this regular outing was vividly evoked in 1938 in the historically accurate novel *All This and Heaven Too,* by Henriette Desportes's grandniece, Rachel Field. It is reminiscent of Ludwig Bemelmans's illustrations for his story *Madeline,* written in the next year, in which the unforgettable Miss Clavel escorts her charges around Paris, and the association is perhaps not too fanciful since Bemelmans himself lived on Gramercy Park.

Each morning in the spring of 1851, Mlle. Desportes and her entourage, all whispering about their romantic new French teacher, passed the houses just then being built by Peter Cooper and Cyrus Field, and also the students coming in and out of Renwick's new Free Academy. Despite the lurid rumors about Mlle. Desportes, Henry M. Field proceeded to marry her in the fall of 1851, and they moved that year to West Springfield, Massachusetts.

By the time Cyrus Field moved into his new house that same fall, his company had so flourished that he was now one of the thirty-three richest men in New York and could, though he was only thirty-four years old, retire from active business. He was looking for a project of some kind when, in January 1854, he met Frederick N. Gisbourne, who had just come from Newfoundland, where he had been attempting to lay a telegraph line. Interest in finding a way to shorten the communication gap between Europe and the United States had long been building. In 1851, the bishop of Newfoundland had proposed that steamers bound for New York be intercepted at the eastern end of his country and their news transmitted directly from there by telegraph. Gisbourne had begun to build the necessary line across Newfoundland, but had got only thirty miles before his backers deserted him.

He found in Cyrus Field the very person he was looking for. Field had money and time, and Gisbourne's proposal interested him right away. What was more, Field's next door neighbor, Peter Cooper, was already president of the North American Telegraph Company. Together, they called a meeting, with three other people of means, at Renwick's Clarendon Hotel early in March 1854. They agreed to raise the forty thousand dollars necessary to back Gisbourne, though at this time there was no formal thought of laying cable between Nova Scotia and Newfoundland—that link was still being conceived of as carried by fast steamer. But the idea and, indeed, the idea of the Atlantic cable itself, was already in Field's mind.

Field had another neighbor, Samuel F. B. Morse, who lived on Twenty-second Street just west of Fifth Avenue, and Morse had, in 1844, not only convinced Congress of the feasibility of the telegraph but predicted that a cable spanning the Atlantic was possible. Field also knew that in February 1854, M. F. Maury had surveyed the ocean floor between Canada and England and found it suitable for the laying of a cable. And Peter Cooper was keen about the idea. When Field proposed it to him, he later wrote, it struck him

as though it was the consummation of that great

> prophecy, that "knowledge shall cover the earth, as waters cover the deep." [There were those who thought the scheme] fitted those who engaged in it for an asylum where they might be taken care of as little short of lunatics. But believing, as I did, that it offered the possibility of a mighty power for the good of the world, I embarked on it.[2]

The meeting at the Clarendon Hotel was followed by four more on successive evenings in Cyrus Field's Gramercy Park library. It was decided that Field, his brother David Dudley Field, and Chandler White should go to Newfoundland and negotiate a deal. They went and returned with a charter, written with a view toward future telegraphic connections with Europe, a fifty-year monopoly on all cables on the island, a bonus of fifty square miles of land, and fifty thousand dollars from the Newfoundland government. The New York, Newfoundland, and London Telegraph Company thus began, with Peter Cooper as the president; on $1.5 million capital they were to span Newfoundland with telegraph wires, and then possibly move on with cable to Nova Scotia.

The work began that summer, as they cut through a road, and hauled in the telegraph poles by donkey; teams of six hundred men worked against the clock until they were stopped by winter. Almost every evening in Field's library with its two prominent globes (Plate 86) the reports of the work were gone over anxiously. When the first snow did stop the work, attention turned to the cable between Newfoundland and Nova Scotia. The next year, that work was plagued with unforeseen problems, but the land lines were finally finished, and by 1856, the St. Lawrence cable was completed. The directors then began to plan the Atlantic cable itself.

It was to be a star-crossed project—with many failures before ultimate success. On August 7, 1857, two side-wheel steamships provided by the United States and British governments set sail from Newfoundland and Liverpool respectively, spooling out the cable and intending to meet at mid-ocean. But four days out, the cable of the American ship broke, and the project had to be postponed for a year. On March 9, 1858, they set out again, this time to meet at mid-ocean, splice the cable, and then sail away from each other. A storm prevented their meeting until June, and when they finally began laying the cable on June 25, the cable broke again. They set out once more on July 17, and again there were cable breaks, storms, and near collisions. But to almost everyone's amazement, this time it finally worked, and 1,950 miles of cable were successfully laid.

A message from Queen Victoria was received on August 16, and for two weeks New York celebrated. There was a procession from the Battery to the Crystal Palace at Forty-second Street and a great torchlight parade. The whole city was illuminated and every window in Gramercy Park had lights in it.

George Templeton Strong, who was in Great Barrington, Massachusetts, wrote on August 24 about a speech typical of those given everywhere in which "the assembled multitudes [were told] that war . . . and other calamities were henceforth impossible, that the millenium had been manufactured by electro-galvanism, gutta percha, copper wire, and Cyrus Field." By September 11, however, the excitement had begun to wane: "People begin to tire of hearing Cyrus called the Great, and of parallels between him and Galileo generally to the disadvantage of the latter."

Although Field and Cooper were everywhere wildly cheered, the joy did not last long. The celebrations were not even over before the signal was apparently beginning to fade and, by October 20, the cable had gone dead. The insulation had been damaged by the sun during preparation and now it failed. To make matters worse, in the financial crisis of 1857, Field's paper business had been suspended and in 1859, its offices were burned to the ground. He was forced to mortgage his house and its contents, and was so discouraged that he was on the verge of giving up, but Cooper refused to let him and said simply, "We will go on." Although the Civil War prevented much from being done for eight more years, finally, in 1864, Field was able to order new cable that weighed less and yet had two and a half times the strength of the old one.

In January 1865, the new steamship *Great Eastern* was procured, and they began laying cable. But again, six hundred miles from Ireland the cable was lost. Another year went by before the work could recommence on Friday, July 13, 1866. That day, the *Great Eastern* set out again and arrived in Newfoundland on July 27, the entire cable having been successfully laid. Then the previous cable was fished up, a difficult operation that took another month, and, on September 7, two cables were in use.

Peter Cooper, at the great public banquet given for Field by the chamber of commerce, declared, "God rewards patient industry." Indeed, Field had crossed the Atlantic forty times before the project was completed, and as the captain of the *Great Eastern* put it, had "worked hard and sacrificed the repose of his home and the repose of everyone who could bear influence on his darling scheme."

After 1869, Field and his family divided their time between Gramercy Park and the estate they had bought at Irvington-on-Hudson. Called Ardsley Park,

Plate 90 *Bills for purchase and repair of the metal swans that floated in the pool around the water nymph fountain at the center of Gramercy Park.*

it comprised seven hundred acres, forty-one dwellings, a church, and a school. Flowers from its gardens were delivered almost every day to the New York house.

The flowering of Gramercy Park itself was being much discussed at this time. In 1874, certain Trustees had suggested that the traditional six hundred dollars per year for Park maintenance was now insufficient and should be raised to eighteen hundred, or thirty dollars per lot. Landscape gardening experts were consulted, but no action was taken. In 1876, it was specifically moved by one of the Trustees that six hundred dollars was quite adequate. The next year, Cyrus Field was elected president of the Trustees. At the same meeting, it was resolved to poll the lot owners concerning an increase in the Park maintenance. The new president was to call an immediate meeting "to receive the resignation of such Trustees as desire to resign." And so, four days later, three Trustees did resign, including the former president, Alexander M. Lawrence, and Charles Kirkland, who had opposed the maintenance increase. On May 5, a printed notice was sent to every lot owner which began:

> The Trustees are embarrassed . . . by the condition of the Park's finances. . . . As it is apparent that a sum of not less than $2,000 per annum is required to keep the Park grounds . . . in suitable order and condition . . . the Trustees solicit an annual due of thirty dollars.

At the bottom of the notice, in small print, it was stated that no new keys would now be issued until all dues were paid. It also announced that "several gentlemen have subscribed in addition to their annual

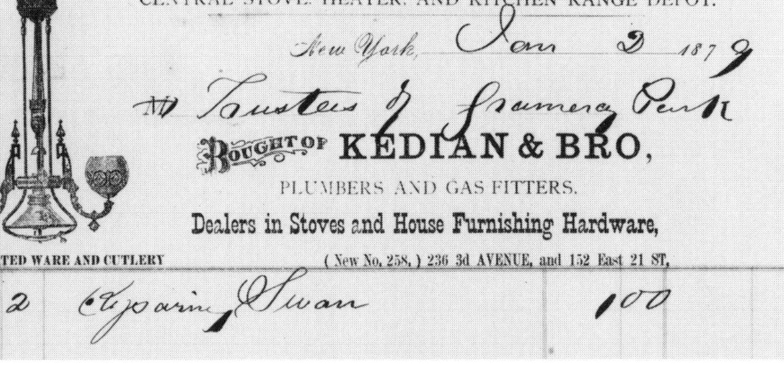

CENTRAL STOVE. HEATER. AND KITCHEN RANGE DEPOT.

New York, Jan 3 1879

To Trustees of Gramercy Park

Bought of KEDIAN & BRO,

PLUMBERS AND GAS FITTERS.

Dealers in Stoves and House Furnishing Hardware,

...ATED WARE AND CUTLERY (New No. 258,) 236 3d AVENUE, and 152 East 21 ST,

2 Repairing Swan 100

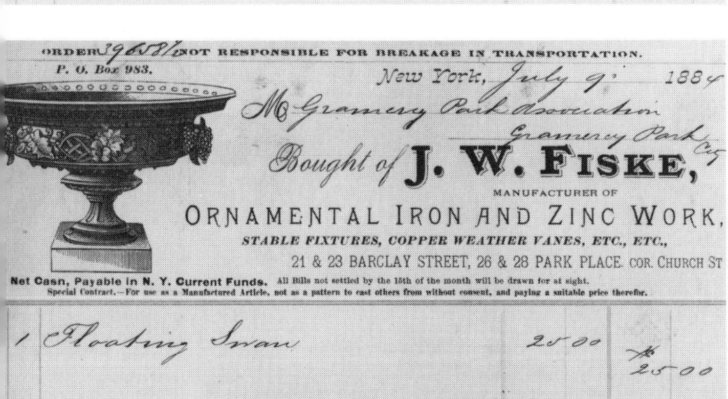

ORDER NOT RESPONSIBLE FOR BREAKAGE IN TRANSPORTATION.

P. O. Box 983.

New York, July 9 1884

Mr Gramercy Park Association
Gramercy Park City

Bought of J. W. FISKE,

MANUFACTURER OF

ORNAMENTAL IRON AND ZINC WORK,

STABLE FIXTURES, COPPER WEATHER VANES, ETC., ETC.,

21 & 23 BARCLAY STREET, 26 & 28 PARK PLACE. COR. CHURCH ST

Net Cash, Payable in N. Y. Current Funds. All Bills not settled by the 15th of the month will be drawn for at sight.

Special Contract.—For use as a Manufactured Article, not as a pattern to cast others from without consent, and paying a suitable price therefor.

1 Floating Swan 25 00 25 00

dues, nearly $1,400 for the permanent improvement of the park grounds."

The next year, 1878, a contract was drawn up that went into the particulars of the new gardens in great detail. It suggested that "Sweet Alysseum Variegated or Pyrethrum Aureum [for instance] might be introduced with good effect." But the issue hung fire until 1885, when the Trustees had to respond to a popular demand to allow croquet and ball playing in the Park. They sent out to the lot owners a proposal countering those who had advocated removing the large ornamental vases on the lawns so that such games could be played. Fearing such an act would "engender disputes and ill-feeling," they submitted instead that the lawns were essentially ornamental, especially when decorated "by carpet-borders and cluster plants [to give] them handsome effects and contrasts."

A general vote was called and the Trustees were upheld against croquet enthusiasts and ballplayers. The votes were tabulated according to the width of a voter's lot, and the talley was 1,243 feet 4 inches against ball playing to 284 feet 2 inches in favor. The question of the assessment for maintenance was not concluded, however, until 1886, when a contract for sixteen hundred dollars was finally signed with a new gardener. Thereafter, potted roses were to fill the beds around the fountain; the pool was to be stocked with goldfish, and a new floating swan was to replace the old one, which often had been repaired (Plate 90). The eight large ornamental vases were to be filled with "pansies of the best modern variety"; and thirty large vermillion tubs with black hoops were to be filled with hydrangeas. In all this, Cyrus Field had taken a major hand, as president of the Trustees, and it is not hard to sense the presence of his wife behind him, given her passion for gardens.

Field's private affairs, however, were increasingly clouded. In the stock market crash of 1887, he lost virtually everything except the two houses, which were fortunately in his wife's name. In 1891, moreover, his son, Edward, was arrested and imprisoned for embezzlement, and then declared legally insane. The insanity was found to have been caused by a horseback-riding injury. After his wife died the same year, Field spent his final days mostly at Irvington. The gardens there, as at Gramercy Park, brought the old man his few final satisfactions.

Notes

[1] Samuel Carter, *Cyrus Field, Man of Two Worlds* (New York: 1968), p. 68.

[2] Edward C. Mack, *Peter Cooper, Citizen of New York* (New York: Duell, Sloan and Pearce, 1949), pp. 220–221.

Plate 91 *Fourth Avenue Presbyterian Church, northwest corner of Twenty-second Street, c. 1890.*

10

Four More Churches and a Meeting House

The rapidly growing population around Gramercy Park occasioned the erection of four religious buildings during the ten years from 1853 to 1863. The first, at the northwest corner of Fourth Avenue and Twenty-second Street, was the Fourth Avenue Presbyterian Church (Plate 91). A Romanesque Revival building with twin towers, it was finished in 1853, together with a chapel adjoining it on the north. Both were demolished in 1909.

Across Fourth Avenue, on the northeast corner of Twenty-second Street, which had been the second site of Calvary Church's wooden building, another church was built in 1863. It was St. Paul's Methodist-Episcopal Church (Plates 96 and 97), designed by an architect about whom nothing is known except that his name was G. Stacy. It had a marble spire over two hundred feet tall, which can be seen in Plate 95 beyond the towers of Calvary Church, and was known as the Cathedral of Methodism. It was demolished in 1891, when its congregation moved uptown.

All Souls Unitarian Church was built two blocks south at the southeast corner of Twentieth Street, between 1853 and 1855 (Plate 98). The church and its parsonage (Plate 101) were designed by the English architect Jacob Wrey Mould (1825–86), who had arrived in this country in 1852; it was his first commission. All Souls was known as the Church of the Holy Zebra or as the Beefsteak Church, because its alternating bands of brick and Caen stone suggested lines of fat running through beef. Officially, it was done in the Anglo-Italianate Romanesque style, drawing as it did on the fourteenth-century Basilica of San Giovanni at Monza in northern Italy.

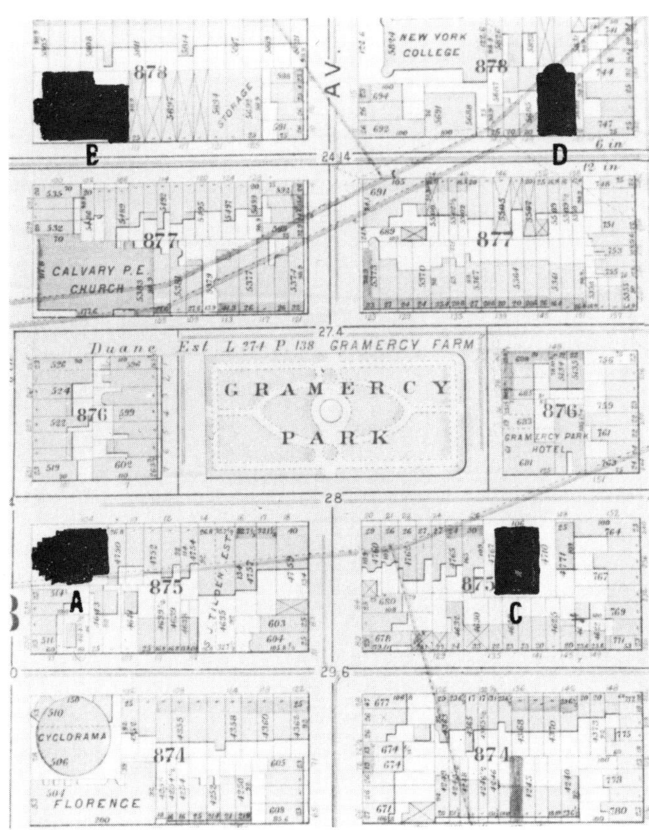

Plate 92 *Map of Gramercy Park area. Shaded buildings are a) All Souls Church; b) St. Paul's Methodist Church; c) Friends Meeting House; and d) Gustavus Adolphus Church.*

Plate 93

Plate 94

Plate 95

Plate 96

Plate 97

Plate 98

Plate 99

Mould was an assistant to Calvert Vaux and Frederick Law Olmsted and did much of the architectural detailing in Central Park. His only surviving building in New York is the former Trinity Chapel School at No. 13 West Twenty-fifth Street; his Church of the Holy Turtle, as the Second Unitarian Church in Cobble Hill, Brooklyn, was called, was destroyed in the 1950's. As one might guess, the Church of the Holy Turtle suggested the carapace of a tortoise.

The first pastor of All Souls was one of the great citizens of New York, Henry W. Bellows. During the Civil War, he was one of the founders of the United States Sanitary Commission, the celebrated predecessor of the American Red Cross, which administered relief to Northern soldiers. Its general secretary and basic organizer was Frederick Law Olmsted, who for many months laid aside all private work and donated his time without remuneration. In all, $15 million worth of supplies, all privately solicited as no government money was available, was distributed to the soldiers.

A huge tower had been designed for the church by Mould (Plate 99), but Charles R. Lamb recalled:

> The campanile . . . was to cost thirty thousand dollars. Then, the great war unfinished, Dr. Bellows called his people together and said, "Don't you think we can do better than build?" They said, "Yes," and the thirty thousand dollars already subscribed for the bell tower went to the sanitary commission for the boys at the front. Wrey Mould said, "That impossible committee. They even wanted to cut down my rose window. I know it is too big, but it is the size that I designed it, even if it makes the front entrance look too small."[1]

All Souls Church was demolished soon after its congregation moved in 1929 to its new building at Lexington Avenue and Eightieth Street.

Plate 100

Plate 93 *Twenty-second Street, looking east from Broadway, c. 1864, showing the south tower of Fourth Avenue Presbyterian Church and the spire of St. Paul's Methodist Church at the corner of Fourth Avenue.*
Plate 94 *Fourth Avenue, looking north from Twenty-first Street, 1894, showing the just-completed Bank for Savings, the original Metropolitan Life Insurance Co. building under construction, and, just visible beyond it, the spire of Madison Square Church and Madison Square Garden.*
Plate 95 *Fourth Avenue, looking north from Union Square, past Samuel B. Ruggles's house, the gable of All Souls Church, the towers of Calvary Church, and, beyond them, the spire of St. Paul's Methodist Church; at the end of the avenue is the 1871 Grand Central Station, c. 1875.*
Plate 96 *St. Paul's Methodist Church, northeast corner of Fourth Avenue and Twenty-second Street.*
Plate 97 *St. Paul's Methodist Church.*
Plate 98 *All Souls Unitarian Church, southeast corner of Fourth Avenue and Twentieth Street.*
Plate 99 *All Souls Unitarian Church.*
Plate 100 *Fourth Avenue, looking north from Nineteenth Street, 1907. Two little boys are sitting on the ledge of the dome of All Souls Church. Behind the oyster store on Nineteenth Street was an outdoor eating area.*

Plate 101 *All Souls Church; parsonage.*
Plate 102 *Friends Meeting House, now Brotherhood Synagogue.*
Plate 103 *Calvary Chapel, 209 East Twenty-third Street, designed in 1859 by William Thomas Beer. After 1873 it was remodeled and became the College of Pharmacy.*

In 1855, the New York Meeting of the Society of Friends decided to move north from their 1840 building on Orchard Street, and acquired four lots at Nos. 27 through 30 Gramercy Park for $24,000. John Kellum of the firm of King and Kellum was asked to design a new building. He was best known for his spectacular cast-iron commercial buildings, especially the 1859–62 A. T. Stewart Store (later Wanamaker's). Kellum's surviving work in New York includes the 1856 Cary Building on Chambers Street, the 1861–72 Tweed Courthouse, and McCreery's Silk Store, at 801 Broadway.

Plate 101

Plate 102

Plate 103

The Friends building committee minutes record that

> in getting up [its] plans, great care has been taken to endeavor to produce such that every person who shall see the house after it is erected will say this is exactly suited for a Friends Meeting, entirely plain, neat and chaste, of good proportions, but avoiding all useless ornament, so as not to wound the feelings of the most sensitive among us.

Construction was begun in 1857 and finished in 1859. The new building was less plain than most meeting houses; its builders were members of the Meeting, and as a later secretary of the Meeting put it, "They couldn't help making it less severe, because they put so much love into it." It was set back sixteen feet from the front building line, when the Park Trustees allowed an exception to the original Deed's requirement that any building other than a private home be forty feet back.

The exterior of the building, while it appears to be brownstone, is, in fact, Dorchester olive stone quarried in Ohio. There was much discussion of the windows, and finally it was decided to let them be more "churchly" than usual: elongated rather than more square. The severity of the exterior is also softened by a curving pediment supported on consoles over the central doorway, which mirrors the curve of the shallow indentation of the whole central panel of the facade and the curving window frames.

Inside, as Ada Louise Huxtable described it, the main second-story hall is a place of "classical, formal elegance and spare simplicity. It is also a superb space, just one foot short of square and two generous stories high, scaled by the tall, clear windows that run nearly full building height."[2] The benches from the Orchard Street Meeting House were installed here; they ascend in a gentle rise beginning halfway back, reached at the rear of the room by semicircular steps. A gallery on three sides is supported by cast-iron Doric columns, another "restrained flourish." The interior is supported by powerful brick basement arches.

At the front of the building is a third floor. Before the Civil War it was used as a refuge and rehabilitation center for fugitive slaves smuggled north by the Underground Railroad. Here, too, later travelers in distress were assisted by a small group of Friends who, in 1905, formed the Travelers Aid Society. Such were the concerns that arose out of the silence of Friends meeting together in this old space. And that silence was carefully protected: when the sessions of the New York Yearly Meeting were held there before 1910, soft, spent bark was laid down on Twentieth Street to allay the rattle of iron tires on the stone paving.

In 1958, the Society of Friends could no longer afford to maintain the meeting house and transferred many of its activities to Stuyvesant Square. The building, just short of a century old, was threatened with demolition. Thanks to the efforts of Douglas Haskell and others, (he spoke eloquently at a community hearing about the danger of cutting off sunlight from the Park) an option which in 1965 had been given to a developer to build a thirty-story apartment house on the site was voted down, and a foundation was created to purchase the building. When this failed, the venerable old meeting house, having been designated a New York landmark, was sold to the United Federation of Teachers; when their plan to use it for meetings and offices did not succeed, it was sold again, in 1975, to the Brotherhood Synagogue, which was looking for a new home. By this time, leaks had caused such interior damage that the main meeting room was ankle-deep in fallen plaster.

The building was put into the careful hands of the architect James Stewart Polshek. His aim was to respect "the conceptual unity of the space,"—not necessarily to restore everything to the way it once was, but to honor the original workable simplicity of the structure, allowing it to be most effective for contemporary use. To the Brotherhood Synagogue goes the credit for saving what Huxtable has called this "truly beautiful building [which is] beautiful both in its sense of space and in its justness of proportion and detail"; one in which "one architect [has taken] another's esthetic pulse, even with a century in between."[3]

The last of the nineteenth-century churches to be built near Gramercy Park was Gustavus Adolphus Church at No. 151 East Twenty-second Street. The oldest Swedish Lutheran Church in New York, it was named for the King of Sweden, 1611–32, who was a great champion of Protestantism. The congregation was organized in 1865 and first used St. James' English Lutheran Church on Fifteenth Street east of Third Avenue; later it purchased Bethesda Baptist Church on Twenty-second Street and, in 1887, razed it to build the present church. The new building, with its picturesque tower, was dedicated in 1889 and has been in active use ever since.

Notes

[1] Charles R. Lamb, "The Tilden Mansion," privately printed, National Arts Club, New York, 1932, p. 15–16.

[2] Ada Louis Huxtable, "Recycling a Landmark For Today," *The New York Times*, June 15, 1975, sec. D, p. 29.

[3] Ibid.

Plate 104 *No. 15 Gramercy Park; entrance to Samuel J. Tilden's house as designed by Calvert Vaux.*

11

Samuel J. Tilden: Bookman and Almost President

Across the Park from the Fields, in a house which is today The National Arts Club, lived another nationally known figure, Samuel Jones Tilden. He was the Democratic nominee for President of the United States in 1876, won the popular vote, and was proclaimed President-elect, until word finally arrived that he had, in fact, lost in the electoral college by one vote. It was the most famous disputed election in American history.

Tilden was born in 1814 in New Lebanon, New York, attended Yale and later the University of the City of New York, and was admitted to the bar in 1841. He became a successful corporation lawyer in New York and was a leader of a radical New York group of Democrats known as the Barnburners, after the celebrated Dutchman who burned his barn to rid it of rats. They believed the only way to do away with corporate corruption was to do away with corporations themselves. They were militantly opposed to the extension of slavery, and they merged with the Free Soil party in 1847. Tilden did not join the newly formed Republican party in 1854 as did many Barnburners, and he was opposed to the Civil War. In his law office, he specialized in railroads, developing great skill at making their necessarily exacting investigations, and over the years, he built up an extremely lucrative practice. In 1863, he bought a house on the south side of Gramercy Park and, in 1874, another house next door. Eventually, he converted both of them into a single Victorian mansion.

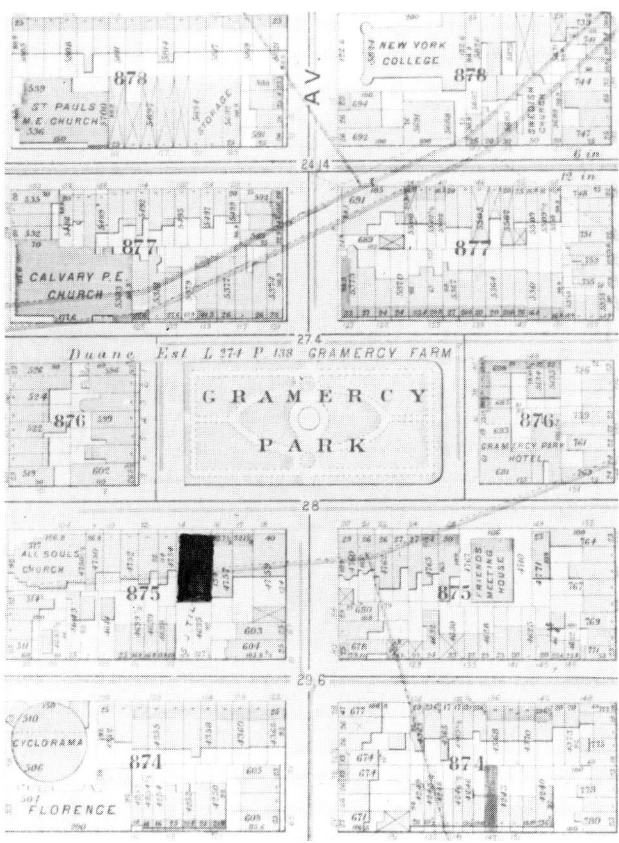

Plate 105 *Map of Gramercy Park area. Shaded building is Samuel J. Tilden's house.*

Plate 106 *No. 17 Gramercy Park.*

In 1863, New York was torn by riots protesting the Civil War draft, and particularly the exemption from the draft of anyone who could pay someone three hundred dollars to take his place. The situation was further aggravated by the resentment of the largely Irish day laborers in New York against the numbers of black freedmen coming up from the South and looking for jobs. From July 13 to 16, there was bloody fighting in the city—robbing, looting, and burning of property—abolitionists and Blacks being particularly under attack. Third Avenue was the scene of the worst fighting after a mob had attacked a recruitment office, driven off the police, and set fire to the building. "The avenue was jammed with human beings who hung over the eaves of buildings, filled the doors and windows, and packed the street from curb to curb."[1] To reinforce the local militia, troops including naval and West Point cadets had to be brought in before order could be restored. The militia, encamped in Gramercy Park itself, did considerable damage.

George Templeton Strong recorded in his diary that Dudley Field, who lived next door to his father, David Dudley, at No. 127 East Twenty-first Street, (this making three Field houses in a row) was prepared for an attack on July 13 and had muskets ready to defend himself. On the sixteenth, Strong related:

> Coming uptown tonight, I find Gramercy Park in military occupation. Strong parties drawn up across Twentieth . . . and Twenty-first Streets at the east end of the Square . . . each with a flanking squad. . . . Occasional shots were fired at them from the region of Second Avenue . . . which were replied to by volleys that seem to have done little execution. . . . This force was relieved at seven by a company of regulars . . . with a couple of howitzers, and there has been but a stray shot or two since dark. The regulars do not look like steady men. I have just gone over to the hotel . . . and ordered a pail of strong coffee to put a little life into them.

By the next day things had quieted down. Strong wrote, "The army of Gramercy Park has advanced its headquarters to Third Avenue leaving only a picket guard in sight. Rain will keep the rabble quiet tonight."

Samuel J. Tilden, who was then thirty-nine years old, had bought the first of his Gramercy Park houses on February 28, 1863. It was No. 15 on the south side and had been built in 1844–45 by Charles and George Belden, and remained in the Belden family. Tilden also bought the lot behind the house on Nineteenth Street, the entire purchase costing $37,500.

The house was one of three (Nos. 15, 16, and 17), all Gothic Revival with cast-iron verandas. Plate 106 shows No. 17, the superstructure of its veranda removed by the time the picture was taken, but still retaining its Gothic porch, which, presumably, all three originally possessed.

The architect Tilden hired to remodel the house was Griffith Thomas (1820–79), and his plans and specifications were ready by that fateful July 1863. Thomas is best known as a designer of cast-iron buildings, in particular the splendid Arnold Constable store that is still standing on Nineteenth Street, with its Second Empire mansard roof and marble front (1868) on Fifth Avenue and an identical cast-iron facade (1877) on Broadway. For Tilden, Thomas took the existing house at No. 15 Gramercy Park and completely redesigned it. The builder, John Meyer, agreed on October 21, 1863,

> [to] erect and finish the new Building with bay window and everything necessary perfectly to enclose it immediately, and make sundry alterations of the present premises . . . the work to begin without delay to be advanced as fast as possible so as to complete the enclosure of said building immediately agreeably to the Drawings and Specifications of Griffith Thomas.

The Gothic porch and veranda were to be removed, the mason's contract agreeing to

> take down front stoop and put up the same in the best manner—new stone where necessary, all cut stone work to be best quality Connecticut brownstone all [to be] polished, [and] to make good to the front whatever damage may be done in taking away the iron verandah [*sic*], and make good to the adjoining verandah. . . . The gates and bars on basement windows to be finished bright-bronze green.[2]

Thomas left the Gothic head molds on the second- and third-floor windows and the Gothic frieze below the cornice. He added a large bay window that Calvert Vaux incorporated into his later renovation, and extended the house at the rear. Inside, the carpenter was instructed to use

> Elizabethan architraves and proper plinths on the windows . . . [to] take down all the present staircase and alter and strengthen the timbers for new stairs, and alter the roof for a large skylight. . . . [Then] to put up a large dome over the center of the staircase. . . . [and] the dining room, anteroom, boudoir and principal library ceilings [were] to be domed. All . . . angles of walls [were to be decorated] with three large reeds and leaves top and bottom. [And the mason was to provide] . . . two verd antique scagliola marble columns and two pilasters, all to have Corinthian capitals and bases and white marble plinths [and here in the margin of the contract has been added "not enough"].[3]

There are carpenters' bills dating from June 1864, and on September 14th, a green marble mantel with bronze ornaments costing eight hundred dollars was installed. Soon after that a pair of plain walnut front doors was put in. The builder's, plumbers', and gasfitters' bills range from March through May of the next year, ending with that for the iron picket fence, dated June 8. The house was ready for Tilden to move in by mid-1865. He had enough means not to have to worry about its cost, and though he was never that interested in art and really didn't care much about what pictures he had on his walls, he had taken pains to provide himself a really comfortable house. The inventory taken at the time of his death showed a man with catholic tastes: it listed framed engravings of such varied subjects as Washington Irving, Christ Walking on the Sea, Lady Jane Grey, Countess Potocka, the Venus de Medici, "Maternal Cares," and the Flight into Egypt. His only valuable painting was "A Hopeless Case" by A. Rotta, which sold at auction for $750.

The library was the most handsome room in the new house because, of all his possessions, Tilden cared most about his books and manuscripts. He had begun by collecting schoolbooks, and later his law library grew to be one of the best in New York. He loved rare books and beautiful bindings, and took great pleasure in acquiring manuscripts such as that of Thomas Jefferson's diary. All his life, he devoured books and journals, and during the final four years of his life alone he read, or had read to him, over seven hundred books.

No. 15 Gramercy Park soon became a mecca for young Democratic politicians and men involved in industry. Business, for Tilden, was inseparable from politics. He had no "regular" law practice as such, but took up a new case "only after finishing an old one." He wrote, "My habit . . . is to make no plans . . . except such as are inevitable . . . and to keep myself as prepared as possible to act. . . . "[4]

As state Democratic chairman, which he became in 1866, Tilden set out to gather evidence of party corruption in New York City. William Marcy Tweed had accumulated absolute power and was able to control all nominations. He and his "ring" ran the city

Plate 107 *Samuel J. Tilden, c. 1875.*

with almost no interference until, finally, they had defrauded it of over thirty million dollars. Tilden was able to have Tweed tried for a felony offense and sentenced to twelve years in prison, of which only one was actually served, the sentence having been reduced by a higher court. Tilden gained great visibility for having "broken the Tweed ring" and was elected governor in November 1874.[5]

Earlier that year, Tilden had bought the house next door at No. 14 Gramercy Park. It was a five-story brick house, not unlike No. 23 today, built in 1844–45; its previous owner was Helen Taylor Varnum, whose father, Robert L. Taylor, having bought it from James Brown in 1863, had deeded it to her in 1864 for "a consideration of $5 and love and affection." When she died in 1873, her husband, acting as her executor, sold the house to Tilden on May 4, 1874. It had already been rented to Thomas E. Turner for eleven months beginning in June for $3,300, but the lease specified that the house was "duly assigned" to Tilden. As at No. 15, Tilden also bought the lot behind the house on Nineteenth Street for his garden and carriage house. As the author of *Old Buildings in New York City* described the garden, it was

> formally laid out with box-edged walks and flower beds. . . . Mr. Tilden, joining with the other owners on the square and the owners of the houses on Irving Place, had all the wooden fences in the angle formed by these houses removed and an open iron fence put in their place. As there were no houses on Nineteenth Street, there remained an unusual effect of greenery and trees for New York City.[6]

Tilden moved in 1874 to Albany, and it was while he was governor that he was chosen, in 1876, to be the Democratic candidate for President, to run against Rutherford B. Hayes. He resigned as governor and was in New York for the final days of the presidential campaign. On October 27, he was cheered by a huge crowd on the steps of No. 15 Gramercy Park at a serenade in his honor.

Election Day, November 7, was cold and rainy. Tilden and Abram Hewitt and others spent the evening at the Everett House on Union Square North, tallying the votes as they came in. By midnight, when they went home, they were convinced that Tilden had won, and on his front stoop he received acclamation as the next President of the United States. The morning papers confirmed his election, except for *The New York Times,* which was the first to suggest that the results were in doubt. Tilden had definitely won the popular vote, and in the electoral college the result was 184 for Tilden and 181 for Hayes, but 185 was the minimum for election. In Florida, a state in which the

Plate 108

Plate 109

Democrats had not had sufficient funds to carry on an adequate campaign, the vote was still unreported. *The Times* not only expected but wanted the state to go Republican.

A telegram was sent to the Republican leaders in Florida early on the morning after Election Day saying, HAYES IS ELECTED IF WE HAVE CARRIED SOUTH CAROLINA, FLORIDA, AND LOUISIANA. CAN YOU HOLD YOUR STATE? ANSWER AT ONCE. It was signed Zach Chandler, the Republican campaign manager, and it served to mobilize carpetbag forces in boss-controlled Florida. In fact, it had not been sent by Chandler; it had come from John C. Reid, the Republican editor of *The New York Times*. Adequate Democratic poll watchers had not been available, due to lack of funds, and there was no way to guarantee a fair count. The scene was wide open to Republican tampering, and the telegram alerted politicians to the closeness of the race.

A challenge to this situation was suggested, and for a while Tilden himself seemed eager to pursue one. There were two sets of returns in Florida, South Carolina, and Louisiana, one tallied by carpetbag Republicans and the other a Democratic recount that gave the victory to Tilden. It could not be agreed which set was valid. But an electoral commission, by an eight-to-seven party-line vote on March 2, 1877, refused to question the returns any further. All the contested southern votes went to Hayes, giving him a majority of one, and he was finally inaugurated. Tilden accepted the decision without further protest, but he always referred to the election as the "crime of 1876."

Not going to Washington meant that Tilden was thrown back upon his own private life, and his books; to Greystone, the country estate he had bought in Yonkers; and most of all to his Gramercy Park house. At last, he could turn his attention to the new adjoining house he had bought in 1874. He decided to combine the two houses into one and, in 1881, hired Calvert Vaux as his architect. Vaux designed a large mansion with a new library worthy of Tilden's growing collection.

Calvert Vaux (1824–95) was one of the leading architects and landscape designers of his day. He was

Plate 108 *Newspaper illustrator's impression of the interior of No. 15 Gramercy Park, during a reception celebrating Tilden's nomination to the presidency, July 1876.*

Plate 109 *Accurate rendering of Nos. 9–16 Gramercy Park. Ex-Governor Tilden was acclaimed on the steps of No. 15 at a serenade in his honor, October 27, 1876.*

born and trained in England, and invited to this country in 1850 by Andrew Jackson Downing, then America's foremost landscape gardener. They worked together in Newburgh, New York, until Downing's untimely death at the age of thirty-six in an 1852 Hudson River steamboat disaster.

In 1857, a competition was held to choose a designer for the huge park that Downing had advocated for New York City. Vaux invited Frederick Law Olmsted to collaborate with him on the project, and they drew the plans for their celebrated Central Park proposal called *Greensward* at Vaux' home at No. 136 East Eighteenth Street. (According to the old system of numbering, this was the second house east of Third Avenue on the north side of the street. Until 1868, when the present system was introduced, by which street numbers recommence at each avenue with the next full hundred [No. 200 at Third Avenue, No. 300 at Second Avenue, etc.] numbering was continuous and uninterrupted by avenues). Downing Vaux, the architect's son, who was a little boy at that time, later remembered his father and Olmsted working away at the project. "There was," he recalled, "a great deal of grass to be put in by the usual small dots and dashes, and it became the friendly thing for callers to help in the work by joining in and 'adding some grass to Central Park.' "[7]

The *Greensward* plan won the competition and the Park was twenty years in construction. Vaux himself designed all the bridges—Bow Bridge and the superb bridle path arches, all in cast iron; and they are among the most beautiful things in New York City.

Vaux also went on to design major public buildings. In collaboration with Jacob Wrey Mould, he produced master plans for the Metropolitan Museum of Art (1874–80) and the Museum of Natural History (1874–77), though only a single wing of each was built according to these designs. At the Metropolitan Museum, all that is left of the original building today is the facade, which is now an interior wall of the Lehman wing. It is Ruskinian Gothic, and it was in this style that Vaux designed the new renovation of Samuel J. Tilden's houses in 1881. He was then working in association with the English-born engineer George K. Radford, and Tilden's house was officially the work of the firm of Vaux and Radford.

The new facade on Tilden's house rose on Gramercy Park at the same time as did a nine-story Gothic apartment house George W. de Cunha designed for No. 34, both radical departures from the surrounding brick or brownstone town houses. A contemporary newspaper article said of the Tilden house, "It is difficult to specify the style, since conventional rules

Plate 110 *Nos. 11–17 Gramercy Park, September 1905. The Vaux entrance to No. 15 was being removed as part of the conversion of the house into the National Arts Club.*

have been largely disregarded. . . . The north exposure compelled high color contrasts to get a good effect, and this has been done with black and red brick, and polished granite arch-stones." Another contemporary writer, the anonymous author of a book called *Artistic Houses,* described the house as

> a free adaptation of the Gothic style of architecture [consisting] principally of Carlisle and Belleville stones, with bands of carved gray granite (which, when polished, presents a surface almost black), and with occasional small columns of Passamaquoddy marble. . . . Medallion heads of Shakespeare, Milton, Dante . . . and Goethe [give] the attention of the passerby something worthy to occupy itself with. The architect . . . seems to have said to himself, "Persons who walk in front of the Governor's house will naturally turn their eyes toward it, and, in order that they may not feel that they are impertinently staring into the windows, I will put before them some pieces of statuary which will invite consideration, and will justify it." These sculptural features are very cleverly wrought, and, that even the wayfaring man may not miss their significance, the names of the celebrities whom they represent are modestly engraved in the narrow bands of gray granite beneath them. Alto-rilievo heads of Spring, Summer, Autumn, and Winter, with surroundings appropriate to each season, appear in Carlisle-stone brackets of the portico.[8]

Vaux designed elaborately carved stone courses for the facade and around the main doorway. They reflect his love of nature, combining leaves and flowers and birds into wonderfully fresh compositions. And a newspaper account of the house described the bust of Michelangelo (now sadly weathered) above the business visitor door at the west side, and the face of Benjamin Franklin (near Shakespeare and the others), chosen because he was "regarded by Mr. Tilden as the typical American. . . . The whole front," he continued "is a marvel of effect in stone while its cost runs up into the thousands at a fabulous rate." As the author of *Artistic Houses* describes it:

> The sky-line of the building . . . being carried higher than that of its neighbors, attracts the attention of the spectator who approaches from Fourth Avenue, long before he reaches the front of the house, Mr. Vaux's long experience with Central Park having given him unusual opportunity for developing and gratifying his taste in the interesting matter of sky-lines. The party-wall on the west side of the house is carried up several feet above the level of the roof, its topmost pediment surmounted by a flagstaff . . . and, in general, it is to be said of the facade as a whole, that its leading features are at the farthest remove from commonplaceness and conventionalism, bearing the impress of a master to whom architecture is the noblest of the fine arts.[9]

Inside the house, many rooms of the Griffith Thomas design were left intact, but the entire parlor floor of No. 14 was turned into a library of real magnificence:

> Stepping from the old library through a richly panelled doorway, the purpose of Mr. Tilden in spending a fortune was at once manifest . . . [the three rooms of the new library] the like of which does not exist elsewhere in this city [could be opened into one]. . . . The floor is of inlaid wood of various colors and intricate designs. Rich oak carving above the cornices encloses a ceiling of blue tiles. Up from the center room rises a light shaft in which is an illuminated stained-glass dome set in bronze framing. . . . Along the bottom of each book case are broad velvet-colored shelves for the rare old folios. . . . The most expensive editions in the richest of bindings alone find place in these shelves. [The windows were curtained in blue satin and fig plush with matching lambrequins.] Above this library is a suite of private rooms which the ex-Governor uses when he does not care to go back to his old quarters in the old house. [Many of the rooms had Shaker chairs in them; New Lebanon, where Tilden was born, was a Shaker com-

Plate 111 *National Arts Club; bay window.*

munity.] The rooms are finished in satin-wood, while the ceilings are ravishments of golden and crimson tint and over the inlaid floors lay Turkish rugs, soft and rare. The bedstead of carved cherrywood faces a fireplace upon which the designer placed the legend "a cheerful blaze for sunless days." . . . [The front windows on the second floor were equipped with sliding metal doors, so that Tilden's privacy was ensured. He also had a secret staircase in the wall of one bedroom through which he could escape to the basement and thence to the rear garden and Nineteenth Street to avoid politicians who might be waiting for him downstairs.] The offices of the residence and quarters for the servants are on a scale of finish commensurate with the entire house. The plumbing is a model in its perfection and its cost. Three years were spent in construction and alterations, and when $50,000 was spent on the bare finish of a single room an idea may be had of the outlay upon the entire residence.[10]

The dome in the central library room was a chief part of the design. It was made in Boston, in 1883, by Donald MacDonald, who had designed the west and north transept windows for Memorial Hall at Harvard. At the four sides of the dome there were, originally, gas jets to illuminate the glass at night; and while its light shaft was eventually closed and artificial lighting installed, the great glass efflorescence was restored in 1970 by the modern glass master Albinas Elskus, and today displays its full radiance.

According to the writer of *Artistic Houses,* the glass in the inner vestibule doors of the main hall designed by John La Farge, was

> the last word of modern art . . . or rather the first word of this later American Renaissance, which our painters, turned decorators, are creating. In this instance, Mr. La Farge has produced some newest and purely artistic results, by an arrangement of varicolored glass of different degrees of thickness, some of the pieces presenting the appearance of the result of pouring molten glass into molten glass, the artist having been guided in the process, not by any formulated recipe, but by the dictates of his own feeling for color. No such work as this latest of our American discoveries was ever elsewhere seen in stained glass; nor could such a piece as that in Governor Tilden's vestibule-doors be duplicated, even by Mr. La Farge himself, so great are the uncertainties of the process of mixing the colors and of firing them in the kiln. At every successive minute of the day, the passage of the daylight through these glowing windows produces its distinctive and inimitable effect. You do not tire of this work of art; its beauty offers fresh significance every time you look at it, and constitutes a direct addition of the purest kind to the sensuous pleasure of life. It tells no story, it shows no forms of men or women, gods or nondescripts, it is not literary at all; it simply brings you face to face with the sweet and subtilest [*sic*] glories of the "bright effluence of bright essence increate"—with light itself, sent back festive and sportive, into its prismatic hues.[11]

Plate 112 *National Arts Club; Donald MacDonald glass dome in what had been Samuel J. Tilden's library.*

It was in the dining room (Plate 113), however, that Vaux lavished his greatest care:

> [He] produced, with complex material, an effect of great richness and perfect unity. The black-walnut wainscoting, four feet high, and several black-walnut bookcases, having been left for him as heir-looms, he proceeded to reconstruct the apartment; and, taking as the key-note of his decorative scheme the ivory tone of old carved satin-wood, he has worked up all the surroundings in harmony with it. . . .
>
> The wall-spaces are paneled in satin-wood, all the principal panels being low-reliefs of birds and foliage in the same firm and hard substance, in the spirit of a free and easy naturalism—the spirit of the Gothic, rather than of the Renaissance. There is no repetition of forms; there is no regular balancing of them—the same form in each corner of the panel—there is no use of geometric forms; but, in their place, such natural forms as birds, leaves, and branches,

Plate 113 *No. 15 Gramercy Park; Samuel J. Tilden's dining room, as designed by Calvert Vaux.*

depicted in that degree of conventionalism which is necessary to an artistic representation, and arranging themselves spontaneously, as it were, without regard to order. Furthermore, the background of these birds and leaves, instead of being flat and spiritless, causing them to appear like *applique*-work, nailed on, is roughened in various ways by the tool of the carver, each panel showing a special sort of roughening, and producing a special effect; and, still further, this irregular background is covered with gold, the very color to set off the satin-wood carvings, to heighten their tone by making it richer and darker. No other color could so well accomplish this result. Each background, therefore, has an artistic individuality as distinct as that of the pictorial representation of birds and leaves thrown out upon it, and gives the spectator the effect of a refinement of individuality as rare as it is pleasing. Moreover, while each panel, when observed closely, presents much precision of detail in its several parts . . . [and] the general treatment of each panel differs from that of any other panel: in contemplating the series you pass from realism to impressionism, through various intervening grades, and, whatever may be your taste, are almost sure to find it gratified.

Of satin-wood, too, is the diapered frieze, every other block or diamond of which is gilded, and, by reason of the irregularity of its background, it gives an impression of flexibility, almost as if it were canvas. In order to blend the black-walnut of the wainscoting with the satin-wood of the walls, the line of molding just above the former is dotted with black-walnut rosettes. The ceiling, thirty-one feet square—and this squareness of dimension adds its own note of fitness to the general effect—is divided transversely, by satin-wood beams, into four parts, each end of the beams terminating in an octagonal panel of the same wood, and each division of the ceiling covered with blue tiles eight inches square, every tile being framed in ribs of satin-wood, and caught by four projections from the center of each rib, and fastened in the back to an iron plate above it. The glaze of these encaustic, turquoise-hued Low tiles gives the ceiling almost a mirror effect, and produces the great charm of changing, shifting tones. Just above the wainscoting, a narrow band of tiles runs all around the room, carrying down to the black-walnut the blue of the ceiling, in a manner precisely analogous to that in which the black-walnut was carried into the satin-wood by the rosettes. The extreme sensitiveness of the design is again manifested by the fact that the lotus-leaf ornamentation which appears on the cove

> of the ceiling is an echo of that which appears on the cove of the porch, outside of the house. One notices, also, that the face of each bracket which adorns the cove is slightly narrower across the bottom than across the top, producing a refinement of effect that invites his sympathetic study. This beautiful room, indeed, abounds in such subtilties [*sic*] of design, and becomes, through them, a banqueting-chamber where the imagination and the eyes alike may feast. The octagonal panel in the center of the ceiling, just above the massive chandelier, is carved in relief, somewhat higher than that of the wall-panels is greater, because the pictorial resources of birds and foliage are larger than those of fruits and berries. These panels, therefore, disclosing, each in turn, its own peculiar loveliness—not wearying by repetition, nor offending by discordancy of tone or disability of drawing, but leading on from one to another—attract and fasten the attention.[12]

When the mansion was finished in 1884, Tilden had only a scant two years to live, much of which was spent at Greystone, his Yonkers estate. For a year or so, however, he was able to enjoy his books in New York in a setting he thought fitting to them. Even then, he was dreaming of a more permanent repository and found Vaux enthusiastic about the idea of a new building somewhere in Central Park.

Tilden's tastes, actually, were "few, simple, and rural"; "his clothes were expensive and clean, but his coat and trousers did not seem to hang becomingly."[13] A friend of his, Mabel Osgood Wright, met him one day in Scribner's Bookstore, which was then around the corner on Fifth Avenue just north of Twenty-first Street (the building is still there), and said he looked

> like an old-time farmer come to a country fair, rather than a New Yorker and politician who had been Governor. An occasional twinkle would flash from his heavy-lidded eyes that at other times seemed closed at the outside corners, as if to prevent anyone from possibly reading his thoughts or getting an opinion in advance.[14]

He was not hesitant, however, to reveal his feelings when it came to something he cared about, like wine. When a caller once drank at one gulp a glass of good wine he had offered him, Tilden said to his butler, "Give him a glass of beer next time."[15]

Though he never married and had a reputation of being something of a recluse, Tilden had many close friends, among them the novelist Sarah Orne Jewett. It was rumored more than once that he might marry: once, in 1876, to Leila Morse, the twenty-four-year-old daughter of Samuel F. B. Morse, whose estate he had settled. When she later did get married, she sent Tilden a picture of herself and her baby inscribed "To Uncle." When Miss Marie Celeste Stauffer of New Orleans visited him with her mother, everyone said an engagement was imminent. But, "when asked, 'Will you marry her?,' Tilden closed his eyes and replied, 'I have compromised with her.' 'What?' 'By leaving her something in my will.' "[16] She received a hundred thousand dollars but complained it was a "paltry sum."

In April 1884, Tilden asked his friend John Bigelow to assist him in revising his will. The bulk of his estate of some five million dollars was to be left to a Tilden Trust to establish a free library and reading room in New York City. Not long after he died, in August 1886, however, his collateral heirs contested the will and, in October 1891, it was held to be invalid. The estate had by now grown to over six million dollars, but just as Tilden had had the presidency within his grasp and had it taken from him, so now the memorial he had planned for himself was taken away. During the litigation, however, Laura Hazard, the sole heir of Tilden's deceased sister, in return for $975,000, surrendered her claim to almost half the estate, and the trust was assured of $2.25 million for the library.

It was proposed that the city erect a new building on Fifth Avenue at Forty-second Street, using stones from the old Croton Reservoir, which had previously occupied the site, for the foundations. In 1895, the Tilden Trust joined with the Astor and Lenox libraries, and the great New York City Public Library system was born.

The mansion on Gramercy Park, however, now deprived of its books, went downhill. It was sold at auction in May 1899. William Ryan, the auctioneer, advertised that it contained "40 rooms, 5 bathrooms, a laundry and drying rooms . . . carved ceilings . . . tapestry walls and two steam heaters." Fewer than twenty years old, it became a rooming house. But then, in 1906, the new National Arts Club, founded by Charles de Kay in 1898, having outgrown its first quarters on Thirty-fourth Street, decided to purchase the wonderful house, and so it was saved. The first president of the club, George B. Post (1837–1913), was the architect of such important buildings as the recently completed New York Stock Exchange and City College. He agreed to design a thirteen-story studio building behind the house on Nineteenth Street. His friend, Charles T. Lamb, one of the charter members of the club, retained as much as possible of the Vaux interiors in his supervision of the remodeling. The main entrance, unfortunately, had to be sacrificed, but as Lamb related,

> I saved the stones we had to take down . . . using them again to avoid a contrast of new against old. The

> only thing actually new is the marble in the staircase and the lower hall. Each time we made a cutting, we saved the carving and used it elsewhere. The mirrors from one place we placed in another. . . . Mr. La Farge's fine doorlights had to be moved to between the stairs and lounge [they were regrouped into the space which had been a doorway. His] secretary wrote to me . . . [that he remembered] having made a pair of interesting doors for Mr. Tilden . . . [and] would be glad to have them back to his studio.
>
> I answered, "I am charmed to know that Mr. La Farge thinks these panels are works of his that he likes to be remembered by, because I have given them a place in the Club where they can be seen by his friends."[17]

Tilden's dining room became the gallery of the National Arts Club and Vaux's marvelous decorations were dispersed. Some of the gilded wood panels now adorn the ground-floor walls of the club, but the room had to be neutralized to function well as a gallery, and so its character was totally changed. Skylights were installed where the blue-glass ceiling panels had been (though these have now been covered up). The room was enlarged to include part of Tilden's middle parlor, and so today one of Griffith Thomas's domed plaster ceilings can be seen next to the portion of Vaux's dining-room ceiling that is left, and the change in the climate of design from 1863 to 1883 is easily read between the two.

Over the years, the club has had such distinguished members as George Bellows, Mark Tobey, Frederic Remington, John C. Johansen, Alfred Stieglitz, Ludwig Bemelmans, Augustus Saint-Gaudens, Daniel Chester French, and Will Barnet. Woodrow Wilson was a member, as was Theodore Roosevelt, who also frequently lunched there. The club has not only encouraged some of the most significant American artists of this century, but has also shown enlightened respect for its celebrated home. The ghost of Samuel J. Tilden, connoisseur of architecture, books, and wine, if not of the other arts, can only be grateful.

Notes

[1] Quoted in John B. Pine, *The Story of Gramercy Park, 1831–1921* (New York: Knickerbocker Press, 1921), p. 44.

[2] Builder's Contract, Tilden Papers, Manuscript Division, New York Public Library, New York.

[3] Ibid.

[4] Alexander C. Flick, *Samuel J. Tilden* (New York: Dodd Mead & Co., 1939), p. 145.

[5] Tweed was defended by David Dudley Field. He was Tilden's neighbor across the Park, and there was little love lost between them. Cyrus Field was also no admirer of Tilden. Their association in the promotion of elevated railways in New York resulted in such discord that Field was quoted in the *New York Times*:

> My feeling toward Mr. Tilden therefore is not so much one of anger as of disgust at the meanness which could take advantage of my confidence to do me an injury. It was to me a revelation of the character of the man. It showed me falseness and trickery, of which I had frequently been warned, but of which I had now my first experience. This will explain my very decided opinion of Samuel J. Tilden, and why I am obliged to regard him as something else than an illustrious statesman.

[6] *Old Buildings of New York City* (New York: Brentano's, 1907), p. 94.

[7] Elizabeth Barlow, *Frederick Law Olmsted's New York* (New York: Praeger Publishers, 1972), p. 21.

[8] *Artistic Houses* (New York: D. Appleton & Co., 1883–1884), p. 61.

[9] Ibid., p. 62.

[10] Contemporary anonymous newspaper account.

[11] *Artistic Houses*, p. 63.

[12] Ibid., pp. 63–65.

[13] Flick, op. cit., p. 478.

[14] Ibid., p. 475.

[15] Ibid., p. 510.

[16] Ibid., p. 478.

[17] Charles C. Lamb, *The Tilden Memoirs* (New York: privately printed by the National Arts Club, 1932), p. 10.

Plate 114 *Vicinity of Gramercy Park as seen from the Latting Observatory, 1855. Engraving by B. F. Smith.*

12

Edith Wharton, Stephen Crane, and Other Writers

The vicinity of Gramercy Park has been home to some of the major American writers of the last 150 years. Some, like Edith Wharton and Stephen Crane, have described life in and around the Park in their work and illuminated our understanding of it. Others have simply lived on the Park or nearby, and it is interesting to document their time there.

Edith Newbold Jones Wharton was born in 1862 at No. 14 West Twenty-third Street. Her father, George Frederick Jones (a college classmate of George Templeton Strong), and her mother had lived previously at No. 80 East Twenty-first Street (Later, No. 119) but in 1858, they moved to the new Twenty-third Street house, which was almost identical to the one on Gramercy Park. As Wharton's biographer, R.W.B. Lewis, has described it, there was the usual high stoop and one then entered

> a vestibule painted in Pompeian red and beyond it, the first of several cramped sitting rooms. The white-and-gold drawing room . . . was rigorously protected from the world outside by two layers of curtains: sashes, lace draperies, and damask hangings. Heavy pieces of Dutch marquetry adorned it, and a cabinet displayed a number of old painted fans and exquisite and never-used pieces of old lace brought back from Venice and Paris. A Mary Magdalene, etched in copper, was on the Louis Philippe table: in the dining room, adjoining, there was an imitation Domenicino; both were nearly invisible in the well-bred gloom. . . . It was a rather cheerless house. The overcrowded rooms, like those of most other New York town houses of the period, were so designed as to lack any clear identity and to make privacy impossible. Each seemed somehow to be a part of the room next to it—the drawing room was part of the hall, the library part of the drawing room. In the latter, inflammable draperies above the mantelpiece made it dangerous to light the fire in the hearth. The ground floor sitting rooms were like the waiting rooms in a dentist's office. The house was expressively but unharmoniously furnished, though among the heavy upholstery were some fine and undervalued colonial pieces.
>
> The Joneses entertained well, even lavishly. . . . [Their] cooks were famous in New York: Mary Johnson, a towering black woman with golden hoops in her ears, and Susan Minneman . . . small . . . and softspoken. . . . For daily fare, they served up corned beef, boiled turkey with oyster sauce, fried chicken and stewed tomatoes; for dinner parties, they provided terrapin and canvasback ducks, soft-shelled crabs and Virginia ham cooked in champagne, lima beans in cream and corn souffle.
>
> . . . [The talk at dinner] was safe, monotonous, and rigidly circumscribed, with scarcely a word about literature or music or art.[1]

From her teens, Edith Wharton remembered two experiences that took place in Gramercy Park. Her best friend was Emelyn Washburn, whose father was rector of Calvary Church. Edith used to love to spend hours with Emelyn in her father's library (Plate 74) at No. 103 East Twenty-first Street (No. 61 Gramercy Park), looking at books on Anglo-Saxon, Icelandic, and Old Norse literature, and when weather allowed, they would climb onto the adjoining roof and read Dante aloud. One Sunday evening, sitting with her friend at a service in Calvary Church, she became so entranced listening to a reading from the King James Bible that she unconsciously plucked bare a place on Emelyn's camel's hair coat.

In 1897, when Edith Wharton published *The Decoration of Houses,* she had few kind words for the New York of her childhood. The book was written in direct opposition to the life-style of affluent society around Madison Square and Gramercy Park that was epitomized by her parents' home.

> Who cannot call to mind the dreary drawing room, in small town houses the only possible point of reunion for the family, but too often, in consequence of its exquisite discomfort, of no more use as a meeting place than the vestibule or the cellar? . . . [Space for a writing table] is generally taken up by a cabinet or console, surmounted by a picture made invisible by the dark shadow of the hangings. . . . The writing table is either banished or put in some dark corner where it is little wonder that the ink dried unused and a vase of flowers grows in the middle of the blotting pad.[2]

Edmund Wilson called Edith Wharton a "poet of interior decoration." She rarely gives lengthy descriptions of places in her work, but her visual awareness allowed her to convey a scene vividly in a few accurate details. Her evocation of well-to-do life as it was carried on in and around Gramercy Park, both in the 1870's and in the early years of the twentieth century, informed as it is by firsthand experience, provides insight into the subtleties and foibles of New York society.

The Age of Innocence begins at a performance, sometime in the 1870's, of Gounod's opera *Faust,* at the Academy of Music on Fourteenth Street and Irving Place, which was the major opera house in the country until the building of the new Metropolitan in 1883. Wharton describes the "shabby red and gold boxes of the sociable old Academy . . . cherished [by conservatives] for being small and inconvenient, and thus keeping out the 'new people' whom New York was beginning to dread and yet be drawn to."[3] Because the social center of the city was always moving northward, one of her characters "already had his eye on a newly built house in East Thirty-ninth Street. The neighborhood was thought remote, and the house was built in a ghastly greenish-yellow stone

Plate 115 *Union Square, looking north on Fourth Avenue, c. 1857.*

that the younger architects were beginning to employ as a protest against the brownstone of which the uniform hue coated New York like a cold chocolate sauce; but the plumbing was perfect."[4]

In *The Custom of the Country* she describes the inhabitants of an old house as being so closely identified with it that

> they might have passed for its inner consciousness as it might have stood for their outward form. . . . As Ralph . . . passed into the hall, with its dark mahogany doors and . . . black and white marble paving, he said to himself that what [was] called society was really just like the houses it lived in: a muddle of misapplied ornament over a thin steel shell of utility. The steel shell was built up in Wall Street, the social trimmings were hastily added in Fifth Avenue; and the union between them was as monstrous and factitious, as unlike the gradual homogeneous growth which flowers into what other countries know as society, as that between the Blois gargoyles on . . . [the] roof and the skeleton walls supporting them. . . . Ralph sometimes called his mother and grandfather the aborigines, and likened them to those vanishing citizens of the American continent doomed to rapid extinction with the advance of the invading race. . . . Before long [they] would be exhibited at ethnological shows, pathetically engaged in the exercise of their primitive industries.[5]

Later in the book, Wharton says:

> From the moment he set foot in Wall Street, Mr. Spragg became another man. Physically the change revealed itself only by the subtlest signs. As he steered his way to his office through the jostling crowd of William Street his relaxed muscles did not grow more taut or his lounging gait less desultory. His shoulders were hollowed by the usual droop, and his rusty black waistcoat showed the same creased concavity at the waist, the same flabby prominence below. It was only in his face that the difference was perceptible, though even here it rather lurked behind the features than openly modified them: showing itself now and then in the cautious glint of half-closed eyes, the forward thrust of black brows, or a tightening of the lax lines of the mouth—as the gleam of a night-watchman's light might flash across the darkness of a shuttered house-front.[6]

In *The House of Mirth* Wharton comments on how "in Mrs. Peniston's youth, fashion had returned to town in October; therefore on the tenth day of the month the blinds of her Fifth Avenue residence were drawn up, and the eyes of the Dying Gladiator in bronze who occupied the drawing room window resumed their survey of that deserted thoroughfare." There are, throughout the book, wonderful details that bring a scene to life, such as when Lily Bart "began to wander aimlessly about the room, fitting her steps with mechanical precision between the monstrous roses of Mrs. Peniston's Axminster [carpet]." Nineteenth-century Gramercy Park front parlors, so remote now and long vanished, are brought into clearer focus in such an accurate image. Or when Lily Bart on the night of her suicide

> continued to sit at [her] table, sorting her papers and writing, till the intense silence of the house reminded her of the lateness of the hour. In the street the noise of wheels had ceased, and the rumble of the "elevated" came only at long intervals through the deep unnatural hush. . . . She felt as though the house, the street, the world were all empty, and she alone left sentient in a lifeless universe."[7]

The very month that Edith Wharton was born on Twenty-third Street, in January 1862, Herman Melville moved into a house at No. 150 East Eighteenth Street, an address between Second and First avenues, according to the old numbering system then still in use. Melville had also been born in New York, forty-two years earlier, but had not been regularly in the city since the three years (1847–50) he had lived at No. 103 Fourth Avenue. He stayed on Eighteenth Street only until the middle of August, however, when he had to move back to Pittsfield, Massachusetts, where he had previously been living. Early the next year though, he returned with his family to New York for good and bought the brick house at No. 104 East Twenty-sixth Street, in a block paved by Samuel B. Ruggles and George Furst in 1837.

Melville made his living thereafter as a district inspector in the Custom House Service, working first at the Hudson River docks, to which he walked every morning. When he was later transferred to the East River docks, he probably took the new Third Avenue El to work. His job, in almost the lowest rank of the service, paid him only four dollars a day, and no raise was ever given him in twenty-one years. When inspecting cargo, the great novelist wore a uniform not unlike that of a policeman. He did virtually no writing during those years except the long poem *Clarel*, which was put down on little scraps of paper in off moments at work.

Melville had been embittered by the lack of recognition *Moby-Dick* had received. In New York, he faded into greater and greater obscurity until, at his death in 1891, the New York *World* could describe him as "Herman Melville, formerly a well-known author." He had been stricken by the death of his two sons, one who shot himself in 1867 when he was only in his teens, and the other who died alone and estranged nine years later. Melville's sorrow and isolation found its way into such lines from *Clarel* as

> that parlor-strain
> Which counts each thought that borders pain
> A social treason.

The poem, which many now consider one of his finest works, was published in 1876, but was described by the critic of the *Daily Tribune* as "hardly a book to be commended, for a work of art it is not in any sense or measure."

In 1887, Melville's publishers closed out his account with a payment of $50.02. Having resigned his job in 1885, he wrote:

> . . . I have entered my eighth decade. After twenty years nearly, as an outdoor Custom House officer, I have latterly come into the possession of unobstructed leisure, but only just as, in the course of nature, my vigor sensibly declines. What little of it is left I husband for certain matters as yet incomplete.[8]

He was referring to the one final task he had been attempting; it was to be one of his best achievements. The year before, he had begun to write *Billy Budd,* the story of a man who is executed but wants first to be reconciled with his executioner. On the manuscript Melville wrote (and later crossed out), "Here ends a story not unwarranted by what happens in this incongruous world of ours." At the end of his life, he had begun to accept his own situation as tragic necessity, and in that acceptance to find some peace.

Melville's widow did not consider *Billy Budd* finished, and carefully packed the manuscript away after his death in 1891. It was not rediscovered and published until 1924. The house they had lived in had been torn down by then and replaced with an office building that is today No. 357 Park Avenue South.

From the back porch of his house, where he had often sat smoking his pipe and looking down at his roses, Melville had been able to look across to the rear of No. 111 East Twenty-fifth Street where, in 1875, another writer lived. His name was Henry James, and he had moved back to New York from Cambridge, Massachusetts, in January of that year, the month that his first novel, *Roderick Hudson,* began its serialization in *The Atlantic Monthly.* He was thirty-one and wanted to "try New York" despite his "irresistible longing" for Europe, saying that he thought it his "duty to attempt to live at home before [he] should grow older, and not take for granted too much that Europe alone was possible." He was making a hundred dollars a month from *Roderick Hudson* and the same for reviews he contributed to *The Nation.* He found two rooms in the house on Twenty-fifth Street (demolished in 1905 for the building of the 69th Regiment Armory). James left an impression of the Twenty-fifth Street he knew in his 1886 novel *The Bostonians.* His character, Basil Ransom, lived nearer to Second Avenue, but the picture of his street must have been drawn from James's own experience in 1875.

> He occupied two small shabby rooms in a somewhat decayed . . . house [with] a red, rusty face, and faded green shutters, of which the slats were limp and at variance with each other. . . . [In the shop window below] savoury wares [were] displayed . . . ; a strong odour of smoked fish, combined with a fragrance of molasses, hung about the spot; the pavement, toward the gutters, was fringed with dirty panniers, heaped with potatoes, carrots, and onions; and a smart, bright wagon, with the horse detached from the shafts, drawn up on the edges of the abominable road (it contained holes and ruts a foot deep, and immemorial accumulations of stagnant mud), imparted an idle, rural, pastoral air to a scene otherwise perhaps expressive of a rank civilisation. . . . One of [Ransom's] rooms was directly above the street-door of the house; such a dormitory, when it is so exiguous, is called in the nomenclature of New York a "hall bedroom." The sitting room, beside it, was slightly larger, and they both commanded a row of tenements no less degenerate than [his] own habitation—houses built forty years before and already sere and superannuated. These were also painted red, and the bricks were accentuated by a white line; they were garnished, on the first floor, with balconies covered with small tin roofs, striped in different colours, with an elaborate iron lattice-work, which gave them a repressive, cage-like appearance, and caused them slightly to resemble the little boxes for peeping unseen into the street, which are a feature of oriental towns. Such posts of observation commanded a view of the grocery on the corner, of the relaxed and disjointed roadway, enlivened at the curbstone with an occasional ash-barrel or with gas-lamps drooping from the perpendicular, and . . . at the end of the truncated vista, of the fantastic skeleton of the [Third Avenue] Elevated Railway, overhanging the transverse longitudinal street, which it darkened and smothered with the immeasurable spinal column and myriad clutching paws of an anti-diluvian monster.[9]

James sat in his little drawing room that winter of 1875 and, as he put it, "scribbled" away, a chapter a month of *Roderick Hudson.* He went to see the annual Watercolor Show at the National Academy of Design, on Twenty-third Street at Fourth Avenue (Plate 160) and wrote a piece on it in the *Galaxy* entitled "On Some Pictures Lately Exhibited." It is interesting to look over his shoulder at that exhibition. He did not

Plate 116 *Free Academy, 1905. In the foreground, the Twenty-second Street annex; in the distance, the 69th Regiment Armory under construction.*

particularly like the Winslow Homers he saw there and thought that Homer

> obviously has no imagination, but he contrives to elevate this rather blighting negative into a blooming and honorable positive. He is almost barbarously simple, and, to our eye, he is horribly ugly; but there is nevertheless something one likes about him. What is it? . . . Not his subjects . . . we detest his subjects—his barren plank fences, his glaring, bald, blue skies, his big dreary vacant lots of meadows. . . . He has chosen the least pictorial features of the least pictorial range of scenery and civilization; he has resolutely treated them as if they *were* pictorial, as if they were every inch as good as Capri or Tangier; and, to reward his audacity, he has incontestably succeeded.[10]

That spring, James often took the "El" uptown and walked in Central Park, which he described as having "lakes too big for the landscape and bridges too big for the lakes." But spring made him long for Italy. When one day he came home and found in his rooms some flowers a friend had left him, he wrote:

> They reminded me . . . of the Roman springtime and I howled, fairly, in spirit when I looked at that enchanting cyclamen and thought of the sheets of it one sees at this time in the villas and on the Campagna—and then saw from my window the hideous driving sleet.[11]

He left New York in mid-July, and by the end of October was in Europe for good. Logan Pearsall Smith reported his saying that in New York "it was impossible to have a picturesque address, . . . that he had gone back to New York to live and be a good American citizen, but at the end [of six months] he had quietly packed up his few belongings and come away."[12] There is no record that he even knew Herman Melville had been living only a few hundred feet from him all the while, and it is unlikely that in 1875 Melville had even heard of James.

Twenty-five years later, when Henry James was firmly established in England, Stephen Crane lived for a while not far away in Sussex. He was about as much younger than James as James had been younger than Melville, but this time the older writer did know and was able to support the younger one. James referred to Crane as "my young compatriot of genius." Seven years before, in 1893, Crane had been living in New York just a few blocks from where James had lived, at No. 145 East Twenty-third Street, and writing about it with a realism that more than equaled that of James.

Stephen Crane was the fourteenth child of a Port Jervis, New York, Methodist minister. After a short stay at Syracuse University, he came to New York in 1892, at the age of twenty, and shared a room with two medical students on Avenue A. What money he lived on came from writing sketches about New York

Plate 117

for various newspapers. In January 1893, he moved in with three friends who shared a studio at the old Needham Building on Twenty-third Street, on the site of the present Kenmore Hotel. The Art Students League had previously occupied the building, but had moved to Fifty-seventh Street in 1892.

Crane and two of his friends slept in the one bed, taking turns in the middle position, and the fourth slept on a cot. They were so poor that they had clothes enough for only one of them to go out looking for work at a time; while the one whose turn it was went out, the other three stayed in. They ate most often at a delicatessen called Boeuf-a-la-Mode, which they nicknamed "The Buffalo-Mud," where one could fill up on a breakfast of potato salad. The upper floors of their building, Crane wrote, "were filled with artists, musicians and writers, young men and women, decent people all, who were glad of the low rents and really congenial atmosphere. The landlord was an artist and as considerate of our financial difficulties as he could be in reason. Our life there was free, gay, hard-working and decent."[13]

In one of Crane's New York sketches, he described the building in some detail:

> This building with its commonplace front . . . once rang with the voices of a crowd of art students who in those days past built their ideals of art-schools upon the most approved Parisian models and it is fact generally unknown to the public that this staid puritanical old building once contained about all that was real in the Bohemian quality of New York. The exterior belies the interior in a tremendous degree. It is plastered with signs, and wears sedately the air of being what it is not.
>
> The interior however is a place of slumberous corridors rambling in puzzling turns and curves. The large studios rear their brown rafters over scenes of lonely quiet. Gradually the tinkers, the tailors, and the plumbers who have captured the ground floor are creeping toward those dim ateliers above them. One by one the besieged artists give up the struggle and the time is not far distant when the conquest of the tinkers, the tailors, and the plumbers will be complete.
>
> Nevertheless, as long as it stands, the old building will be to a great many artists of this country a place endeared to them by the memory of many an escapade of the old student days when the boys of the life class used to row gaily with the boys of the "preparatory antique" in the narrow halls. Everyone was gay, joyous, and youthful in those blithe days and the very atmosphere of the old place cut the austere and decorous elements out of a man's heart and made him rejoice when he could divide his lunch of sandwiches with the model.
>
> Who does not remember the incomparable "soap slides" of those days when the whole class in the hour of rest, slid whooping across the floor one after another. The water and soap with which the brushes

Plate 117 *Twenty-third Street, looking west to Lexington Avenue, 1905. The Free Academy is on the left, and across Twenty-third Street from it, beyond the sign reading Signs, is the Needham building, where Stephen Crane lived.*

were washed used to make fine ice when splashed upon the floor and the hopes of America in art have taken many a wild career upon the slippery stretch. And who does not remember the little man who attempted the voyage when seated in a tin-wash basin and who came to grief and arose covered with soap and deluged the studio [with] profanity.

Once when the woman's life class bought a new skeleton for the study of anatomy, they held a very swagger function in their class room and christened it "Mr. Jolton Bones" with great pomp and ceremony. Up in the boy's life class the news of the ceremony created great excitement. They were obliged to hold a rival function without delay. And the series of great pageants, ceremonials, celebrations, and fetes which followed were replete with vivid color and gorgeous action.

The Parisian custom exhaustively recounted in "Trilby" of requiring each new member of a class to make a spread for his companions was faithfully followed. Usually it consisted of beer, crackers and brie cheese.

After the Art Student's [*sic*] League moved to Fifty-Seventh St., the life class of the National Academy of Design school moved in for a time and occasionally the old building was alive with its old uproar and its old spirit. After their departure, the corridors settled down to dust and quiet. Infrequently of a night one could pass a studio door and hear the cheerful rattle of half of a dozen tongues, hear a guitar twinkling an accompaniment to a song, see a mass of pipe smoke cloud the air. But this too vanished, and now one can only hear the commercial voices of the tinkers, the tailors, and the plumbers.

In the top-most and remotest studio there is an old beam which bears this line from Emerson in half-obliterated chalk-marks: "Congratulate yourselves if you have done something strange and extravagant and broken the monotony of a decorous age." It is a memory of the old days.[14]

Crane thought of buildings as metaphors for people. In his first book, *Maggie: A Girl of the Streets,* he described the shutters of tall buildings as "closed like grim lips" and a saloon door as "an open mouth." In another of his New York sketches he wrote that the Needham was

a mournful old building [that] stood between two that were tall and straight and proud. In a way, it was a sad thing; symbolizing a decrepit old man whose lean shoulders are jostled by sturdy youth. The old building seemed to glance timidly upward at its two neighbors, pleading for comradeship, and at times it assumed an important air derived from its environment, and said to those who viewed from the sidewalks: "we three—we three buildings."

It stood there awaiting the inevitable time of downfall, when progress, to the music of tumbling walls and chimneys would come marching up the avenues. Already, from the roof one could see a host advancing, an army of enormous buildings, coming with an invincible front that extended across the city, trampling under their feet the bones of the dead, rising tall and supremely proud on the crushed memories, the annihilated hopes of generations gone. At sunset time, each threw a tremendous shadow, a gesture of menace out over the low plain of the little buildings huddling afar down.

Once this mournful old structure had been proud. It had stood with its feet unconcernedly on the grave of a past ambition and no doubt patronized the little buildings on either side.[15]

Crane left Twenty-third Street in May 1893, but came back in October and lived in a little room near the Needham Building. One afternoon, he turned up at the door of his old room there, in a rainstorm, but with no overcoat and shaking with cold. His friends insisted he stay, and it was then that the manuscript of *The Red Badge of Courage,* which he had been working on for a year or so, was finished. He took it to the writer, Hamlin Garland, the following April 1894, and as Garland described the experience:

He handed it over to me with seeming reluctance, and while he went out to watch my brother getting lunch, I took my first glance at [it]. It was a bit soiled from much handling. It had not been typed. It was in the clearly legible and rather handsome script of the author.[16]

While Crane ate lunch, Garland looked at his "sallow, yellow-fingered guest" and was

unable to relate him to the marvelous manuscript of images so keen and phrases so graphic and newly coined that [I] hardly dared express openly [my] admiration.

The first sentence fairly took me captive. It described a vast army in camp on one side of a river, confronting with its thousand eyes a similar monster on the opposite bank. The finality which lay in every word, the epic breadth of vision, the splendor of the pictures presented—all indicated a most powerful and original imagination as well as a mature mastery of literary form. Each page presented pictures like those of a great poem, and I experienced the thrill of the editor who has fallen unexpectedly upon the work of genius. . . . [Crane] confessed that all his knowledge of battle had been gained on the football field.[17]

The book brought considerable fame to Stephen Crane, but the social obligations of a famous author were alien to him. In the spring of 1896, he was staying at No. 33 East Twenty-second Street and wrote to a friend that he had just come from a social weekend:

> After I had sat before twelve fireplaces and drunk 842 cups of tea, I said, "I shall escape." And so I have come to New York. But New York is worse. I am in despair. The storm-beaten little robin who has no place to lay his head, does not feel so badly as do I. . . . If there is a joy of living I can't find it. The future? The future is blue with obligations and trials and conflicts.[18]

The next year, however, he fell in love with Cora Howorth and moved with her to England. They lived extravagantly in an old Sussex manor house, entertained wildly, and became friends not only with Henry James, but H. G. Wells and Joseph Conrad. Crane wrote desperately in a futile attempt to get out of debt, but never succeeded. By 1900, he had contracted tuberculosis, and when he was dying, the writer Ford Madox Hueffer recalled how Henry James was forever considering devices for his comfort. He even telegraphed Wanamaker's for a whole collection of New England delicacies "from pumpkin pie to apple butter . . . and soft shell crabs, so that the poor lad should know once more and finally those fierce joys."[19]

Two authors are especially associated with Irving Place—O. Henry and Washington Irving, for whom Ruggles named the street. O. Henry believed that Irving had lived at No. 122 East Seventeenth Street, the house at the corner of Irving Place that bears a plaque that announces this, and many others have assumed as much. But the truth is that he did not. He did live for a short time in Colonnade Row, Nos. 428–434 Lafayette Street.

O. Henry lived in the front parlor of the rooming house at No. 55 Irving Place from 1903 to 1907. Born in North Carolina as William Sydney Porter, he had once lived in Texas, where, as a teller in an Austin bank, he was accused of embezzlement and imprisoned for three years. It was there that he began writing short stories. On his release he moved to New York; he loved the area between Madison Square and Irving Place, loved going to Scheffel Hall, the *brauhaus* at No. 190 Third Avenue (now Tuesday's), and could often be found sitting on benches in Madison Square. He spent a lot of time at Healy's pub (now Pete's Tavern). During his years on Irving Place, his habit was to sit at his window, watch people passing by, and write stories about them. Lonely little people, hopeful, beaten-down people were the ones he wrote most successfully about—those who had come to the big city and were bewildered by it. (O. Henry came to understand their plight in prison, and he even took his pen name from a prison guard he had known named Orrin Henry.) In the scope of only a few pages, he was able to lift the poignancy of their lives into sharp focus. He described the inhabitants of a rooming house like his own in a story called "The Skylight Room" with an accuracy born of close observation and great empathy.

The two remaining authors about whom more should be said here are Hart Crane (1899–1932) and Nathanael West (1903–40). Hart Crane came to New York from Cleveland at the end of 1916 with a view toward entering Columbia College the next year. His parents were estranged, and his mother and grandmother joined him in New York in May 1917, and all three found an apartment—two rooms, really—for the summer in a house at No. 44 Gramercy Park (No. 135 East Twenty-first Street). Crane was just getting his first poems published in magazines, but there was, as yet, little hint that he would become one of the most original American poets of the twentieth century. He made a valiant attempt at studying for the Columbia entrance exams, but in the end he gave up. When the lease expired at the end of the summer, his mother and grandmother returned to Cleveland, and he moved elsewhere in New York.

Nathanael West, whose real name was Nathan Weinstein, was born in New York in 1903. After graduating from Brown University and spending two years in Paris, he returned to New York and made his living as a hotel manager, first at the Kenmore Hotel on East Twenty-third Street, just two blocks from Gramercy Park. It was while he was there that he began to write and produce his first novel, *The Dream Life of Balso Snell* (1931). The people he observed in the hotel, the bitter, alienated victims of the depression, were his real subject. He presented them most powerfully in his next book, *Miss Lonelyhearts* (1933), which is a tragic lament for people who apply for advice in a newspaper's "lovelorn" department. In 1935, West moved to Hollywood on the strength of *Miss Lonelyhearts* and became a scriptwriter. Only five years later, however, at the age of thirty-seven, his career and life were cut short when he died in an automobile accident.

Among the other authors who have lived in the vicinity of Gramercy Park are William Dean Howells (No. 241 and No. 330 East Seventeenth Street), Ezra Pound (No. 270 Fourth Avenue, for a brief period before 1907), Elinor Wylie and William Rose Benét (No. 142 East Eighteenth Street, 1923–24), John Steinbeck (No. 38 Gramercy Park, after his arrival in New York in 1925), W. H. Auden and Christopher Isherwood (George Washington Hotel, after coming to New York in 1939), Booth Tarkington (Hotel Irving, during the 1920's), Mark Twain (two stays at The Players), and S. J. Perelman (Gramercy Park Hotel, where he died in 1979). Perelman, toward the end of his life, decided he had had enough of America and wanted to end his days in less-frantic England. He left but, before too long, came back. One of his reasons: while he loved the English countryside, to him even more beautiful than the most beautiful country sunset was the glow of a Third Avenue deli on a cold New York night.

Notes

[1] R. W. B. Lewis, *Edith Wharton: A Biography* (New York: Harper & Row, 1975), pp. 22–23.

[2] Edith Wharton and Ogden Codman, Jr., *The Decoration of Houses* (New York: W. W. Norton & Sons, 1978), pp. 20–21.

[3] Edith Wharton, *The Age of Innocence* (New York: Charles Scribner's Sons, 1970), p. 3.

[4] Ibid., p. 72.

[5] Edith Wharton, *The Custom of the Country* (New York: Berkley Books, 1981), pp. 47–48.

[6] Ibid., p. 78.

[7] Edith Wharton, *The House of Mirth* (New York: Bantam Books, 1984), p. 309.

[8] Leon Howard, *Herman Melville* (Berkeley: University of California Press, 1951), p. 328.

[9] Henry James, *The Bostonians* (New York: New American Library, 1979), pp. 150–151.

[10] Henry James, *The Painter's Eye* (Cambridge, Mass.: Harvard University Press, 1956), pp. 96–97.

[11] Leon Edel, *Henry James, vol. 2* (New York: Avon Books, 1978), p. 189.

[12] Ibid., p. 190.

[13] R. W. Stallman, *Stephen Crane,* (New York: George Braziller, Inc., 1968), p. 81.

[14] R. W. Stallman and E. R. Hageman, *The New York Sketches of Stephen Crane and Related Pieces* (New York: New York University Press, 1966), pp. 14–16.

[15] Ibid., pp. 16–17.

[16] Stallman, op. cit., pp. 92–93.

[17] Ibid., p. 92.

[18] Stephen Crane, *Love Letters to Nellie Crouse* (Syracuse, New York: Syracuse University Press, 1954), p. 53.

[19] Stallman, op. cit., pp. 500–01.

Plate 118 *No. 122 East Seventeenth Street; Elsie de Wolfe's dining room, 1898. To assess how avant-garde this room was, one need only contrast it with Stanford White's dining room of the following year (Plate 133).*

Plate 119 *No. 121 East Twenty-first Street; the 150-foot vista from the drawing room to the music room of Stanford White's house.*

13

Stanford White: Designer For a Gilded Age

Of all the architects who have done work in the vicinity of Gramercy Park, the one who had the greatest impact was Stanford White (1853–1906). Ironically, however, he never had the opportunity to design a single new building here, as he had at Washington Square, where his Judson Memorial Church and Washington Arch still exert such a strong presence; in Gramercy Park his work had to do with the transformation of existing houses.

He took the interiors of ordinary brownstone buildings and turned them into palatial extravaganzas. When he had finished, one then could enter quite unassuming front doors and find oneself in a world of Renaissance luxury. Single-handedly, he created a rich fin de siècle chapter in the history of the Park. It was a chapter, however, that lasted a scant thirty years, and, when it was over, it vanished, leaving scarcely a trace. Of all his major work here, only The Players remains.

Stanford White was born on Tenth Street and grew up in Brooklyn, on the Narrows near Fort Hamilton, and then on Stuyvesant Square. Though his formal education was minimal, White learned a great deal at home about music and the fine arts. His father was a Shakespearean scholar, and writers and artists were constantly his parents' guests. As he was growing up, he wanted to become a painter, but he was discouraged by his father's friend John La Farge, who told him it was too uncertain a career, so he decided to become an architect.

In mid-nineteenth century America, architecture was a profession that required no formal training; architecture schools didn't yet exist, and one learned only by being apprenticed to a practicing architect. Therefore, in 1872, when he was nineteen, at the suggestion of another of his father's friends, Frederick Law Olmsted, White was apprenticed to the great architect Henry Hobson Richardson. He learned his art from Richardson and from working alongside Charles Follen McKim, who was also employed in Richardson's New York office at the time. In 1874, when Richardson moved to Brookline, Massachusetts, White followed and did renderings there for two of Richardson's major works, Trinity Church in Boston and the Senate Chamber in Albany.

Plate 120 *Stanford White, 1880.*

White left Richardson in 1878 and traveled in Europe with McKim and with his sculptor friend, Augustus Saint-Gaudens. He had met Saint-Gaudens one day, probably during the summer of 1875, "on the way up the cast iron stairs of the German Savings Bank Building at Fourth Avenue and Fourteenth Street." He "heard someone singing loudly . . . the Andante from Beethoven's Fifth Symphony. This was followed by the Serenade from Mozart's *Don Giovanni,* with raucous words in French. . . . He knocked at a studio door, the singing stopped and Saint-Gaudens appeared."[1] They became friends for life.

When White returned to New York in the fall of 1879, it was to a city described by his biographer, Charles C. Baldwin, as

> of two, three and four stories . . . with perhaps a dozen passenger elevators in the downtown business and financial districts. The New York telephone directory was a card listing 252 names; there were no telephone numbers; you simply gave the operator the name of the person you wanted; service . . . was slow, inadequate, and limited to persons of wealth. Electric lights were unknown. Kerosine and gas supplied what . . . illumination there was. Matches, made with brimstone, and used to light the vilest cigars, almost choked you with their poisonous fumes. Offices, stores and residences . . . were kept warm with big round stoves called Base Burners. The streets and avenues were lined with sycamores, poplars and telegraph poles. The trains and carriages were horse-drawn—with an extra horse to help going over the hills. Men wore paper collars . . . coats stopped abruptly at the hips: trousers were skin-tight.[2]

White was invited, when he returned, to become a partner with William Rutherford Mead and McKim in a new firm to be called McKim, Mead and White. One of his first pieces of work was at No. 4 Gramercy Park for James Thorne Harper. This was the son of James Harper, the founder of what is now Harper & Row, who had bought the house in 1847 and been its first occupant. James Harper, Sr., had also been mayor of New York in 1844–45, and mayor's lamps such as had lit the steps of his Rose Street house when he was mayor were now installed in front of the Gramercy Park house. As mayor, he had seen to it that pigs were no longer allowed to roam the streets of New York or cattle driven below Fourteenth Street. He was also credited with having put all of New York's two hundred policemen into uniform. After Harper's death in a Fifth Avenue carriage accident in 1869, his family had continued to live in the house.

The one change James Harper, Sr., had made in the house was to have the original front door replaced with the present doors and vestibule. In December 1879, his son and daughter commissioned Stanford White, then only twenty-six, to construct a new dining room at the rear of the parlor floor (Plate 122). White designed windows with window seats, half-domed corner shelves, and mahogany paneling. The work was decorated with cupids and bowknots, but these "excrescences" (as the *Gramercy Graphic* put it in the summer of 1952) were removed in the 1930's and

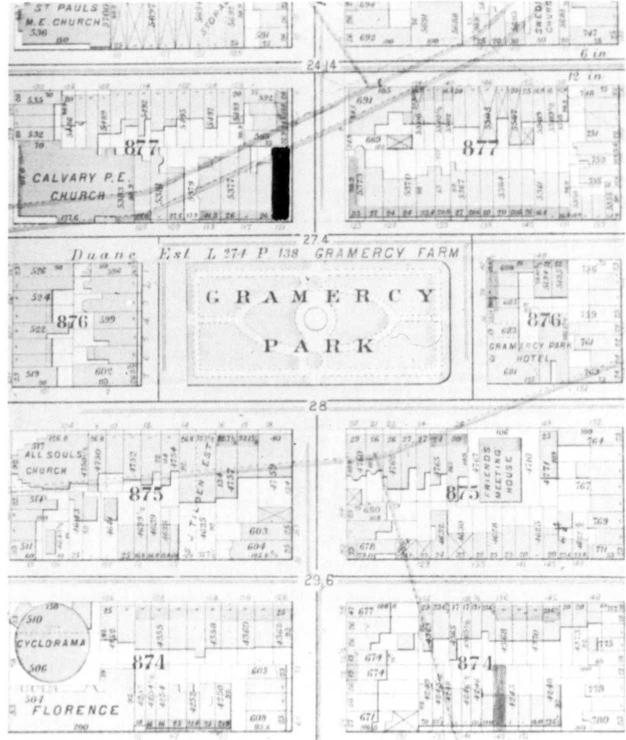

Plate 121

the room painted white. The entire addition by White, as listed in McKim, Mead and White records, cost only $350.

In February 1884, Stanford White married Bessie Springs Smith, and their six-month honeymoon in Europe, as far as Constantinople, was also a glorious buying spree. They brought back tapestries, paintings, huge majolica jars, rugs, statuary, and furniture.

In 1891, the offices of McKim, Mead and White moved up from 57 Broadway to Fifth Avenue and Twentieth Street, and then, in 1894, a block farther north to 160 Fifth Avenue (the building is still standing) where they occupied the entire fifth floor for the rest of White's and McKim's lives, in fact until 1913. An account of what it was like to walk into that fifth-floor office was given by the sculptress Janet Scudder. Stanford White had bought a fountain from her,

Plate 122

Plate 121 *Map of Gramercy Park area. Shaded building is the house of Stanford White.*
Plate 122 *No. 4 Gramercy Park; Mrs. James Harper's dining room, c. 1885, added to the house by Stanford White.*
Plate 123 *No. 4 Gramercy Park; corner of the Stanford White dining room today.*

Plate 123

Plate 124 *No. 121 East Twenty-first Street; former house of Alexander M. Lawrence, for sale sometime after his death in 1883. (The For Sale sign has been whited out on this copy of the photograph.)*

which he had used in his Chapin house on Long Island, and she subsequently received a letter inviting her to come to his office. About this visit, she wrote:

> I was there at the hour named . . . and was given a comfortable chair in the outer offices. Whoever gave me that comfortable chair . . . probably knew what I was in for. I waited one hour and a half before there was the least sign of my presence being noticed. Then one of the doors suddenly burst open and Stanford White rushed into the room, shook my hand vigorously and said: "Oh, Miss Scudder, I wanted to . . ."
>
> He got no further, for close on his heels appeared his secretary to say that Chicago was calling on the telephone. He rushed out and I sank back again into my comfortable chair.
>
> Another half hour and he burst into the room again.
>
> "Oh, Miss Scudder, I wanted to . . ."
>
> Again the secretary at his heels with some murmured words that carried him away without further explanation.
>
> By this time my anxiety and curiosity to know what he really did want was getting the best of me. The comfortable chair was no longer comfortable. I had to leave it and walk about a bit to keep calm. The third time Mr. White appeared, he had his hands full of sketches which he thrust into mine before anyone could possibly call him away.
>
> "Designs for two fountains," he said breathlessly, "Yes, take them along. Make sketches for the figures. I've indicated what I want. . . . Bring them back as soon as you can. Work out your own ideas for them. . . .
>
> Again that bothersome secretary appeared, and over his shoulder Mr. White called to me: "Bring in

Plate 125 *No. 121 East Twenty-first Street, during residence of Stanford White. A horse-drawn Steinway piano van is parked in front.*

the sketches the moment you have them ready. We can talk them over. Good-by."

I haven't the slightest idea how I got out of that office. If I'd fallen out the window or down the elevator shaft I'm perfectly sure I should not have been hurt.

Stanford White's existence was the most hectic anyone could have lived; and yet he always knew exactly what he wanted and was able to explain his ideas in the most clear, distinct and inspiring manner.[3]

As Charles Baldwin, who was his friend as well as biographer, described him,

[He was intense, and driven by a passion for beautiful things. He was tall, red-haired, and always in a hurry. He was adored by his friends. The story is told about another visitor to 160 Fifth Avenue, a painter he had once known, now] grown old and outmoded, who came . . . with a dirty, unframed canvas under his arm . . . at the busiest hour of a busy day. White looked up to see him standing in the doorway. The painter began some mumbled apology; but White interrupted him, taking the canvas to set it against the wall on his desk. Wiping the dust from it with his handkerchief, he began: "Why it's bully . . . I had forgotten . . . of course . . . you always knew how to use color." He wanted to forestall the hard luck story which, perforce, accompanies every request for a loan. Still talking, he began to empty his pockets. "This is just a retainer," he said. As was his habit, he had crumpled bills tucked away in vest, coat and trouser pockets. Out they came, to be hastily smoothed and turned over to the painter. "Just a retainer . . . come back tomorrow . . . I'll see what I can do."[4]

Plate 126

Plate 127

From 1885 to 1888, White had redecorated Abram Hewitt's house at No. 9 Lexington Avenue and, in 1894, had renovated the old stable entered at No. 5. In 1888, he also had made changes at No. 19 Gramercy Park for Stuyvesant Fish, and completely redesigned Edwin Booth's house at No. 16 to become The Players, (see Chapter 14). He himself had rented No. 119 East Twenty-first Street, doing minor renovations to the house, and then No. 121, (on the site of the present Gramercy Park Hotel) both houses owned by Henry A. C. Taylor. The four houses, Nos. 115 through 121, had been built in 1846–47, and No. 121 had first been owned by Alexander M. Lawrence, the fruit merchant and shipowner. (The exquisite designs for the front door to his house, dated March 17, 1847, survive, having been carefully copied from a book published in Glasgow in 1845.) Lawrence, like his neighbor across the street, Cyrus Field, had kept a cow in his Lexington Avenue stables and grazed it every morning in the neighborhood. He later replaced the stables with a ballroom at the rear of the house in which he hung part of his sizable art collection. When the collection was auctioned in 1883 after his death, it included 171 paintings and sculptures, among them works by Velazquez, Poussin, Veronese, Rubens, Van Dyck, and Bassano. He also added a rounded solarium to his dining room.

Stanford White substantially redesigned No. 121 though he never owned the house; the work began in the fall of 1898 and was completed by early 1900. Lawrence's ballroom was turned into a gold-and-white music room (Plate 135), and above it, White built a picture gallery (Plates 126 and 139) with skylight and projecting window seat (Plate 125). He added a window in the dining room, removed the front stoop, and replaced the old parlor-floor entrance with one directly into the ground floor, a few steps below grade. The walls separating off the stair hall were removed, allowing the entrance room to be the full width of the house. A glassed-in alcove above the entrance opened off of the drawing room, which, with the removal of the former entrance-hall wall, was now also opened up to have the full house width.

The Renaissance furniture, walls, ceilings, and artworks that White had been collecting were lavished on the new interior. His major design principle was that the best of any period went well with the best of any other period. White had taste: he had an educated eye that could recognize quality that had gone unnoticed by others. At first sight, his interiors often appeared to be improbable mixtures: eclecticism run wild. He loved things like Robert Chanler's huge depiction of silver giraffes plucking golden oranges from birch trees, which hung in the music room,

Plate 128

Plate 126 *No. 121 East Twenty-first Street; Stanford White's picture gallery, looking north.*
Plate 127 *No. 121 East Twenty-first Street; drawing room, looking northeast.*
Plate 128 *No. 121 East Twenty-first Street; drawing room, looking south.*

defying a more timid taste that would have considered it inappropriate. The critic John J. Chapman chided him for "his too great reliance on festive ornament."[5] But he had already responded to this in the motto his firm had chosen for itself in 1879—"*Vogue la galère!*"—which Brendan Gill has suggested can mean "Come what may" or even "what the hell!"[6]

The definition of good taste attributed to White's almost exact contemporary, Oscar Wilde—that it was the "refuge of the untalented"—could never have been applied to Stanford White, however. At the same time that he was transforming Peter Cooper's severe old interiors for Abram Hewitt and buying up all the Renaissance furniture he could get his hands on in Europe, he and McKim were also busy designing some of the great houses of their day. In three successive years, from 1884 to 1886, they produced the Tiffany house at Madison and Seventy-second Street, the celebrated Villard houses, and, for William G. Low in Bristol, Rhode Island, a house with lines so clean, so powerful, so elegant that it must rank with the most important ever built in this country.

White felt no need to be "original."

> He knew that the Greeks had borrowed from the Egyptians; that the Gothic cathedral had been inspired by the Crusades and by social contact with the East; that the Renaissance—that breathless period of unexampled artistic achievement—had been a rebirth . . . that every great age is a revival, demanding the best that tradition has to offer. He would take his good where good could be found, translating the historic idioms of the past and recreating them to suit his purpose.[7]

Plate 129

Plate 130

Plate 131

The front door to White's house opened directly from the street into a wide entrance room (Plate 129). This was presided over by a French-carved Caen stone mantel dating to Henry II. Before it was an antique Italian madonna and child with saints, and to its left an imposing antique throne chair upholstered in cardinal red velvet. Across the room was an Italian marble sarcophagus and next to it a Renaissance refectory table with elaborately carved claw feet. Between the front windows was a sixteenth century Italian fountain base, on which stood an early nineteenth century marble crouching Venus. On the floor was a large lion-skin rug with mounted head.

From the entrance hall, guarded by a pair of three-foot-tall wooden lions, one antique, one a copy, and flanked by antique Spanish Corinthian columns, French doors opened through a curving wall into a reception room (Plate 131) dominated by a huge early-sixteenth-century tapestry of a nobleman presenting a heron to a lady. It was made in the Loire

Valley and was later owned by Andrew Mellon before being presented, in 1964, to the Metropolitan Museum, where today it can be seen in the Fleischman Gallery. It is a rare example of *mille-fleurs* design on a pink background and measures seven feet eight inches by ten feet eleven inches. The lady in the tapestry has a pained expression on her face, perhaps because the falcon she is holding has dug its talon into her left hand.

The main staircase of the house rose from the entrance hall into the first-floor hall (Plate 136). Here, on the west, or staircase, side were two 10-foot 11-inch antique red Verona marble columns, highly polished, with white-and-gray marble plinths and bases, and composition capitals. Between them stood an Italian Renaissance marble table with carved claw feet. The antique Italian newel posts of the stair, here and at the ground floor, were in the form of carved

Plate 129 *No. 121 East Twenty-first Street; entrance hall, looking southeast.*

Plate 130 *No. 121 East Twenty-first Street; entrance hall, looking north into reception room. The tapestry had been removed.*

Plate 131 *No. 121 East Twenty-first Street; reception room showing* mille-fleurs *tapestry. In front of it is a Russian sledge seat.*

death. In front of the tapestry is a Russian sledge seat.

Plate 132 *No. 121 East Twenty-first Street; drawing room, looking northwest.*

Plate 132

Plate 133

Plate 134

Plate 135

and gilded lions clutching cornucopias, standing erect on spheres supported by bases elaborately carved with cherubim, leaves, and garlands. These had been "arranged for electric light." The Istrian stone mantel and overmantel of the hall (seen through the doorway in Plate 127) were Italian Renaissance, twelve feet high and surmounted by a bust of Henry IV. They were flanked by live palm trees. The ceiling contained a gilded wood sunburst with cherubs, and on the floor was an old-rose antique Persian carpet.

The drawing room opened off the south side of the hall. On the far side near the windows on the Park (Plate 128) was an eighteenth-century Louis XIV-style Italian settee, with gilded wood frame upholstered in green-silk damask, with a green-velvet panel on the back, appliqued with the papal coat of arms and gold-bullion embroidery. At the center of the room was an octagonal antique Florentine table with mother-of-pearl inlay and four wing-shaped legs with lion feet; and behind it a first-century Greek marble vase, fifty-three inches high, with scroll handles. The Portuguese wing chair near the alcove was upholstered in ruby-red velvet. On the floor to its right was a royal Bengal tiger-skin rug with mounted head. Continuing along the west wall (Plate 132) was a red-velvet davenport, its ball feet incased in gilded brass and, above it, an early Spanish School portrait of the Earl of Dorset, his hat in his right hand and a falcon in his left. Farther on was Sir Joshua Reynolds's portrait of Kitty Fisher, her light-brown hair bound in a blue ribbon. On the north wall was a sixteenth-century full-length portrait of Mary Tudor by Federigo Zucchero. To its left was a School of Clouet portrait of a young lady, and to its right a portrait of a burgomaster by Christoph Amberger, a sixteenth-century Dutch painter. The walls of the drawing room were covered in antique cardinal-red Genoese velvet, and on the floor was an eleven-by-seventeen-foot Khorassan rug, its center panel natural camel's hair with a yellow and old-rose medallion; its corner pieces had floral scrolls on a pale-green ground.

Over the fireplace was a black-and-gold Spanish doorway with twisted columns supporting a gold Italian Renaissance entablature, with a cartouche at the center of the frieze inscribed "Silentium." On the mantel was a maquette of Saint-Gaudens's *Diana*, designed for the top of the tower of White's Madison Square Garden.

The ceiling of the drawing room was Italian Baroque painted wood, its large circular central panel depicting the angels at the Nativity in a frame with alternating shields and female heads between which hung garlands. This was all encased in a square red-

and-gold frame surrounded by eight painted panels of biblical subjects in Baroque gold frames.

From the drawing room there was a 150-foot vista through to the music room at the rear of the house (Plate 119). Crossing the first-floor hall, one next entered the dining room (Plate 133), with its imposing late–Italian Renaissance ceiling. Polychromed wood with added plaster ornament, the ceiling's central painted panel was a coronation of the Virgin Mary; the two side panels had paintings of Mary Magdalen with a skull, and a shepherd with his crook; the four corner panels were the four evangelists. Its overall dimensions were thirty by seventeen feet.

In the curved glass solarium, which Alexander Lawrence had added to the room, White installed an antique Florentine alcove ceiling of carved and gilded wood in high relief. The alcove was dominated by an Italian Renaissance fountain, with the figure of Silenus emptying a water bottle into a shell-shaped carved marble basin. Trout swam in its pool. To the right of the alcove was an antique Italian marriage coffer, gilded, with painted panels illustrating "The departure and return," "A lover bidding good-bye to his sweetheart; returning to find his sweetheart dead," and "A man setting fire to their united funeral pyre." At the ends were paintings of a lake and of mountain scenery. The entrance from the hall was a carved-wood Italian Renaissance doorway with richly ornamented columns and Corinthian capitals reproduced across the room as the entrance to the music room. The table and chairs were Henry II-style reproductions.

The dining-room mantel was French Renaissance in carved-gray stone, and on the west side of the room stood a large Empire side table supported by two large carved spread eagles. At the corners of the room these eagles were reproduced as console tables. Along the west wall hung a series of four Italian Renaissance tapestries, and in the windows Flemish tapestries were draped. On the floor was an antique

Plate 136

Plate 137

Plate 133 *No. 121 East Twenty-first Street; dining room, looking north.*
Plate 134 *No. 121 East Twenty-first Street; dining room, alcove.*
Plate 135 *No. 121 East Twenty-first Street; music room, looking north.*
Plate 136 *No. 121 East Twenty-first Street; first-floor (parlor) stair hall, looking southwest.*
Plate 137 *No. 121 East Twenty-first Street; second-floor sitting room, looking east.*

Afghan rug, predominantly rose colored, its designs in green, blue, ivory, and brown.

The music room (Plate 135) contained a large collection of guitars, lutes, and harps, and an early-eighteenth-century harpsichord formerly belonging to a Roman noble family, the Colonnas. An elaborate Louis XVI chandelier hung in the room, and behind the stage was a seventeenth-century Grand Gobelins tapestry, bearing the coat of arms of the Prince of Orange and commemorating the opening of commerce with the Orient.

Returning to the main hall and staircase, one went up to the intimate second-floor sitting room/library (Plate 137) overlooking the Park, with its Robert V. V. Sewell painting of a bacchante over the mantel. At the rear of the second floor was the stair lobby to the picture gallery (Plate 138). Lit by skylights shielded by lattice, the walls of this lobby were covered with antique Rhodian, Damascus, and Tunisian tiles—blue and green, orange and iron-red, fire-red and turquoise—436 in all. To the left of the stair was an Italian Renaissance marble wall fountain and basin, carved with leaves and birds. From the ceiling hung an antique metal *écusson* containing a standing figure, with a large silvered-ball pendant.

The picture gallery itself, with its wonderful window seat (two others had been planned on the other side), trimmed lemon trees, comfortable red-velvet davenports, elaborate Henry II mantel and overmantel, Baroque Spanish doorway, and iron gate, was the only new addition to the house. The clean, massive beams of its roof, made bolder by being directly lit from the skylight above, contrasted effectively with the eclectic scene below. Some of the major paintings in White's collection hung here. To the left of the fireplace was an early-seventeenth-century, School of Ravesteyn, Dutch full-length portrait of a gentleman in full court costume, holding his lance, standing against a red curtain; to the right a seventeenth-century Spanish portrait of a lady, attributed to Claudio Coello, wearing a black-velvet robe over a brocade petticoat, her face framed by an elaborate ruff. The west wall was crowded with paintings, pieces of tapestry, antlers, and other objets d'art; and on the floor was a magnificent fifteenth-century Hispano-Mooresque rug, its two ruby-red medallions on a sapphire-blue ground, the whole covered with floral scroll designs in yellow, turquoise, and ivory. In front of the fireplace was a large cinnamon bear rug. A royal *écusson* in the form of a gilded lion within a laurel wreath hung from one of the roof beams.

The placement of furniture in this room was significant. At first sight it appeared quite unplanned, but this was not the case. One of the guiding princi-

Plate 138

Plate 139

Plate 138 *No. 121 East Twenty-first Street; stair lobby of picture gallery, looking north.*
Plate 139 *No. 121 East Twenty-first Street; picture gallery, looking south.*

ples of White's interior decoration was the desire to activate the space and allow people to move freely around a room. He rarely arranged furniture along a wall or let it be merely part of the pattern of a wall surface. Rather, he placed it out in the open, inviting people to sit all around a room, not just in conventional groupings. Many of the pictures were not on the walls, but out in the room on easels or leaning against furniture. The chairs, therefore, were placed primarily for viewing pictures and arranged to give a maximum number of different points of view. The two large wing chairs were not placed haphazardly out in exposed space, unrelated to each other or to the other furniture, as at first it might have seemed, particularly as they even backed at quite close range onto other chairs. They were precisely located for looking at certain pictures. And the small random chairs, placed every which way, invited being moved around, allowing one to sit as close to a particular picture as desired.

Stanford White's next large interior, the reconstruction for Henry W. Poor of the two Field houses was directly across the street (where No. 1 Lexington Avenue now stands). The two houses had opened into each other before; but now White made them one house. The work began in 1899, just as White's own house was reaching completion, and was finished in 1901 at a cost of $137,844.

Mr. Poor wrote to the architect on March 18, 1901, to express his own and his wife's pleasure at the new house, enclosing the final payments and concluding,

> Any excess of cost over the original estimates amounts to nothing in view of the result obtained, and to say that I am satisfied with it, puts it mildly! *I am enraptured*, and feel that we have the most beautiful house in the world. But—charming as it is to live in—the greatest delight that Constance and I feel in it, is that it embodies so much of your own personality and charm. It will be a perpetual reminder to us of the many happy hours you have spent with us during its construction, so full of sympathy and artistic delight.[8]

This time, a new entrance was created at the Lexington Avenue side of the old house (Plate 140). One entered into a wide-open hall (Plate 141), punctuated only by a huge Renaissance wellhead with ferns. Opening off this hall was a reception room whose walls White covered in light-colored leather, arranged in rigorous squares by the use of upholstery tacks. The main stairs rose into the parlor-floor hall, again essentially free of furniture, being a place designed exclusively for moving through. There was, however, a stopping-off place, a "palm nook" whose furniture hugged the floor and invited one to lie down before the huge hearth and relax under the palm trees as in an oasis. From the hall one entered the drawing room (Plate 143). Most of the furniture here was placed in the middle of the room, allowing its proportions to be clearly seen. White had great respect for proportion in a room and for the correlation between furniture, walls, and ceiling. Here he

Plate 140

Plate 141

Plate 142

Plate 140 *No. 1 Lexington Avenue; Henry W. Poor house.*
Plate 141 *No. 1 Lexington Avenue; entrance hall, looking west.*
Plate 142 *No. 1 Lexington Avenue; first-floor stair hall, looking northeast.*

used a geometrically pronounced Italian Renaissance bronze, red, and gray-blue ceiling with fifteen coffered panels, and architectural wall detailing that related the walls to the ceiling. A sixteenth-century Ispahan carpet in rose and dark blue, not unlike the ceiling panels in tone, whose shape was emphasized by being isolated on the large expanse of polished floor, related the floor to the ceiling and to the huge central table, also covered in carpet. This interplay of similar rectangles reinforced the basic rectangular proportions of the room itself. Chairs, too, were included in this scheme, their embroidered backs picking up the patterns of the floor and table carpets. Despite the ornateness of the components of this room, they were actually quite few in number and clearly articulated either against the plain wood of the floor or the darker unlit backdrop of the walls. At both ends of the drawing room were huge fireplaces with marble mantels and overmantels.

The drawing room opened through huge floor-to-ceiling, indented windows onto Gramercy Park (Plate 144). The area also served as a large winter garden of trees and plants, with an Italian carved-stone fountain and other large outdoor sculpture. This indoor/outdoor porch was supported by Irish green-marble columns with gilded capitals.

On the opposite side of the main hall from the drawing room was the open and uncluttered dining room. Its Lexington Avenue windows projected out from the building, thereby linking them with those of the drawing room and giving the effect of massively thick walls in keeping with the huge Renaissance fireplace.

The main feature of the dining room, however, was the breakfast alcove, which opened from it at the northeast corner (Plate 146). For this, White had adapted Mrs. Field's former "greenhouse," adding extra windows and introducing, dramatically, a great thirteen-foot twelfth-century Italian marble ciborium. It had come from the Church of San Stefano at Fiano Romano where it was the high altar canopy until 1889. (It can be seen today in the chapel from Notre-Dame-du-Bourg, Langon, at the Cloisters.) When White installed it in the Poors's breakfast room, he had to remove its top, and instead of an altar, it housed a Renaissance wellhead with ferns.

Along the Gramercy Park side on the second floor of the house was the library (Plate 145). A visitor to the house described the view of the Park from the library windows:

> Magnolias blossom in the spring, and flowers under

Plate 143 *No. 1 Lexington Avenue; drawing room, looking northeast.*

Plate 144 *No. 1 Lexington Avenue; drawing room, looking southeast.*

> arching trees bloom all the summer through. To one who enters here, the quiet stretches of the square and the sky beyond seem suddenly and somehow to belong to libraries, so great is the sense of repose and refreshment they inspire.[9]

Henry W. Poor was one of the country's foremost railroad authorities and president of *Poor's Railroad Manual* and *Poor's Handbook of Investor's Holdings.* He was no mean scholar and was able to read Greek and Latin, Sanscrit, Hebrew, Icelandic, and Russian. he had a large collection of rare books, including such treasures as a first edition of Thomas à Kempis's *Imitatio Christi,* which were kept in this library.

While few of the individual elements of the house, except for the drawing-room ceiling and the great ciborium, were in themselves of any real distinction, it was the way Stanford White combined them that was the important thing. It demonstrated his unerring eye for correct proportions, for combinations and juxtapositions that exceeded the interest of any of their components.

In 1909, however, the wonderful house was demolished. All that remains of it today is the iron fence that White had had designed for it, which was used by Herbert Lucas for his new building at No. 1 Lexington Avenue. The squash court and garage into which White had turned an old stable at No. 134 East

Plate 145 *No. 1 Lexington Avenue; library, looking northeast.*

Plate 146

Plate 147

Plate 148

Twenty-second Street for Henry Poor (at the noble cost of $22,344) have also disappeared.

In 1905, a fire in his own house destroyed a number of Stanford White's best paintings. It was a terrible blow to him, but then, in just a year, his life itself was abruptly ended. One of his mistresses, Evelyn Nesbit, a beautiful woman whom he had met when she was in her teens, had married a ne'er-do-well Pittsburgh millionaire named Harry K. Thaw in an attempt to further her career as an actress. He was wildly jealous of her relationship with White. On the evening of June 25, 1906, Thaw and his wife were at Madison Square Garden and, just as the comedian Harry Short was finishing a song called "I Could Love a Thousand Girls," Stanford White walked in and sat down at his regular table. He had just come from taking his son and a Harvard classmate to dinner. Harry Thaw walked up to him, took out a gun, and shot him dead.

Thaw was declared insane but was later released; (he lived into the 1940's, Nesbit until 1966.) White was immediately described in the press as a satyr and menace to society. The journalist Richard Harding Davis was one of those who sprang to his defense. He replied to the charges that:

> To answer [them] by saying that he was a great architect [was] not to answer . . . at all. He was an architect. But what is more important is that he was a most kind-hearted, most considerate, gentle and manly man, who could no more have done the things attributed to him than he could have roasted a baby on a spit. Big in mind and body, he was incapable of little meanness. He admired a beautiful woman as he admired every other beautiful thing that God has given us: and his delight over one was as keen, as boyish, as grateful as over any of the others. Described as a voluptuary, his greatest pleasure was to stand all day waist deep in the rapids of a Canadian river and fight it out with a salmon. . . . [10]

If people were not supportive of Stanford White after his death, they did turn up for the auction of his possessions that was held the following year at his Gramercy Park house. Among those who came was William Randolph Hearst, who bought one of the carved wooden lions for $170, and one of the first-floor Baroque ceilings for $3,000. John Wanamaker paid $4 for a tambourine; David Belasco, $430 for an early-eighteenth-century harpsichord; and Isaac Newton Phelps Stokes, $30 for a short Italian Renaissance stone frieze, $11 for a carved stone capital, and $520 for the gilded lion *écusson* that had hung in the picture gallery.

At subsequent sales of White's possessions held in November and December 1907, Louis Comfort Tiffany bought three open-work trays for $6, a Spanish plaque for $7, an ecclesiastical statuette for $22, and three French armchairs for $21. Joseph Pulitzer bought two stuffed crocodiles for $5; Daniel Chester French, a lamp for $22; Bertram Grosvenor Goodhue, an early Italian school Madonna and Child for $27.50; and John D. Rockefeller, Jr., an antique marble garden seat for $120, a terra-cotta water jar for $75, an old Italian Corinthian capital for $35, and a marble sarcophagus for $125. Also, many things were bought by the Metropolitan Museum.

And so the house was stripped of all its riches and taken over by the Princeton Club, and after that by the United Service Club. It was torn down in 1923, and a residential hotel, Fifty-two Gramercy Park North (now the Gramercy Park Hotel), was built and opened on the site in 1925. Its furnishings were supplied by W. & J. Sloan, its linens by B. Altman & Company, and its silver by Gorham. All that remained of the wonderful house that once had stood there were three black-marble fireplaces, probably dating to Alexander Lawrence. They are still to be seen in three suites of the Hotel today.

Notes

[1] Louise H. Tharp, *Saint-Gaudens and the Gilded Era* (Boston: Little, Brown & Co., 1969), p. 101.

[2] Charles C. Baldwin, *Stanford White* (New York: Dodd, Mead & Co., 1931), p. 109.

[3] Ibid., pp. 282–84.

[4] Ibid., p. 5.

[5] John J. Chapman, "McKim, Mead and White," *Vanity Fair,* September 13, 1919. Frederick Law Olmsted once expressed his opposition to White's treatment of the entrance to Prospect Park in Brooklyn by referring to his "cockney taste."

[6] *Macmillan Encyclopedia of Architects*, (New York: The Free Press, 1983), vol. 4, p. 392.

[7] Baldwin, op. cit., p. 174.

[8] Ibid., p. 271.

[9] John B. Pine, *The Story of Gramercy Park, 1831–1921* (New York: Knickerbocker Press, 1921), p. 29.

[10] Baldwin, op. cit., p. 309.

Plate 146 *No. 1 Lexington Avenue; dining room, looking northeast into breakfast room.*
Plate 147 *Metropolitan Museum, The Cloisters; Romanesque chapel showing twelfth-century Italian ciborium formerly in the Poors' breakfast room.*
Plate 148 *Mammoth antique Japanese bronze lantern belonging to Stanford White, placed in Gramercy Park.*

Plate 149 *Gramercy Park; statue of Edwin Booth.*

14

Edwin Booth: The Great Hamlet of His Time

At the center of Gramercy Park is a life-size bronze figure of a man. He is not, as many have thought, Samuel B. Ruggles, logical though this might seem. He is wearing medieval clothes and standing in front of a medieval chair because he is, in fact, Hamlet, as played by one of the first great American actors, Edwin Booth. The sculpture by Edmond T. Quinn was erected in the Park in 1918, replacing the earlier fountain, the once-gilded water nymph of which was then moved to another section of the Park. "Hamlet" was presented by members of The Players, the club that Edwin Booth founded in 1888 at No. 16 Gramercy Park.

Of all the roles Booth played, Hamlet was his most celebrated, and so it was in this guise that he was depicted. His contemporary, the critic William Winter, wrote that Booth's interpretation "was the simple, absolute realization of Shakespeare's haunted prince. . . . It was dark, mysterious, afflicted, melancholic, sympathetic, beautiful—a vision of dignity and of grace, made sublime by suffering, made weird and awful by 'thoughts beyond the reaches of our souls.' "[1]

It is, nevertheless, difficult today to appreciate the greatness of Booth's art. His biographer, Eleanor Ruggles, drawing on contemporary accounts of how he acted Hamlet, particularly in the famous hundred-night run of 1864–65 at the Winter Garden (on Broadway at Bond Street), describes it as follows:

> "From his first entrance . . . every eye was riveted on that forward-drifting, small, lithe, elegant, saffron-faced figure in shabby black with the dark hair hanging to the shoulders. . . . Left alone, [he] roved from side to side
>
> O God! O God!
> How weary, stale, flat, and unprofitable
> Seem to me all the uses of this world.
>
> On the midnight battlements . . . Hamlet stood apart from his friends and questioned the air with rolling glances. He seemed a figure created by the night: shadowy, fantastic, moonstruck. A few years before, Booth had sometimes worked himself up so in this scene that he was incoherent, but since then he had learned restraint. His acting had a quiet ease now, an intensity of emotion without rant; yet breaking every so often into what seemed a spontaneous explosion of tragic power, as when he commanded Horatio and Marcellus to swear by his sword—they standing resolutely on either side of him while he held the crossed hilt high, his head thrown back, his face dazzling and impassioned under the [flare of the calcium lights]:

> Never to speak of this that you have seen,
> Swear by my sword.

> Booth gave the great speech on suicide sitting near the footlights, his chin in his hand, his solitariness intensified by the sweep of the empty stage. The touches of emotion were so slight, yet . . . suggested such depth of feeling, that the least touch more would have been unbearably crude. He began almost in a whisper:

> To be, or not to be.

> The audience sat rapt, its thousand faces as immovable in the half-light as a painted backdrop; its thousand minds alert, while the six words on which the actor had lavished as many weeks of labor seemed to be spoken not to but within each separate consciousness, as though each man and woman . . . heard his own thoughts speak.[2]

Booth never lost the name he had made at the Winter Garden. *The Times* called his Hamlet "a part in which he has no living equal." Louis Comfort Tiffany was commissioned to make a gold medal to be presented to him. But before the presentation could take place, disaster struck Booth down. April 3, 1865, General Grant took Richmond, and six days later, Robert E. Lee surrendered the Confederate Army to him. Edwin Booth was in Boston at the time, and on April 14, Good Friday, he played Sir Edward Mortimer in *The Iron Chest or The Mysterious Murder.* In Washington that same night, Booth's bearded twenty-six-year-old brother Johnny, their mother's particular favorite, himself a brilliant actor and also an ardent Confederate sympathizer, did his deed in Ford's Theater.

Edwin Booth's life was never the same. He wrote, "Oh how little did I dream . . . when on Friday night I was as Sir Edward Mortimer exclaiming, 'Where is my honor now? Mountains of shame are piled upon me!' that I was not acting but uttering the fearful truth."[3]

The country reacted with real anger. Crowds gathered around stage doors and shouted, "Arrest all the actors!" For months, it was not safe for Edwin Booth to go outdoors during the day; only at night could he slip out of his house at No. 28 East Nineteenth Street and walk around disconsolately. He swore never to act again, and for a long while he didn't. When he did finally return, in January 1866, the New York *Herald* asked, "Will Booth appear as the assassin of Caesar? That would be, perhaps, the most suitable character." He reappeared as Hamlet, again at the Winter Garden, and the audience rose to its feet when they saw him on the stage. There was a deafening ovation, and slowly Booth stood up and bowed deeply to the crowd, his eyes streaming with tears.

He had himself encountered Abraham Lincoln only once, when he had played Shylock at Ford's Theater early in 1864. Lincoln had been there, and had afterward commented that it had been "a good performance, but I'd a thousand times rather read it at home if it were not for Booth's playing."[4] A year later, about a month before Lincoln was assassinated, Booth shared an experience that is best described in the following extract from a letter, dated February 17, 1918:

> I being a student at Harvard, was on my way to Washington. . . . On the night of my journey from New York, I, with other passengers, crossed the ferry and went to the waiting train at midnight in order to get a berth in the sleeping car. . . . The train was in the station with the platform of its cars level with the passengers' platform of the station, just as is the case now in all large stations, but it was [then] a new thing with us. . . . While waiting, I was pressed against the car by a bunch of people . . . and while in this position, the train began to move slowly. There was a little commotion which resulted in my being so tightly pressed against the car, that its movement screwed me off my feet and they dropped down into the space between the car and the platform and I was for a few seconds in a dangerous position from which I could not rescue myself. I was seized from behind by the collar and . . . brought to my feet on the platform without my having sustained any injury. I turned to thank my rescuer and in doing so recognized [Edwin] Booth, whom I never knew personally, but whom I had often seen on the stage.[5]

The letter was signed by Robert T. Lincoln, the President's son. The experience was one that never failed to comfort Booth in his later life.

When President James Garfield was assassinated in 1881 by "another mad killer," Booth felt that "that terrible business will never be buried."[6] He wrote to an inquirer:

> Dear Sir,
>
> I can give you little information regarding my brother John. I seldom saw him since his early boyhood in Baltimore. He was a rattle-pated fellow, filled with Quixotic notions. . . . We used to laugh at his patriotic froth whenever secession was discussed. That he was insane on that one point, no one who knew him well can doubt. . . . He was of a gentle, loving disposition, very boyish and full of fun,—his mother's darling,—and his deed and death crushed her spirit. He possessed rare dramatic talent, and would have made a brilliant mark in the theatrical world. . . . All his theatrical friends speak of him as a poor, crazy boy, and such his family think of him.[7]

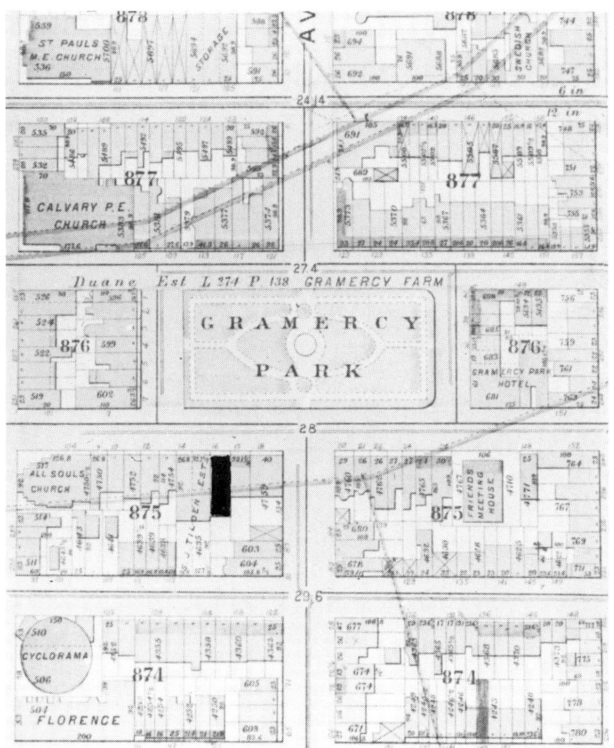

Plate 150

Plate 151

Plate 152

Plate 153

Plate 150 *Map of Gramercy Park. Shaded building is The Players.*
Plate 151 *Edwin Booth, 1889.*
Plate 152 *The Players, c. 1910.*
Plate 153 *The Players; lamp designed by Stanford White, reminiscent of those at the Palazzo Strozzi in Florence.*

Booth's first wife, Mary Devlin, had died in 1863, leaving him with a daughter, Edwina. He was married again, however, in 1869, to Mary McVicker, but she never held the place in his affections that Mary Devlin had. They had a son, Edgar, who lived only a few hours after birth, and the second Mrs. Booth soon suffered from periods of derangement and died after a long illness in 1881.

Booth continued to act into the 1880's, touring with a troupe of actors for whom he cared deeply. He wrote to his friend William Bispham about one of these actors, Dave Anderson, and the note reveals Booth's sense of loyalty and kindliness. He asked Bispham to look out in New York for four or five "cozy rooms" for

> a poor player, who struts, etc., but one I love with all the tenderness a son might bear for a father—one of the oldest and the dearest of duffers the good God ever made. He approacheth now the time when the oil burneth low and the wick waxeth brief. He wants to settle in New York—his dear old wife and he—and I want them to settle near me.[8]

Booth and his troupe traveled around the country by train—he and his daughter, Edwina, in a private hotel car with a piano and their books, and the others in a Pullman car. Edwina would play the piano as the train rolled along and the two old Andersons would nod while one or another of the troupe sang songs. Early in 1883, Booth played Hamlet in Berlin, in English to the German of the rest of the cast. The performances turned out to be some of the brightest moments in his entire career. The German critics fell over him with praise, and he said he felt more like acting than he had for years.

In 1885, Edwina married Ignatius Grossmann, a Hungarian professor and stockbroker. She had been briefly engaged, three years before, to Downing Vaux, the son of Calvert Vaux, but the engagement had been called off when he contracted an incurable disease of the nervous system. After her marriage, Booth was left very much alone. Charles Townsend Copeland, the great Harvard professor, passed him once on a Boston Street not far from his Chestnut Street house and described how Booth seemed "to be looking in, not out, with the curious introverted gaze of his own Hamlet. . . . I thought then that I had never seen so sad a face."[9]

Booth was only fifty-two years old in 1885, but his health had already begun to fail. He felt, when he sold his house in Boston, that he now had no real home, and it was not long before he began to think of founding a club for actors like himself that could also be his home. This hope materialized, and on January 7, 1888, The Players was incorporated by Booth and thirteen others, including Mark Twain and General William Tecumseh Sherman. He bought No. 16 Gramercy Park for $75,000 as the clubhouse.

The house was one of three with Gothic porches and cast-iron verandas built in 1844–45 for the New York banker Elihu Townsend. Booth bought it from the widow of Clarkson Potter, a Democratic congressman from New York in the 1870's. Another of the original members of The Players—Stanford White—offered to redesign the house as a contribution to the new club, and his plans were completed by July 2, 1888. He removed the old front stoop and veranda and replaced them with a new covered stone porch and street-level entrance lit by huge lanterns. There were to have been square green boxes with bushes, but many around the Park felt this would have the look of a German beer garden, so the club was obliged to relinquish this plan.

On the inside, walls were removed and spaces opened up that flowed gracefully into one another. At the front of the main floor a writing room was given a raised floor, which not only lent it intimacy but allowed greater headroom to the entranceway below. At the center of the building the broad stairs led into an elegant hall. Here, on New Year's Eve, 1888, at the official opening of the club, Booth stood in front of the huge marble fireplace and offered the members the silver loving cup from which they have drunk on each successive New Year's Eve since. The new interior was warm and inviting, and as Professor Brander Matthews of Columbia said, so adroit was the skill of Stanford White that "the house appeared to be mellow from the very beginning." Thanks to Booth's munificence, it seemed to have come into being "fully armed for the struggle for existence—not enfeebled by debts and deficiencies."

Soon trophies and mementos began to proliferate, together with pictures and playbills. John Singer Sargent was commissioned to paint Booth's portrait, and, in fact, his face soon looked down from nearly every wall, in one guise or another. When yet another portrait was once offered, he protested. "Please don't! Even now I can't go anywhere in the house without bumping into a Booth."

The clubhouse was also his home. Above the large second-floor library, the third floor was reserved for him, and there were also rooms there for him to lease to his fellow actor, Lawrence Barrett, when he was in town. His bedroom, which overlooked Gramercy Park (Plate 155), was sparsely furnished; among his pictures was one of his brother, John. On summer nights, he would eat his supper on the porch outside the grill at the rear of the club, and then, back in his

Plate 154 *The Players; main hall, 1907.*
Plate 155 *The Players; Edwin Booth's room, 1907.*

Plate 154

Plate 155

Plate 156 *Dedication ceremony of the Edwin Booth statue in Gramercy Park, November 13, 1918*

Plate 157 *The cast-metal water nymph, repositioned with a fountain and pool in 1918.*

Plate 158 *The Edwin Booth statue. Photographed in Edmond T. Quinn's Brooklyn studio.*

own room, lie on the sofa by the open window and listen to the lingering sounds from the street. Often, when he couldn't sleep, he would stare out into the tops of the Park trees all night. Such sleepless nights he called his "vulture hours." When someone suggested he travel, he said, "I've been traveling all my life. What I want now is to stay in one place with things I like around me. . . . Here is my bed, and here is the fire, and here are my books. . . . I suppose I shall wear out here."[10]

He did just that. By the age of fifty-nine, he seemed an old man. He stayed more often in his room, and his usual walk around the Park became slower and slower. Henry Noble MacCracken, the president of Vassar who, as a small boy, often played marbles around the Park, remembered seeing Booth occasionally stop to watch a game or two. He later described how sad he always looked, and he recalled his father telling him that the great actor forever bore his family's tragedy. Booth lingered on until 1893, gradually growing weaker, and finally, after suffering a cerebral hemorrhage, he died on June 7, just as a midnight thunderstorm threw all the lights out.

His room was kept just as he left it, and it remains this way today. Downstairs, the house again was altered in 1904 and 1906 by McKim, Mead and White. A bay window was added to the dining room at the back, and the covered porch was extended around three sides of the rear yard, leaving, at one place, a tree growing through its deck. Later, the porch and yard were replaced to make room for a new theater hall.

Sarah Bernhardt once visited the all-male club on one of its ladies' days to see the apartment where Booth had died, and because of her wooden leg, used the little elevator that had been installed for the actor. When it broke down, she cried, *"Laissez sortir!"* for she suffered from acute claustrophobia. A full-length picture of Madame Bernhardt now dominates the little elevator cage, and it has even been known as the Bernhardt Room.

In 1906, Augustus Saint-Gaudens was asked to make a memorial to Booth, showing him as Hamlet. Before a contract could be signed, however, the sculptor died, and the commission was given, in 1909, to Frederick MacMonnies. Disagreements led to his giving up the project in 1913, and, finally, a competition for the commission was won by Edmond T. Quinn, the pedestal to be made by Edwin S. Dodge. The figure was finished in 1917, but the arrival of the granite base from New Hampshire was held up by a World War I railroad embargo. The memorial was at last dedicated on November 13, 1918, Booth's birthday, two days after the armistice (Plate 156).

Today the club maintains its marvelous building to a large extent on an endowment set up by Booth. His collection of books became the nucleus for the Walter Hampden Library, one of the outstanding theater collections in the country. The list of people who have been associated with The Players is an impressive one and ranges from Winston Churchill to George Burns. Such luminaries have been in no small part drawn there by the club's celebrated home, which today is as glowing as when Stanford White first designed it.

Notes

[1] *Gramercy Graphic,* April, 1951, p. 10.

[2] Eleanor Ruggles, *Prince of Players* (New York: W. W. Norton & Co., 1953), pp. 166–68.

[3] Ibid., p. 185.

[4] Ibid., p. 157.

[5] *Valentine's Manual,* no. 6, New Series (New York: Valentine's Manual, Inc., 1922), p. 182.

[6] Ruggles, op. cit., p. 291.

[7] Ibid., p. 291.

[8] Ibid., p. 296.

[9] Ibid., pp. 309–10.

[10] Ibid., p. 362.

CANDY

15

Augustus Saint-Gaudens, Louis Comfort Tiffany, Richard Morris Hunt Et Alii

In 1861, the National Academy of Design held a competition for a new building to be built on Twenty-third Street at Fourth Avenue. It was won by Peter B. Wight (1838–1925), with a polychromed and elaborately embellished Venetian palazzo, inspired by the alternating colors of All Souls Church three blocks to the south. It was built between 1863 and 1865 (Plates 160 and 161) and stood on the site until 1902, providing an intimate scale to the intersection.[1] It was in this little palazzo that Henry James saw the spring painting exhibition of 1875 that he reviewed in *The Nation*, and it was also here that two artists, who were both born in 1848 and lived close to Gramercy Park, showed their early work: Augustus Saint-Gaudens and Louis Comfort Tiffany.

Though he was born in Dublin, Saint-Gaudens grew up in New York from the age of twelve. His family lived in rooms at No. 304 Third Avenue, and his father was a tailor whose shop was at No. 268 Fourth Avenue, across the street from Calvary Church. Augustus went to the Twentieth Street School and, after classes, delivered shoes for his father. At thirteen he left school and was apprenticed to a cameo cutter on Broadway at Eleventh Street, who made pins and brooches, often with animal heads cut from amethyst and malachite. Augustus had to be at work at seven and usually walked there for lack of bus fare, though sometimes he hitched rides on the backs of horse-drawn wagons. He enrolled in Peter Cooper's new Union, and worked there after supper until eleven o'clock, which left him so exhausted he had to be dragged from bed in the morning. Among his most vivid early memories was of the 1863 draft riots. He was fifteen, and on Monday, July 13, he was let off work early, found Broadway quite deserted, its stores closed, and he ended up running all the way home. He remembered seeing the two cannons set up at the northeast corner of Gramercy Park.

When he was sixteen, Saint-Gaudens found work with a shell cameo cutter named Jules Le Brethon, a generous man who taught him how to cut a cameo portrait and gave him time to model in clay. He transferred from Cooper Union to the new Academy of Design and was able to save enough of his wages to go to Paris in 1867 to study at the Ecole des Beaux-Arts. He studied there and in Rome until 1872, when he returned to New York and took a studio in the German Savings Bank building at the southeast corner of Fourth Avenue and Fourteenth Street. There, he made his model for the sculpture of Admiral Farragut, his first major work, which was finally erected in Madison Square, in 1881, on a base that was also the first such work of Stanford White.

It had been in the spring of 1875 that he and White had met, when, on the stairs of the German Savings Bank, White had heard Saint-Gaudens sing-

Plate 159 *Stuyvesant Apartments, No. 142 East Eighteenth Street, c. 1935.*

Plate 161

Plate 160

Plate 160 *National Academy of Design, 1865–1902, northwest corner of Fourth Avenue and Twenty-third Street.*
Plate 161 *National Academy of Design; entrance stairs.*
Plate 162 *Fourth Avenue, looking north from Twenty-first Street. Bernard Saint-Gaudens's shoe shop was at No. 268 Fourth Avenue, where, in this 1905 photograph, the sign reads D. L. Cella.*
Plate 163 *No. 103 East Fifteenth Street, formerly Samuel B. Ruggles's stable and later the home of Richard Watson Gilder.*
Plate 164 *Augustus Saint-Gaudens's relief of Richard Watson Gilder; his wife, Helena De Kay; and son, Rodman, 1879.*

Plate 162

ing in his studio. Soon afterward, coming down those same stairs, Saint-Gaudens had been introduced by an artist he knew to Richard Watson Gilder, then the editor of *Scribner's Monthly.* He and his wife, the artist Helena de Kay, at that time were forming a new organization for young artists and asked if Saint-Gaudens would like to join them. Having just submitted a piece to the academy's annual show, Saint-Gaudens paid little attention to the offer. When his sculpture was rejected by the academy, however, he immediately sought out Gilder and rang the bell of his little carriage house at No. 103 East Fifteenth Street (just behind the house at No. 24 Union Square where Samuel B. Ruggles was still living and whose stable it once had been. Gilder wrote that "It was noon and I was at home for lunch. I ran down to the gate and . . . there was a high wind blowing. Saint-Gaudens was 'mad as hops' because they had just thrown out his piece of sculpture . . . and he was ready to go into the new movement. I told him to come around that evening."[2] The organization was called the Society of American Artists, later the American Art Association, and by its third meeting, not only Saint-Gaudens but Louis Comfort Tiffany had joined.

Stanford White redecorated the Gilders' old carriage house in 1881. He suggested a design for the facade whereby the third story was to be covered with the outspread wings of two peacocks done in colored glass. Gilder rejected this, fearing that "there would always be a crowd out on the sidewalk waiting to see the peacocks flap their wings."[3] White bowed to the opposition, but in the decoration of the third story he placed round pieces of peacock-colored glass, and glass mosaic in a fan-shaped pattern over the doorway (Plate 163). For the second story, Saint-Gaudens

Plate 163

Plate 164

made terra-cotta reliefs of the Gilders's children. Inside, was a marvelous bronze bas-relief of the family, also by Saint-Gaudens. (Plato 164) As a wedding present, John La Farge, had designed a large glass fire screen with "H[for Helena] 1874 R[for Richard]" in its central panel. The house was always a haven for artists, and Walt Whitman once said of the Gilders, "At a time when everybody else in their set threw me down, they were nobly and unhesitatingly hospitable. They were without pride and without shame—they just asked me along in the natural way."[4]

Louis Tiffany grew up in New York at No. 212 Fifth Avenue and, in his teens, exhibited at the Academy of Design. Like Saint-Gaudens, in 1868–69 he was studying in Paris and traveled in North Africa, where he became interested in Islamic textiles. When he returned to New York, he took a studio in Renwick's new YMCA on Twenty-third Street, directly across from the academy. (His 1875 painting called "Duane Street," which was exhibited there, anticipated the later Ash Can School painters in its realistic treatment of city slums.) He was made an associate member of the academy in 1871, and an academician in 1880, but was nevertheless one of the founding members and, by 1878, the treasurer of Gilder's rebel American Art Association.

In 1879, Tiffany set up a partnership known as Louis C. Tiffany and Associated Artists and took space at the top of what had been an old hotel at No. 333 Fourth Avenue at the corner of Twenty-fifth Street. Later, Associated Artists separated from him and moved to No. 115 East Twenty-third Street, but he continued on in his studios. In his experiments with color, his associate Candace Wheeler recalled, he was always

> . . . working out his problems with bits of old iridescent Roman vases which had lain centuries underground; or finding out the secrets of tints in ancient cathedral windows, and the proportions of metal and chemicals which would produce certain shades of color. The actual melting and mixing was done in the laboratory underneath his own apartments [around the corner at No. 48 East Twenty-sixth Street], but the results of the study and the effects of juxtaposition were tried in the glass-loft.[5]

Tiffany worked in tiles, stained glass, mosaic, and eventually, in the particular blown glass that made his name almost a household word. He maintained his studios in the Fourth Avenue building until 1902, when he moved them to Madison Avenue at Forty-fifth Street.

In the 1870's, two architects of real stature were also at work in the vicinity of Gramercy Park. One was Bruce Price (1845–1903), whose great shingled houses at Tuxedo Park are among the best of their

Plate 165

Plate 166

Plate 165 *YMCA, southwest corner of Fourth Avenue and Twenty-third Street, c. 1890. Behind it the Fourth Avenue Presbyterian Church.*
Plate 166 *YMCA; library.*
Plate 167 *Stuyvesant Apartments, No. 142 East Eighteenth Street, not long before demolition in 1959.*

Plate 167

kind. He built a private house at No. 21 East Twenty-first Street in 1878. It is an interesting departure from the uniform brownstone houses that were then lining these blocks—brick, with a three-story curving front and delightful cast-stone details.

Almost directly across the street from it was the atelier of Richard Morris Hunt (1827–95) at No. 28 East Twenty-first Street. Hunt was recognized in the latter half of the nineteenth century as the dean of American architecture and, in 1857, was one of the founders of the American Institute of Architects. In 1871, he bought the Twenty-first Street house and used it for his office and studio until 1877, when he moved to a new building of his own on Courtlandt Street.

Hunt may ultimately be remembered less for his actual architecture than for his major role in making architecture a respected profession. His own work was best when he took his inspiration from the Renaissance châteaus of the Loire Valley, as in the Vanderbilt mansions on Fifth Avenue and at Asheville, North Carolina. But there is no disputing the grandeur of the Great Hall at the Metropolitan Museum or the solid rectitude of the Statue of Liberty base, which are among the few existing examples of his work in New York.

Hunt had two commissions in the vicinity of Gramercy Park. The one that survives is his 1883 town house built for Sidney Webster at No. 245 East Seventeenth Street on Stuyvesant Square. The other was at No. 142 East Eighteenth Street, where he designed the first apartment house, not only in New York but in the United States. It was called the Stuyvesant Apartments, having been commissioned by Rutherfurd Stuyvesant, a nineteen-year-old great-nephew of Peter Gerard Stuyvesant, whom Hunt had met in Paris. Stuyvesant had been born Stuyvesant Rutherfurd, but at the age of five, when his great-uncle drowned at Niagara Falls, he had inherited a third of the old Stuyvesant farm, Petersfield, on condition that he change his surname to Stuyvesant. This had been done simply by reversing his two names. In Paris, he had been impressed with the addition to the Louvre designed by Hunt and had suggested to him building an apartment house on Eighteenth Street similar to those that were springing up all over Paris.

New York had already seen the construction of tenement housing on a large scale, mostly on the Lower East Side and now crowded with foreign immigrants. The very idea of multiple-family dwellings for "respectable" people was highly suspect. It was assumed that such buildings quickly degenerate into slums. Even though the Eighteenth Street experiment was to be styled "French flats" and called the Stuyvesant Apartments, it was first known as Stuyvesant's Folly. And yet the idea was such a natural one, particularly given the soon-to-be-developed elevator, that it quickly caught on, and it has been estimated that within thirty years there were over forty thousand apartment houses in New York City.

No. 142 East Eighteenth Street (Plate 159 and 167) was a five-story building with two symmetrical halves, each side with its own entrance, tiled Romanesque-style lobby, concierge, and basement laundry connected by a dumbwaiter to individual drying areas on the roof. At the rear was a formal garden. There were four apartments per floor, each of them having from four to nine rooms, and on the high-ceilinged fifth floor were four studios. Rents were about a hundred dollars a month. The facade of the building was awkward: the Mansard studio floor made it look top heavy, and its stone ornamentation, lacking any structural significance, appeared fussy. But the new French flats were an instant success, attracting such tenants as publisher G. P. Putnam, Calvert Vaux, and Edwin Booth, who rented an apartment for his mother. The apartment of the editor Mary Fanton Roberts and her husband was a salon where Nijinsky, Isadora Duncan, and Mary Garden, among others, often came. The Stuyvesant Apartments were not demolished until 1959.

Of the early apartment houses engendered by them, one of the first, two blocks north at No. 34 Gramercy Park is still standing. It was built in 1882/3 and its height, twice that of the Stuyvesant, was possible because of the recent development of the elevator. Its site had previously been occupied by part of a five story hotel built in 1853/4 along the entire east end of the Park, where there had once been an old

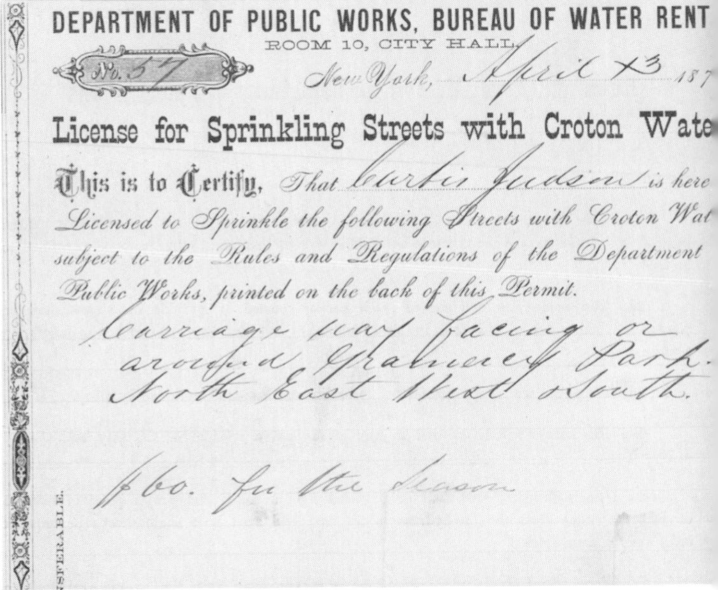

DEPARTMENT OF PUBLIC WORKS, BUREAU OF WATER RENT

ROOM 10, CITY HALL

No. 57 New York, April 23 187

License for Sprinkling Streets with Croton Wate

This is to Certify, That Curtis Judson is here

Licensed to Sprinkle the following Streets with Croton Wat

subject to the Rules and Regulations of the Department

Public Works, printed on the back of this Permit.

Carriage way facing or around Gramercy Park. North East West & South.

$60. for the Season

Plate 168

Plate 169

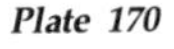

Plate 170

Plate 168 *License allowing Gramercy Park House to sprinkle the east carriage way, 1877.*
Plate 169 *Gramercy Park House, east side of Gramercy Park, c. 1875.*
Plate 170 *Gramercy Park House.*
Plate 171 *No. 34 Gramercy Park, c. 1890. The center section of the old Gramercy Park House, next door, then called the Gramercy Park Hotel, had been refaced with stone to match No. 34 and its central pediment removed.*

Plate 171

Plate 172

Plate 174

Plate 173

marble yard. It was listed with the City in 1854 as the Sanderson Hotel but, in 1856, became the Gramercy Park House, which until 1863 was operated by Henry Crocker and, thereafter, by the pioneer hotelier Curtis Judson; the hotel was much frequented by southerners and Cubans. Judson was a Trustee of the Park, and the Trustees often met at the hotel to discuss such issues as ball playing in the Park, croquet, and lawn tennis. When the Gramercy Park House closed in 1880, the center section was bought by Arthur G. King, renovated and opened as the Gramercy Park Hotel (which was unrelated to the present day hotel of the same name). Then, in 1882, the southern section of the old Gramercy Park House was torn down and replaced with No. 34 Gramercy Park. Arthur King's hotel apparently flourished, for around 1890, he bought the northern section of the old Gramercy Park House and, by 1903, planned to erect a fifteen-story hotel and was offering to buy No. 34 as well.

The name of No. 34 was originally to be the Gramercy Family Hotel but, before being completed, the building was sold to the Gramercy Company, a group of investors led by Judge William H. Arnoux. Sixty-five hundred shares were sold at a hundred dollars a share, each apartment equaling a certain number of shares. The Gramercy was incorporated on March 28, 1883, as the first cooperative apartment house in New York.

The turreted building has a magnificent foyer decorated with stained glass and Minton tiles; even its interior brick walls are up to twenty-four inches thick and floors are flushed with tin to keep out mice; all stairs are iron, marble, and tile. Window awnings once relieved the somewhat severe exterior. The building is most celebrated for its three hydraulic elevators, one passenger and two freight (one being outdoors in an air shaft). They were installed in 1883 by Otis Brothers and Company—the sons of Elisha Graves Otis, who had invented the first safe hoist and produced the world's first passenger elevator in 1857, but who had died at age forty-nine in 1861. These are the oldest such elevators still in operation today, and operate as follows: a cable that runs through the elevator is connected to a valve on a roof water tank. When pulled, it opens the valve and allows water to flow down a pipe, turning a cylinder that hoists the lifting rope attached to the elevator. When pulled in the opposite direction, it opens another valve, releasing the water in the pipe into a basement tank, gradually unwinding the lift rope. The water was originally pumped to the roof by a steam-engined pump; now it is electric. The elevators can travel at fifty feet a minute; as the Otis Elevator Company now describes it, "The residents still float up and down . . . in touch with the stately pace of yesterday."

One early feature of the building was the Louis Sherry restaurant on the eighth floor, placed high up in the building so that residents would not be disturbed by kitchen smells. (Only servants and bachelor quarters were above it. It was announced that persons desiring dinners, ice creams, or other delicacies could "have the same furnished satisfactorily, and in the best manner, by sending word to Mr. Sherry at The Gramercy." The lease specified that it would be "a first class Restaurant equal in style and quality to Delmonicos and [the proprietor] will fit it up properly with linen, china, silver and table para-

Plate 175

Plate 172 *Homeopathic Medical College, northwest corner of Third Avenue and Twentieth Street, c. 1860.*
Plate 173 *Chancellor Walworth Lodge (Gramercy Hall), northwest corner of Third Avenue and Twentieth Street, c. 1875.*
Plate 174 *No. 34 Gramercy Park; entrance.*
Plate 175 *Gramercy Park, c. 1905. The Gramercy Park Hotel next door to No. 34 had been demolished; the site was a vacant lot until the erection of No. 36.*

Plate 176 *Fourteenth Street, looking east toward Irving Place. In the foreground, Steinway Hall and at the corner of Irving Place, the original Academy of Music Building, 1866.*

phernalia." The wine list ran from fifty cents for a half bottle of St. Julien red wine to a top price of five dollars for a bottle of Clos de Vougeot; a pony of Chartreuse or Curacao cost twenty cents. The restaurant failed in less than a year, however.

No. 34 has, over the years, had its share of famous residents. Emma Thursby, the coloratura soprano, whom Walter Damrosch called the Jenny Lind of America, was one. When she sang in Haydn's *Creation* with the New York Oratorio Society under his direction at Steinway Hall in 1877, *The New York Times* referred to her "exquisite fidelity," and to her "electrifying the house with the . . . power of her higher notes." She lived at No. 34 from the time it was built until her death in 1931, and her regular Friday-morning classes, known as "Thursby Fridays," though often complained about by neighbors, were often attended by Caruso, Mary Garden, Nellie Melba, and her own pupil Geraldine Farrar.

Movie actors John Carradine, James Cagney, and Mildred Dunnock have all lived at No. 34, and when neighborhood children stop at the door to ask, "Does the witch live here?" they are referring to Margaret Hamilton, who played the Wicked Witch of the West in *The Wizard of Oz*. And she did live at No. 34 for many years.

The house records contain documents such as the two-page, closely typed complaint of a tenant and wife of a Park Trustee, Mrs. J. P. Day, who on May 21, 1902, had her skirt caught in the elevator gate before she could pull it in behind her; she called the elevator man, who did not come until he heard the ripping noise made as she was forced to pull the skirt over her head. That was not all: she also complained that the hydraulic elevator pipes had been leaking and soaking her kitchen floor so that her servants had been getting their skirts wet. She submitted a bill for her fourteen-dollar-a-yard silk skirt, which "being of the very heaviest kind had probably been good for a number of years' wear."

Also interesting is the 1908 note that read, "You are no doubt aware that on Monday, July 27, the horse attached to your wagon ran away and damaged about sixteen feet of the railing in front of our building. Kindly let me know what action you are taking." Or the reference on May 17, 1907, to the large open lot adjoining No. 34: since the old hotel building next door had been taken down "over 1½ years ago," it had become a "universal dumping ground."

Then there is the August 31, 1904, demand to have a Mrs. Cridge's woman servant barred from using the hall telephone, which she had used out of turn, for servants were not to use it if tenants were waiting; Mrs. Cridge contended, however, that the woman was not so much a servant as a companion.

Until the Metropolitan Opera House was built in 1883 and Carnegie Hall in 1891, the center of musical life in New York, in fact in the country, was only a few blocks from Gramercy Park, at the Academy of Music on Irving Place at Fourteenth Street (where the Consolidated Edison Building replaced it in 1925). It was built in 1854 and opened with a production of Bellini's *Norma*. In 1859, Adelina Patti made her triumphant debut there in *Lucia de Lammermoor.* When the old house burned in 1866, it was rebuilt the next year, with seating for twenty-seven hundred; the 1867 season opened with Gounod's *Romeo and Juliet.*

The Academy of Music was also the home of the New York Philharmonic. George Templeton Strong, who was a member of the board of the Philharmonic, went regularly to its rehearsals and concerts there. His diary entry for December 15, 1871, reads:

> To Philharmonic rehearsal this afternoon. . . . The Raff symphony grows on one. But how infinitely below good, honest, old Joseph Haydn (in G) in freshness, spontaneity, geniality, and inspiration. It is like a volume of Robert Browning after Shakespeare's songs.[6]

On November 16, 1872:

> The great [Anton] Rubinstein did a concerto of his own and certain Preludes by Chopin with amazing delicacy, power, and prestidigitation. He seems to me beyond all question the most skilful pianist or pianizer I ever heard.[7]

And on April 18, 1873:

> To Philharmonic rehearsal this afternoon. Academy was packed. The illustrious Wieniawski played a prettyish concerto by Spohr quite as well as it deserved, and the illustrious Rubinstein conducted his own *Ocean Symphony* without the score. He is a most magnetic conductor. His pantomime, or gesture, expressed p, pp, ppp, sf, fff, staccato, and the like. . . . The orchestra was on its mettle, and never played better. But the symphony is nothing more than a piece of scholarly, careful work, never offending good taste and signifying nothing at all.

Philharmonic boxes were regularly auctioned at the Academy of Music. Strong recorded that on Mon-

Plate 176

day, November 13, 1871, from three to four-thirty, with A. H. Mueller as the auctioneer, the attendance was large, the bidding spirited, and the proceeds larger than the year before.

A few doors to the west, at No. 109–11 East Fourteenth Street, was Steinway Hall (Plate 176), built in 1866 by the founder of the piano firm, Henry E. Steinway, and for many years the foremost concert hall in the country. Anton Rubinstein played there, as did Rafael Joseffy and pianists of the golden age such as Moriz Rosenthal. Great violinists such as Wieniawski, Vieuxtemps, de Sarasate, and Kreisler gave recitals, as did Lilli Lehmann, Marcella Sembrich, and other singers. Leopold Damrosch, Theodore Thomas, Arthur Nikisch, and Anton Seidl often conducted in the beautiful hall.

At the corner of Irving Place and Eighteenth Street was the National Conservatory of Music, founded in 1885; its director from 1892 to 1894 was Antonín Dvořák, who lived at No. 327 East Seventeenth Street, where he began is symphony *From the New World*. Also on Seventeenth Street, at Irving Place, lived Victor Herbert, who had come to this country in 1886 to be first cellist of the Metropolitan Opera Orchestra, when his wife, Theresa Herbert-Foerster, was engaged to sing there. They had lived first at the Belvedere House on Fourth Avenue at Eighteenth Street. With his lifelong friend the great music critic James Huneker, who lived in a small family hotel at the northeast corner of Irving Place and Seventeenth Street, Herbert was a member of Dvořák's faculty at the National Conservatory. He wrote his Second Cello Concerto on Irving Place and played it with the Philharmonic in 1894. It was later, however, when he had become conductor of the Pittsburgh Symphony, that he began to write the operettas for which his name is most famous. At the southwest corner of Irving Place and Seventeenth Street lived Elsie de Wolfe whose interior design was radically modern in its day. (Plate 118)

Finally, mention must be made of Sir Arthur Sullivan, who during the winter of 1879/80 stayed in a rooming house at No. 45 East Twentieth Street. He and William Gilbert had come to this country to conduct an authorized version of *H.M.S. Pinafore* (because there was no copyright agreement between England and the United States, anyone was free to steal and give first performances of their works, thus depriving them of any royalties). American publishers were making fortunes from *Pinafore;* one newspaper announced, "At present there are forty-two companies playing *Pinafore* about the country. Companies formed after six P.M. yesterday are not included."

The authorized performance took place on December 1, 1879, at the Fifth Avenue Theater (at Twenty-eighth Street), with Sullivan conducting. The pirated versions suddenly paled before its authentic orchestration. But the piracy had also suggested a new operetta called *The Pirates of Penzance*. Gilbert had completed its libretto before leaving England, and Sullivan had sketched out most of the music. Although he had brought the second act with him, he had forgotten to bring his sketches for the first, so he had to rewrite them from memory in New York. All December, what with public dinners, rehearsals, and performances, he rarely got to bed before dawn. He finished his new work at five A.M. on December 31. Six hours later he rehearsed it; that night, more dead than alive, he conducted its first performance. It caused a sensation.

Thereafter, to avoid pirated scores from being produced, audiences were searched for hidden music paper. The scores used were locked in safes every night. Eventually, various stolen versions did appear, however, but this time the true version had preceded them, and numbers of authorized casts were trained and sent out on tour. The strain of all this work told on Sullivan, and he once bitingly commented that "A free and independent American citizen ought not to be robbed of his right to rob someone else."

Both he and Gilbert had to put up with the American public at close range, but they rarely let it get the best of them:

> "Oh, Mr. Gilbert," said a wealthy lady at some dinner party, "your friend Mr. Sullivan's music is really too delightful. It reminds me so much of dear Baytch [Bach]. Do tell me: what is Baytch doing just now. Is he still composing?"
>
> "Well, no, madam," Gilbert returned, "just now, as a matter of fact, dear Baytch is by way of decomposing."[9]

Notes

[1] When the building was taken down in 1902, its facade, though modified, was reerected, together with James Renwick's original east end of St. Patrick's Cathedral and John Kellum's Marble Palace for A. T. Stewart, as the exterior of the Church of Our Lady of Lourdes, on West 142nd Street.

[2] Louise H. Tharp, *Saint-Gaudens and the Gilded Era* (Boston: Little, Brown & Co., 1969), p. 113.

[3] *Gramercy Graphic*, October, 1946, p. 9.

[4] Ibid.

[5] Robert Koch, *Louis C. Tiffany, Rebel in Glass* (New York: Crown Publishers, 1966), p. 50.

[6] Alan Nevins and M. H. Thomas, eds., *The Diary of George Templeton Strong* (New York: Macmillan Publishing Co., 1952), vol. 4, p. 404.

[7] Ibid., p. 457.

[8] Ibid., p. 477.

[9] Hesketh Pearson, *Gilbert and Sullivan* (London: Penguin Books, 1954), p. 93.

Plate 177 *John and Grace Bigelow, on their way to the opening of the New York Public Library, 1911 (the year of his death).*

16

Nineteenth-Century Memoirs

Perhaps the most detailed and informative of the many memoirs that have been written about nineteenth-century life in Gramercy Park are those of Caroline Pryor Pine. She was born in 1856 at No. 25 on the south side of the Park, grew up there, and was married to John B. Pine, the Park historian and a Trustee. Though written in 1929 and never published, her memoirs are largely about life in the 1860's, 1870's, and 1880's.

Mrs. Pine's grandmother and two great-aunts lived in three adjoining houses, Nos. 24, 25, and 26 Gramercy Park. The easternmost great-aunt at No. 26 was married to Morris Ketchum; they had five boys and a girl and, because the great-aunt at No. 25, Mrs. Samuel Mitchill, had no children when their two houses were built in 1849–50, she gave a foot of her property to her sister so she could have a slightly wider house. When her other sister, Mrs. Pine's grandmother, who lived to the west, died at an early age leaving her husband, Judge Sylvanus Miller of the New York Surrogate Court, with more children than he could handle, Mrs. Mitchill took in two of them to live with her. Mrs. Pine's mother was one of these children, which accounts for her having been born at No. 25 and not at her grandfather's house at No. 24. She writes:

> Our own house, where my mother and father first met, and were married, was not so pleasing in its proportions as the larger one adjoining. It and No. 26 were built of Nova Scotia stone, which did not harmonize with any others on the Park. . . . The contractor who built [it] was a Mr. Hennessy, who lived and had

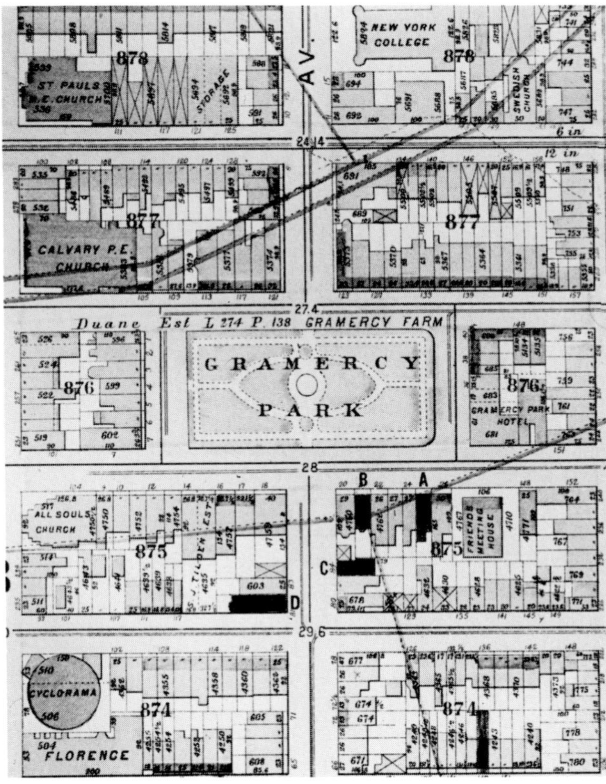

Plate 178 *Map of vicinity of Gramercy Park. Shaded buildings are a) No. 25 Gramercy Park, the home of Caroline Pryor Pine; b) No. 21 Gramercy Park, the Bigelow house; c) No. 84 Irving Place, the home of Henry Noble MacCracken; and d) No. 81 Irving Place, the home of Gladys Rice Brooks.*

his little shop below his dwelling quarters, directly across Nineteenth Street, on which our garden opened.

An event of . . . interest and excitement was my mother's wedding on a lovely day in May, when certain boys who lived in nice little houses on or near Third Avenue wished to attend via the board fence. The gate did not open to their attempts, but one of the wedding attendants, of which there were ten, bridesmaids and groomsmen, all little nephews and nieces of my mother, managed to collect a pailful of refreshments. They were served rather informally over the fence. . . .

The owners of the lots on the other side of ours had built on their rear lots very good stables, which made comfortable dwelling places for their coachmen's families. As we could not afford to keep horses, our rear property was more of a garden, with two different levels, and a few marble steps, and many wisteria and rose vines climbing on the adjacent brick walls. Our garden had connected with the Ketchums' by a gate, which could be opened, but after the wedding episode, my grandmother had this permanently closed. In contrast to playing within the vine covered walls of our 19th Street garden, were the winter days when we children made orange sherbet out of snow, and I think, partook of it then and there. . . .

After my grandmother's death . . . the property was sold to Mr. Albert Gallatin, who lived and died in the house. During the last few years when we still owned, but rented it furnished to friends, our tenants included the widow of Samuel Morse, and Mr. Thomas Edison.

The east end of the Park was occupied chiefly by the Gramercy Park Hotel (1856–80)—a most exclusive and expensive house where families, in many cases, had their own private dining room, as well as occupying one or more floors in the house. . . . Two or three years ago, I chanced to meet . . . a very old lady who recalled the days when it was a marble-yard. . . . [She] lived just around the corner on Fourth Avenue, and used, occasionally, to play truant from school, upon which occasions she and her little brother spent long hours enjoying themselves in the marble-yard, while their family thought they were safely at school. . . .

In my early days, the freight and passenger cars ran down Fourth Avenue, and I shall always remember the noise they made.[1]

As a child, Caroline Pryor played in the Park, and at night, she and her friends were even known to have thrown stones at the tin swans that floated in the pool around the water nymph fountain, in some instances even sinking them. (Plate 90 shows the bills for their repair and replacement).

Once Theodore Roosevelt's mother (who lived on the other side of Fourth Avenue) came to the house to ask for a cook's reference. "My mother was not well and sent me down, although I was still a young school girl, to give the information to Mrs. Roosevelt."

Theodore Roosevelt was born in 1858, two years after Caroline Pryor Pine, two blocks away at No. 28 East Twentieth Street in a house built in 1848. His *Autobiography* is a source of interesting glimpses of a boyhood spent in the neighborhood of Gramercy Park.

He speaks of how

> . . . the black haircloth furniture in the dining room scratched the bare legs of the children when they sat on it. The middle room was a library, with tables, chairs, and bookcases of gloomy respectability. It was without windows, and so was available only at night. The front room, the parlor, seemed to us children to be a room of much splendor, but was open for general use only on Sunday evening or on rare occasions when there were parties. The Sunday evening family gathering was the redeeming feature in a day which otherwise we children did not enjoy—chiefly because we were all of us made to wear clean clothes and keep neat. The ornaments of that parlor I remember now, including the gas chandelier decorated with a great quantity of cut-glass prisms. These prisms struck me as possessing peculiar magnificence. One of them fell off one day, and I hastily grabbed it and stowed it away, passing several days of furtive delight in the treasure, a delight always alloyed with fear that I would be found out and convicted of larceny. There was a Swiss wood-carving representing a very big hunter on one side of an exceedingly small mountain, and a herd of chamois, disproportionately small for the hunter and large for the mountain, just across the ridge. This always fascinated us; but there was a small chamois kid for which we felt agonies lest the hunter might come on it and kill it. There was also a Russian moujik drawing a gilt sledge on a piece of malachite. Some one mentioned in my hearing that malachite was a valuable marble. This fixed in my mind that it was valuable exactly as diamonds are valuable. I accepted that moujik as a priceless work of art, and it was not until I was well in middle age that it occurred to me that I was mistaken.[2]

For a few months, Theodore Roosevelt went to Professor McMullen's school on Twentieth Street, but most of his education was with tutors. He recalled:

> While still a small boy I began to take an interest in natural history. I remember distinctly the first day that I started on my career as zoölogist. I was walking up Broadway, and as I passed the market to which I used sometimes to be sent before breakfast to get strawberries, I suddenly saw a dead seal laid out on a slab of wood. That seal filled me with every possible

Plate 179 *No. 21 Gramercy Park, c. 1900.*

feeling of romance and adventure. I asked where it was killed, and was informed in the harbor. I had already begun to read some of Mayne Reid's books and other boys' books of adventure, and I felt that this seal brought all these adventures in realistic fashion before me. As long as that seal remained there, I haunted the neighborhood of the market day after day. I measured it, and I recall that, not having a tape measure, I had to do my best to get its girth with a folding pocket foot-rule, a difficult undertaking. I carefully made a record of the utterly useless measurements, and at once began to write a natural history of my own, on the strength of that seal. This, and subsequent natural histories, were written down in blank books in simplified spelling, wholly unpremeditated and unscientific. I had vague aspirations of in some way or another owning and preserving that seal, but they never got beyond the purely formless stage. I think, however, I did get the seal's skull, and with two of my cousins promptly started what we ambitiously called the "Roosevelt Museum of Natural History." The collections were at first kept in my room, until a rebellion on the part of the chambermaid received the approval of the higher authorities of the household and the collection was moved up to a kind of bookcase in the back hall upstairs. It was the ordinary small boy's collection of curios, quite incongruous and entirely valueless except from the standpoint of the boy himself.[3]

Theodore Roosevelt's family took him to Europe to live in 1872. When they returned in 1874, they moved into a new house at No. 6 West Fifty-seventh Street. However, Roosevelt returned to Gramercy Park in 1885, at the age of twenty-six, to act as godfather to his brother Elliott's daughter, Eleanor, when she was baptized in Calvary Church, and he often came back when he belonged to The Players. In the meantime, Twentieth Street became increasingly commercial, and eventually even the old Roosevelt house was taken over for business use. In 1916, it was demolished and replaced with a two-story commercial building, which was itself razed in 1923 to make way for the replication of the original Roosevelt house, which stands there today.

In 1881, one of the important citizens of New York moved into a Twentieth Street house at No. 21 Gramercy Park. He was John Bigelow, and the house was his winter home until his death in 1911. John B. Pine remembered:

> [his] venerable figure and massive gray head, the very embodiment of the dignity of age, and [I] recall the keen sympathy and quick intelligence with which to the very last, he greeted his many visitors. Few, however, recall the important part which he played at a most critical period in the history of the nation,

Plate 180 *No. 22 Gramercy Park, c. 1900.*

> when in 1865, by appointment of President Lincoln, he represented the United States as Minister Plenipotentiary at the Court of France. . . . Previous to his going abroad, Mr. Bigelow had been associated with his intimate friend, William Cullen Bryant, on the *Evening Post,* and while abroad, he devoted all of his literary skill and ingenuity to counteracting the propaganda actively conducted on behalf of the Southern Confederacy. . . . He was richly entitled to describe his life as "active," for when not engaged in national service he gave the greater part of his time to matters of local interest and importance and held numerous public positions, from that of a member of the Tilden Commission, which broke up the Canal Ring, to the presidency of the New York Public Library. It was a tribute to his remarkable virility that he was elected president of the Century Club in his eighty-ninth year and he held that office until his death [at the age of ninety-four].[4]

From 1850, when Bigelow had married, he and his family had lived at No. 188 West Twenty-second Street (which, according to the old numbering, was beyond Ninth Avenue and opposite the house of Clement Clarke Moore, the author of "'Twas the Night Before Christmas.") After 1857, however, much of each year was spent at their house in Highland Falls, New York. In 1881, Samuel J. Tilden, presented his great friend Bigelow with the house on Gramercy Park, taking the precaution of deeding it to his daughter, Grace, in order to forestall Bigelow's protests.

A convinced Swedenborgian, a believer in homeopathy, and a stalwart individualist, John Bigelow cannot have been an easy person to live with. He disapproved of hot-air furnaces, so the Gramercy Park house, in the dead of winter, was heated only by coal-burning fireplaces, and the family was taught to take cold baths every morning as did he. He had a horror of stimulants of any kind: tea, coffee, and even vanilla! He looked down on "society," and by contrast with the lavish parties of his next-door neighbors, the Stuyvesant Fishes, he gave regular dinner parties at which the guest list rarely varied and the menu never did. Yet it was he who, in 1882, invited Oscar Wilde to dinner after his New York reading, and who took him to the Century Club. He disapproved of Wilde's epicureanism, but when he was imprisoned, Bigelow condemned it as persecution.

His granddaughter, Grace B. Cook, in her unpublished memoirs, remembered:

> [When he] grew to be very old, his birthday became a very important day for us. There were numerous visitors always and among them Andrew Carnegie, who had a mysterious admiration for him. He always presented him with Scotch products such as oatmeal, which he never ate, and whiskey which he never drank. Grandpa used to laugh about it, and say that Carnegie's interest in him was entirely on account of his long life which he was interested in emulating. Carnegie was inordinately afraid of death.
>
> When in New York in the winter, accompanied by one or another of his feminine family, he went for a drive in an open carriage every single day in all weathers, literally. Many was the afternoon that I cowered shivering under the fur robe at his side. He in a top hat and fur coat with a high sealskin collar. Nevertheless, I love to look back on those drives, the policeman saluting him as he drove up Fifth Avenue, and the long talks we had together. Talking with him was like drinking from an inexhaustible fountain.[5]

John Bigelow's daughter, Grace, never married. She had once fallen in love with a German officer, but her father had forbidden her to marry him and "removed her to Italy . . . to cure her broken heart. . . . Her life then came to be more and more centered about her father."[6] She was, however, obsessed, even into her old age, by the very subject of marriage; Irene Abdusheli, her step-grandniece, remembers her saying, "Get married, Irene, get married!" as she tapped her walking stick commandingly on the floor. She was an austere person, but possessed of a de-

Plate 181 *John Bigelow, in his Gramercy Park parlor.*
Plate 182 *Grace Bigelow and her friend Helen Lawrence, 1906, before the erection of No. 36 Gramercy Park.*

Plate 181

Plate 182

Plate 183

Plate 184

lightful wit and a razor-sharp mind; she had great common sense. She wore a black-ribbon choker around her neck and long white-lace dresses; she was, in fact, very much a grande dame (Plate 182). In 1916, she was the first woman to become a Trustee of Gramercy Park, and, in 1932, at the age of seventy-nine, she was elected president of the Trustees. Early that year, she was busy seeing to it, among other things, that the "Gramercy Park Valet," which had illegally set up shop at No. 60, was made aware of its being in violation of the Trust Deed, which prohibited the conducting of business on Park lots. She remained active in matters concerning the Park right up to her death that same year.

Among the most vivid descriptions of life in Gramercy Park in the 1890's are the memoirs of Gladys Brooks and Henry Noble MacCracken, who grew up across the street from each other on Irving Place. Gladys Brooks's father was a doctor who lived and practiced medicine in the high-stooped brick house at 81 Irving Place at the northwest corner of Nineteenth Street. There was a separate office entrance around the corner at No. 123 East Nineteenth Street, and above the office was the library. "From its curving seat in the bow window," Mrs. Brooks remembers, "I often went to read or study my spelling, now and then looking down into the adjoining backyard which belonged to The Players." There was a tall ailanthus tree in the next garden, and a huge wisteria

Plate 183 *Grace Cook's friend Elinor Lee, with two children and their nanny in Gramercy Park, 1906.*
Plate 184 *Grace Cook and Elinor Lee in Gramercy Park. The turrets of the Free Academy can be seen in the distance.*

Plate 185

tree. Occasionally there would be a dinner party, and the house

> was taken over by the florist and the caterer's man who arrived soon after I got home from school. . . . We children loved to sit on the stairs in our night clothes, ready for bed, looking down from our hiding place onto the table below, on the white cloth trimmed with smilax, the silver candy dishes filled with almonds and Turkish Delight, the open work silver candle shades lined with India silk that cast a pink glow over everything.[7]

Mrs. Brooks went to the Brearley School then on West Forty-fourth Street. To get there, she took a Fourth Avenue horse car at the corner of Nineteenth Street. Along Nineteenth Street, she remembered passing a row of small houses

> at the back of their neat front yards. Each morning, I stopped for a moment, to look over the fence that bound them, thinking how pleasant and friendly they seemed . . . the wrought-iron balconies beneath French windows beckoned me and in one of the houses I had a glimpse of flames vividly lighting the hearth within, and bright flowers on the mantel above it. At the corner, I had to wait. The streetcar was down at Union Square and the horse was slower than ever today because [it had snowed and] the snow was piled between the tracks. . . . Behind me four big stallions were coming near, slipping along the cobbles as they pulled a tray piled with barrels from the brewery down the street. . . . The horses were almost at the corner now, drawing the narrow swaying car on the rails behind them. The driver stood moving from side to side on the outer platform, stamping his feet in the cold, slapping his free arm across his chest. As I stepped on board, he turned and slid the door back for me, closing it again after I had gone in. I sat down on a long hard bench covered with red carpeting, worn and raveled at the edge, and pulled a nickel from inside my mitten to hand it to the conductor when he came in from the rear platform.

Plate 185 *Irving Place, west side, looking north from Eighteenth Street, March 1909. Gladys Rice Brooks's house (No. 81) can be seen at the northwest corner of Nineteenth Street.*

She also remembered being in New York in September when it was hot and the dusty rooms of the house "seemed almost a part of the late summer streets and the shrill, grinding sound of the brakes on the Third Avenue Elevated as the trains slowed down for the Eighteenth Street Station, came in through the open window as I lay awake at night."

Her mother took great interest in the children's music. "She founded a Children's Orchestra that met in our dining room . . . on Saturday afternoons with Mr. [David] Mannes to conduct us." There were also Sunday-evening musicales at which such pianists as Ossip Gabrilovitch played. There, the guests

> [walked] around the corner to our house for a Sunday supper of scalloped oysters and chicken croquettes and Rhine wine from Bohemian glass goblets, going

Plate 186

Plate 187

Plate 186 *Irving Place, east side, looking north from Eighteenth Street, March 1909. Healy's pub, now Pete's Tavern, is in the foreground, and Henry Noble MacCracken's house is the third house north of Nineteenth Street. Mailboxes have not changed to this day, but they must have appeared daringly modern in 1909.*

Plate 187 *Irving Place, looking north to Gramercy Park, c. 1880.*

Plate 188 *No. 101 East Nineteenth Street, 1913.*

later into the drawing room to gather around the large Steinway below the *verdure* tapestries and the ceiling of Japanese gold rice paper which was gently illumined by the glow of the hearth fire. . . .

[In the library] above the bookshelves were majolica pharmacy jars and copper pots [which] caught the rays of the afternoon sun, while the tawny velvet of buttoned furniture covering and the gold of silk curtains from Liberty's of London enhanced the far promise of peace. All this was my mother's doing—who delighted, on a spring day, to thrust daffodils into a copper bowl or crisp tulips into a pottery jar . . . and who spent many quiet moments here reading to me from a book that she loved.

My own particular portion of the library was the wide bay window. From here I watched the first signs of spring . . . in the ailanthus tree. [Here, also, I] was introduced to death through the tears of one of my school friends whose mother had died [and who] beside the library fire had sobbed out her grief, head buried in the broad sofa arm.[8]

Henry Noble MacCracken, Gladys's neighbor across the street, remembered playing "tipstick" in Gramercy Park South:

We made a little stick about six inches long . . . and a bat made of an old barrel stave. [You] slammed the bat down on the end of the tipstick and . . . it went up in the air [and you] ran across the street to

Plate 189 *Fourth Avenue horse car passing Union Square, 1892.*

Mr. Tilden's house and touched base. . . . Of course you had to dodge the express wagons . . . they made noise though, so you could tell when they were coming. . . . I was scared of grocery horses. They hit you when you went by, even if you were walking on the curbstone.

The old men that lived around the park liked to come out and watch us play. . . . There was old Mr. Cyrus Field and Mr. Edwin Booth. . . . And one time Mr. Hewitt, who used to be mayor. . . . Mr. Booth was the best, because he let us play tag on his steps, and climb up the porch, and drop off. . . . Then he had Mr. Stanford White take away the stoop . . . put in columns and a balcony and alot of fancy ironwork. It was completely spoiled for tag. . . . Tilden tag was more fun though, because Mr. Tilden had two front doors and a yard between and we could run down one steps and up the other and race along the sidewalk, or vault over into the front yard.

In June the ailanthus was all sticky. Peddlers yelled "Strawberries" up and down Irving Place, and flower-pot wagons sold geraniums and begonias. Vegetable men from Long Island came with scallions and peas; old clothes, and knife grinders—it was a noisy street. Electra Nilsson was a girl who lived at No. 1 Gramercy Park. . . . I got to know her one afternoon when I was chased by the Calvary Choirboys when they were coming out of rehearsal, and I ran into her yard and slammed the iron door under the stoop. She and I did some Five Cent Saturdays. We went down Third Avenue on the L to South Ferry and transferred to the Second Avenue line and went up to Harlem. We got in the front car and watched the little [steam] engine.[9]

The El had replaced the street tracks of the Third Avenue Railroad Company which had begun operation on July 2, 1853 and was the second such transportation company in New York. The first, in 1832, was the New York and Harlem Railroad, which ran from Prince Street to Twenty-sixth Street and Fourth Avenue, on rails that were flat strips fastened to stone blocks embedded in the ground. The first two cars of the New York and Harlem had been built by the pioneer designer, John Stephenson, and were like stagecoaches, with three compartments, each seating ten people. They were well upholstered on the inside, and brightly painted on the outside. The Third Avenue cars, however, had single compartments, with seats in figured plush upholstery along the sides. Collection of fares in some cars was by means of a groove slanting from rear to front, down which passengers would slide their nickels. At night, smoky oil lamps gave a flickering light, and sometimes there were oilstoves for heat. In 1871, a grander "Palace Car" was inaugurated, costing ten cents, but it was discontinued when the public appeared indifferent to its charms.

The Third Avenue El was the last of the elevated

Plate 190 *Gramercy Park, September 1905.*

lines to be built. Construction began in November 1877, and the line was formally opened on August 26, 1878, from South Ferry to Grand Central station. (Steam engines showered sparks and belched smoke along Third Avenue, until 1900.) The elevated lines in New York had been promoted by such investors as Cyrus Field and Peter Cooper, and they were greeted with great enthusiasm. *Leslie's Illustrated Weekly Newspaper* described the Third Avenue El approvingly:

> The interiors of both the ladies' and gentlemens' waiting rooms are very tastefully furnished throughout, in what is known as the Eastlake style of decoration.
>
> The general style of the stations with their many gables, finials, etc., might be properly classed as modification of the Renaissance and Gothic Styles of architecture, presenting somewhat the appearance of a Swiss villa. The glass ventilators are . . . in variegated colors [Grace Cook wrote in her memoirs of "the beauty of the red and blue glass windows"] and ornamental bay windows in the waiting rooms . . . afford a view of the street below. . . . The woodwork of the doors, seats, and sides of the cars is of mahogany and the ceiling is paneled with oak and mahogany. The seats are furnished with flexible backs of maroon morocco for winter use and, in summer, to be covered with woven rattan. The floors are covered with heavy Axminster rugs and carpets.[10]

Henry MacCracken went to school at No. 5 East Twenty-second Street. One of his memories of the school was of the lunch recesses during which students regularly took long walks, eating as they walked. These walks took two alternate routes: one went down Broadway to Union Square and Fourteenth Street and then back by Fourth Avenue (it was just a mile); the other went up to Thirty-first Street. When one got back, one slammed the classroom door hard and "yelled 'Union' or 'Thirty-first,' as the case might be." The teacher wrote it down in a book and every month paid you two cents a mile.

> On Fridays he would count up the walks the school had [cumulatively] taken, and then measure [the total distance] on a big map of the world on the wall behind his desk. It would be Kansas City or somewhere after a while. By the end of the year we would be in China. We walked around to China by Canada and the Bering Strait. We got alot of geography that way.[11]

MacCracken's most vivid memory of the Calvary choirboys concerned the day they got into a snowball fight with MacCracken's Gramercy gang. It was Sunday evening and almost service time, and when the choir had been unable to make it to the church because of the battle lines—trying to shove past but

Plate 191 *Steam-drawn train on the Third Avenue El.*

Plate 192 *Third Avenue El station at Twenty-third Street.*

Plate 193 *Hotel New Amsterdam, southeast corner of Fourth Avenue and Twenty-first Street. Bay windows at the rear of No. 1 Gramercy Park show from behind the hotel.*

Plate 194 *Cyclorama, in the distance at the southeast corner of Fourth Avenue and Nineteenth Street; All Souls Church in the foreground, c. 1895.*

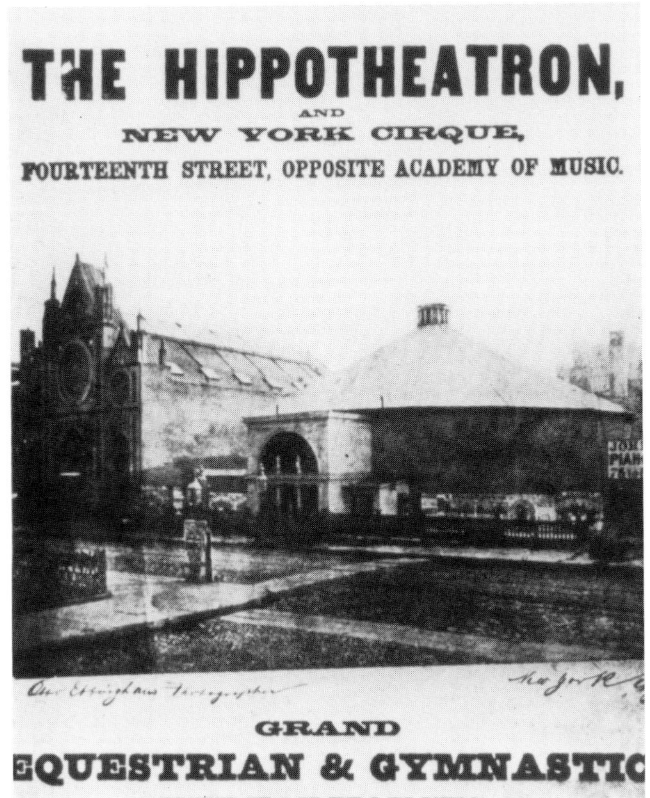

Plate 195 *Hippotheatron (almost identical to the Cyclorama) on Fourteenth Street, across from the Academy of Music at Irving Place, c. 1880.*

getting rolled in the snow—the rector, Dr. Satterlee, appeared at the door and called to them. One of the Gramercy gang, not a choirboy, answered, "'We're not coming in tonight, Dr. Satterlee. The snow's too good, and we're having fun.' 'How dare you talk like that, you little vagabond,' said Dr. Satterlee," and grabbed the boy and dragged him into the church. There, he was told to vest and was thrust into a procession (the only boy among the men). When the service was over, he was taken in to talk to Satterlee, to whom he explained that he wasn't even in the choir, but was only going home "'and first thing I knew I was in a snowball fight. Then you came, and grabbed me, and pulled me in here'. . . . So, for once, Calvary didn't have its famous boy choir," but only one lone member of the Gramercy gang.[12]

One of the most popular entertainments in the neighborhood in the 1890's was the Cyclorama (Plate 194) at the southeast corner of Fourth Avenue and Nineteenth Street. In the circular corrugated iron structure was a fifty-foot high, four-hundred-foot long painting, its ends joined to make a complete circle. It was painted by a French artist named Phillipotteaux and was a bird's-eye view of Niagara Falls. This was the second Phillipotteaux painting to be displayed in the building, the first being a scene of the Battle of Gettysburg, described in *The Illustrated New York: Metropolis of Today* as being so realistic that the artillery could "almost be heard to thunder," and its "fierce charges of cavalry and masses of infantry [presented] the grandest dramatic spectacle of modern times." An 1890 volume of the *Annals of the New York Stage* claimed that people were flocking to see it. By 1897, however, the Cyclorama was gone, replaced by the huge Parker Building.

Notes

[1] Caroline Pryor Pine, *Recollections,* privately printed, in collection of the Museum of the City of New York, pp. 6, 8, 10.

[2] Theodore Roosevelt, *An Autobiography* (New York: Charles Scribner's Sons, 1926), pp. 5–6.

[3] Ibid., p. 14.

[4] John B. Pine, *The Story of Gramercy Park, 1831–1921* (New York: Knickerbocker Press, 1921), pp. 37–39.

[5] Grace B. Cook, "Highland Falls," *Memoirs,* (unpublished,) pp. 38–39.

[6] Ibid., pp. 13–14.

[7] Gladys Brooks, *Gramercy Park, Memoirs of a New York Girlhood* (New York: E. P. Dutton & Co., 1958), p. 49.

[8] Ibid., pp. 32–33, 46, 87, 88, 213–14.

[9] Henry Noble MacCracken, *The Family on Gramercy Park, A New York Boyhood at the Turn of the Century* (New York: Charles Scribner's Sons, 1949), pp. 11–13, 33, 38–40, 124.

[10] Quoted in *Gramercy Graphic,* September, 1962, pp. 11–12.

[11] MacCracken, op. cit., p. 85.

[12] Ibid., pp. 193–194.

Plate 196
No. 1 Lexington Avenue, c. 1910.

17

The Twentieth-Century Park: Endangered, Saved, and Lively

Among Samuel Tilden's papers there is a small handbill dated 1864, announcing the proposed Lexington Avenue Railroad and describing in detail how it would be built up Fourth Avenue to Fourteenth Street, over to and up Irving Place, and around Gramercy Park (southbound taking the West Carriageway, northbound the East), and then up Lexington Avenue to Sixty-fourth Street. Fortunately, nothing came of this scheme, but it was only one of a series of threats to the Park. In 1890, the state legislature passed a bill permitting the construction of a cable car route, not around the Park but through it. This time, the governor refused to sign the bill. Then, in 1912, it was proposed that a new line of the subway system be tunneled under Gramercy Park, and Irving Place be extended through the Park to connect with Lexington Avenue. Fortunately, the danger was averted and the Lexington Avenue line, opened in 1904, continued to run under Fourth Avenue.

In 1902, a crisis developed over the proposed Hotel Irving. The question was whether it was to be a hotel or a private dwelling, the latter being all that was specifically allowed by Ruggles's Deed. Heated discussions took place at two meetings held in January at the Friends Meeting House, with John Bigelow, at age eighty-four, in the chair. Because the plans had been filed for a hotel, and because there was to be only one kitchen, a hotel it seemed to be; Bigelow was particularly concerned about the clause in the Deed prohibiting "anything that is dangerous or offensive" to one's Park neighbors. He pictured "hacks standing at the [new hotel] door and carriages coming in at all hours of the day and night and upon the arrival of every train and steamboat at all parts of the island, and the class of hangers-on that naturally beset a hotel [which] would not only be an interference with the general quiet of this place but would be offensive."

He launched into a courtly discourse on the word *offensive.* Asking whether it really were up to a judge to decide what was offensive, he declared,

> The question that is raised is not what is offensive to the judge, but what is offensive to the neighbors, and if we all agree in saying what is offensive to us, how is it possible for the court to go behind it? I think that is what was intended by Mr. Ruggles—to leave to us to decide. . . . Why should a court undertake to decide what is offensive to us? . . . We are the judges, and we do not leave open any contingency in which the opinions of anybody else are of any importance.[1]

The "we" to which Bigelow referred was simply, as he put it, "the seventy odd riparian owners" of property on the Park ("riparian" presumably referring to Crommessie Vly, not to the East or Hudson rivers). He also worried that if the Trustees did not object to a forbidden structure, the Deed itself might

Plate 197 *Gramercy Park South, looking east from Irving Place, September 1905. A street sweeper, dressed entirely in white, stands at the corner. Stuyvesant Fish house is at the corner.*

Plate 198 *Postcard of Gramercy Park, 1905. East birdhouse is not in its present position. Iron urns, as in the west quadrants of the Park today, are also at this time in the east quadrants. The tall building on the horizon, right, is the Fuller (Flatiron) Building, 1902.*

be forfeited and the Park returned to Ruggles's heirs. Henry B. Anderson, who had been retained as counsel, assured him that this was well nigh impossible. It was also pointed out that Gramercy Park House had been allowed to operate for twenty-four years as a hotel on the east side of the Park, and the technicality that it had not been built as such hardly seemed to carry much weight.

The real world was thrust upon the meeting when "a voice," later identified as that of Charles Buek, said:

> If you gentlemen will look about you in this great city and will notice . . . what is going on, why should Gramercy Park be exempt? Is there any indication that anything better than apartment hotels will be built here? Here is a neighborhood that is becoming antiquated; where are the new families coming here to take the place of the old ones? Not any. The residences are becoming old, and they are being turned into boarding houses and when the boarding houses become unprofitable from competition of bachelor apartments [the term used for apartment hotels of two-room suites] the result will be that your property will depreciate. The only consolation is that such [bachelor apartments] can be built here profitably; private houses cannot. It will have to be apartment houses of this kind, or it will have to be something worse; and we know what usually comes after boarding houses, when boarding houses become unprofitable. Therefore I think it very unwise to take any action to prevent it.[2]

In the end, as John Bigelow himself finally suggested, the matter was decided in court and it was established that a private family hotel was not a violation of the Deed. The house at No. 26, built for Caroline Pine's great uncle, Morris Ketchum, and later owned by William Steinway (one of the "sons" in the firm of Steinway & Sons), had been torn down in 1901; the suit, brought by Albert Gallatin, who lived at No. 25, claiming the hotel to be in violation of the Park Deed, was ruled against, and the Hotel Irving was built in 1902.

The following year, the city, reversing its 1832 decision that said that so long as the Park was ornamental it was tax exempt, proceeded to assess it for purposes of taxation at $750,000, though this was later reduced to $500,000. In 1852, the Common Council of New York also had tried to assess the Park for taxation, and even offered it for sale, for unpaid taxes, but later remitted the tax. Now the Trustees protested again that the higher taxes levied on the surrounding lots because they are enhanced by the Park, more than compensated for the loss of taxes on the Park itself. A bill was introduced into the legislature again exempting the Park, but met with no success: assessment again was made, and taxes actually paid, in 1904 and in the succeeding years.

Only after seven years of litigation were the assessments vacated. The Appellate Division of the Supreme Court held that the lot owners had an easement on the Park, and that the assessed value of their land was "several hundred dollars per front foot in excess of the value of other lots in the same part of the City." The total excess, it was held, was $660,000. John B. Pine has described the results of this ruling in a way that cannot be improved upon:

> The conclusion of the Appellate Division was that the City, having added to the market value of the surrounding lots a sum equal to the estimated value of the easements, which exceeded or equalled the value of the Park itself, it could not assess the value of the Park a second time against either the Trustees, who held the fee, nor by necessary consequence, against the owners of the land benefitted by the easement. This decision, which was affirmed by the Court of Appeals . . . furnishes a complete answer to the not infrequent . . . attacks which are made upon the Trustees and lot owners for maintaining the "privacy" of the Park, as it is a judicial finding that in so doing they are merely exercising the right which every property owner has to the enjoyment of property which he has bought and paid for. As such owners, they are fortunate in possessing a "front yard" as well as a "back yard" and their right to the exclusive use of the one can no more be questioned than their right to the exclusive use of the other.[3]

The taxes that had been paid for the seven years, amounting, with interest, to $105,067.48, were refunded and distributed to the lot owners, less the cost of litigation and the sum of approximately $12,000, which was retained as an endowment fund for the maintenance of the Park.

Among the Trustees who had to deal with this trying situation was Stuyvesant Fish, the son of Hamilton Fish, a governor of New York, a United States senator, and the secretary of state under President Grant. Stuyvesant was married to Mayme Fish, one of the formidable (not to say frightening) leaders of New York society (Plate 201), and had become president of the Illinois Central Railroad before he was thirty. In 1887, the Fishes bought the house at No. 19 Gramercy Park, which had been built in 1845 for the lawyer William Samuel Johnson and owned after 1850 by Horace Brooks, a paper merchant who added the stable (Plate 200) at the rear of the property and, in the 1860's, a mansard-roofed fifth floor to the house. The Fishes had Stanford White redesign the house in 1888, adding a splendid white-marble staircase, the entire renovation coming to a cost of $120,000. Soon, it became the scene of some of New York's fanciest dinner parties. Fay MacCracken Stockwell, who grew up next door at No. 84 Irving Place, remembered as a child looking from her house into the Fishes' dining room, where the butler would raise the shade and open a window to air the room, revealing

Plate 199

Plate 200

Plate 199 *Postcard of Gramercy Park, photograph altered by the removal of the top three floors of No. 24 to give it the same height as the Hotel Irving, and the squaring of the southeast corner of the Park fence. The new No. 251–255 Fourth Avenue, built in 1909, appears in the distance.*

Plate 200 *Southeast corner of Irving Place and Gramercy Park South, November 1909. No. 24 Gramercy Park is under construction.*

Plate 201 *Mrs. Stuyvesant Fish late in life.*

one of Mrs. Fish's famous centerpieces: a cherry tree and hatchet, or the replica of a building, each made of spun sugar.

Mayme Fish is reputed in Park lore to have bought the first automobile on Gramercy Park, a little boxy electric car. According to the story, when she first took the wheel (or, more probably, the lever), she immediately knocked down and ran over a man on the street. Flustered, she put the car into reverse and ran over him again. Now, completely at her wits' end and not knowing what she was doing, she drove forward again and over him a third time, whereupon he jumped up, ran away in terror, and was never seen again. Another time, she is said to have given a sit-down dinner for her dog and its friends, insisting they serve themselves from the sideboard.

Stuyvesant Fish was made a Trustee of the Park in 1893 and became its president in 1906. He remained reliably in the chair until his death in 1923, though in 1899 he had moved out of the neighborhood to a new house Stanford White had designed for him at Seventy-eighth Street. His contribution to the Park was beautifully recalled by George Zabriskie, his successor as president:

> . . . He was genial and kindly and always gave some sparkle of merriment to our meetings by a jest or a tale. He had taken part in large affairs of railroads, banks, and other enterprises of business. He was deeply interested in this city and the State of New York which, so long, has been the home of his ancestors, . . . He loved flowers, trees, green fields, and the pleasant landscapes of Putnam County, where he and his father before him had dwelt. He was studious of books, especially of history. He was, all his life, an earnest member of the Episcopal Church, and for a long time a vestryman of Trinity Church. Thus, he was deeply interested, by tastes and by habits, in Gramercy Park; and all the years he was a Trustee, he attended conscientiously to the duties of his trust. [Within twenty-four hours of his last meeting of the Trustees, Fish suddenly] "fell down dead in the National Park Bank."[4]

No. 19 Gramercy Park continued to be owned by the Fish estate. In 1909, a builder who had leased it razed the stable and built on its site a six-story red-brick apartment house that became Stuyvesant Chambers. This building, designated No. 20, was later opened into No. 19 at several levels. Over the years, among the people who had apartments in the double building were Cecilia Beaux, the figure and portrait painter, and Ludwig Bemelmans.

In 1931, Benjamin Sonnenberg and his family moved into the first two floors and began the long process of returning the old house to its former, and perhaps more than its former, glory. They acquired such a wonderful collection of paintings and sculpture, furniture, brass, and other rare artworks, that, in Brendan Gill's words, it became "a work of art in its own right." Of Sonnenberg and his house, Alistair Cooke wrote:

> Ben Sonnenberg, who was to become the Richelieu of American public relations, was twelve years old when he arrived at Ellis Island from Brest Litovsk with no English, two sisters and a mother in a shawl. Six years later, he was stumping through rural Michigan in his only suit selling small picture frames. Four years after that, he was married to a girl he'd known since boyhood on the Lower East Side. They had a two-room apartment and Ben was up and out each morning offering to turn obscure actors into living legends by squeezing their names into gossip columns. . . . From them he moved on to big actors and . . . then to corporations. Many another poor immigrant has struck it rich and remained a poor immigrant with a large bank account. . . . But Sonnenberg began in his early twenties to groom himself as a *grand seigneur,* and nobody ever did it better.
>
> He must have had taste, and he had the good sense to marry a woman whose matching visual taste created the fabrics, the colors, the rooms—the stage, for the incomparable Sonnenberg performance as the grandee of Gramercy Park. . . . Two of Queen Elizabeth's equerries [once] stayed the night there. They were ravished by the uniform style and grandeur of

> the place, by the absence of any seedy nook or cranny. "Buckingham Palace," one of them said, "was never like this." . . . For over forty years he roamed through England (mostly) plucking a Sargent or a Sickert here, an Ingres or an Old Master drawing there, combining in his head, with the skill of a jig-saw champion, an Irish hunt table, a Welsh dresser, a Caroline silver tankard, a set of Chippendale, . . . an exquisite Queen Anne . . . chest to bring them home to their proper setting.[5]

Plate 202 Benjamin Sonnenberg.

Sonnenberg, too, gave lavish dinner parties and, at the top of his house, had a fifty-seat theater in which he gave his guests previews of movies his friend Sam Goldwyn had sent him. He wore a walrus moustache, a derby, an overcoat of the most wonderful shade of tan, and every day a Rolls-Royce in that same tan was waiting outside his door. He had one servant who did nothing but polish brass. The house struck one as the coziest, most colorful, most opulent place one had ever seen. Its myriad possessions were lit in the warmest, most intimate way. Yet when one looked for a masterpiece, or even an extraordinary piece of furniture, it was almost as if one looked in vain. There were no masterpieces, there was only the marvelous ensemble. And after Ben Sonnenberg died in 1978 (ironically, for the greatest public relations man of them all, without an obituary, because he died during a newspaper strike), one had to agree sadly with Robert Hughes that "the greatest masterpiece the house had contained—ebullient, wry, kindly, vain and shrewd—was the old man himself."

Plate 203 Fish-Sonnenberg house, 1984.

The house at the other corner of Irving Place and the Park was not so fortunate in finding a twentieth century owner. It, too, had four stories and was built in 1845, but it was even larger, with four bays on the Park instead of three and the conventional high stoop. It, too, had an added mansard fifth story and a stable at the rear of its even larger garden. The two mansions flanked the southern entrance to the Park like grand ladies in huge Victorian hats.

In 1905, the Clark family who had lived there since 1853 sold the house to the Columbia University Club. One entered the house into a small foyer from which rose a circular stairway. To the right, when it was the club, was a long room with pool tables under droplights with colored-glass shades. To the left was the lounge and main dining room, painted Columbia blue. There were thirteen bedrooms, a library, and card rooms upstairs, and on the roof of the kitchen extension at the rear was an outdoor summer dining place, awninged and screened from the street by clematis vines. The old coach house was converted into squash courts; the bar was in the basement. Club

Plate 204 *Fish-Sonnenberg house; Stanford White staircase. Portrait is of the Duchess of Sutherland by John Singer Sargent.*

Plate 205

life was sedate, and in the register were such names as Nicholas Murray Butler, Bishop Manning, and Edward S. Harkness.

The club outgrew the Clark house by 1918, however, and it was sold to the Army and Navy Club. The library was filled with a huge collection of military books, brought there by a series of horse-drawn wagons. But the Army and Navy Club did not stay long, either, and soon the house became a professional woman's club. In 1926, it was torn down and The Parkside—a residence hotel for women—was built and later taken over by the Salvation Army.

Another of the great private houses on the south side of the Park is No. 11, for years the home of Samuel L. M. Barlow, an entrepreneur, composer, poet, and Trustee of the Park. He and his wife, Ernesta, for years held elegant, serious musicales on alternate Wednesday evenings at which the Juilliard Quartet often played. For the music one sat in tight eighteenth-century gilt chairs in the marvelous drawing room, and at eleven, a buffet supper was served in the dining room at the rear of the house. Then, at midnight, the music would resume, and Mr. Barlow occasionally would move through the room tapping those who had dropped off to sleep.

The night Joan Sutherland made her New York opera debut in 1961, the Barlows held a party afterward. The present writer has the following recollection of that evening. Having recently rented the front

Plate 206

Plate 205 *Gramercy Park South, looking west from Irving Place, c. 1905. The Clark house at the corner was at this time the Columbia University Club; its awninged dining terrace can be seen at the rear of the house.*
Plate 206 *No. 11 Gramercy Park.*

Plate 207

Plate 208

parlor floor of No. 10, the house next door, and not yet having met the owners of No. 11, I stood on my little balcony just above the Barlows' front door and brava'd Sutherland and Leontine Price as they went in. Then I sat down glumly, uninvited. In the silence I heard faint music. It seemed to be coming from the fireplace, and as I went closer to the fireplace it became louder. When I put my head into the fireplace, it got louder still. Unable to resist, I climbed into the fireplace, put my head in the flue, and heard Joan Sutherland sing quite perfectly.

When I finally met the Barlows and was invited to a musicale, I went in through the little foyer at the street door and suddenly remembered friends of mine on Washington Square. One Christmas Eve they had been offered, by someone they knew in the circus, the use of a camel. Singing "We Three Kings," they had ridden up Fifth Avenue to visit their friends, the Barlows, on Gramercy Park. When Ernesta Barlow, tall, elegant, and forbidding, had answered her front doorbell, she had found herself face-to-muzzle with a camel. I doubt that it fazed her, but the memory of the story caused me to smile as I crossed her threshold.

The twentieth century has seen more than half of the original houses on Gramercy Park inevitably torn down to make way for the apartment houses that all stem from Richard Morris Hunt's first French flats on Eighteenth Street. Some of them have architectural distinction, especially No. 36, designed in 1908 by James Riely Gordon and replete with guardian knights, gargoyles, and cherubs. It often looks, in fact, as though Gordon had been trying to depict the children's crusade, because beneath each window group over the whole building are cherubic loin-clad children, their arms resting on shields, and at an upper floor, four cowled monks grinning jovially.

David Chester French lived there, as did John Ringling, of the circus family, who had had an organ installed in his apartment. Roger Rosenblatt, of *Time* magazine, grew up there and remembers delightfully from his childhood that there were three maiden ladies who lived together on the floor above him: Miss Prescott, formerly a librarian at Columbia, was then in her eighties; Miss Jourdan, "who dressed like a man and had the voice of a bass violin," had been a novelist and journalist and was in her seventies; and Miss Cutler was a sculptress of the same vintage. "On the evening of December 23, each year, without fail, the three of them would hire a car to take them on a tour of the Fifth Avenue shops. They liked to see the windows lit up, and they liked to see them from a car."[6]

Rosenblatt also remembers Sidney Homer, the son of Louise Homer, the great Metropolitan Opera contralto. Homer, whose apartment contained, among other treasures, four works by Augustus Saint-Gaudens, to whom he was related, would al-

Plate 207 *Gramercy Park, east birdhouse.*
Plate 208 *Union Square birdhouse, c. 1859, on which the Gramercy Park birdhouses were modeled. Such birdhouses were built in New York City parks in the mid-nineteenth century when English sparrows were first introduced into this country.*

Plate 209 *Gramercy Park Hotel, 1925, when first built.*

ways address Rosenblatt in a booming voice as "young man" and would ask when he planned to enroll at Harvard.

No. 24 Gramercy Park, built in 1909, and No. 1 Lexington Avenue, built one year later, were both designed by Herbert Lucas. Both are cooperative apartment houses with duplex layouts of considerable individuality. No. 24, which was planned by Richard Watson Gilder, has, in the apartment that still belongs to his illustrious family, a beautiful fireplace and overmantel Stanford White designed for their house on Eighth Street; and around No. 1 Lexington Avenue is the elegant iron fence designed for White's Henry W. Poor mansion, which preceded it on the site.

The Gramercy Park Hotel replaced Stanford White's own house at the other corner of Lexington Avenue in 1925 (Plate 209) as well as that of Robert G. Ingersoll, the great agnostic and humanist, which was two doors to the west. Shortly after the hotel opened, Joseph P. Kennedy and his entire family occupied the second floor for a number of months, prior to their move to London, where he was United States ambassador. John F. Kennedy was eleven, went to school in New York, and spent a good deal of time playing in Gramercy Park.

Farther along the block, at Calvary Church, the old Renwick rectory was torn down in 1927 and replaced with what is today Tracy House. The rector of the parish at this time, and until 1952, was Samuel M. Shoemaker, who was instrumental in the conception of Alcoholics Anonymous. Bill Wilson, one of the cofounders, said of him, "He gave us concrete knowledge of what we could do about our illness . . . he passed on the spiritual keys by which we were liberated."[7]

Immediately south of Gramercy Park on Nineteenth Street are two blocks between Park Avenue South and Third Avenue that contain much that is of interest; indeed, the "block beautiful" between Irving Place and Third Avenue is one of the most varied and attractive blocks in New York. Many of the nineteenth-century buildings are now gone, of course, such as William Steinway's stable at No. 133, which, together with his house at No. 26 Gramercy Park, was replaced by the Hotel Irving. At the southeast corner of Park Avenue South, the Cyclorama disappeared as long ago as 1897, and the little late 1840's house with its added Victorian mansard roof shown in Plate 00 lasted only until around the time of World War I. The small brick houses built in the same period that were east of it, which Gladys Brooks passed on her way to school, with their iron balconies and inviting windows set back behind gardens, were also there in the 1840's, but were torn down before 1900. (There had originally been a row of six.) The brownstones at Nos. 109 through 117 date from the mid-1850's.

No. 113 was bought in 1898 by William Rhinelander, whose father-in-law, Judge Oakley lived directly behind at No. 12 Gramercy Park. It was later the office of the architects Henry Beaumont Herts (1871–1933) and Hugh Tallant (1869–1952), and its interior details reflect their taste. Herts and Tallant designed some of the best theaters in New York, including the Folies Bergère, now the Helen Hayes (1911); the Lyceum (1903); the New Amsterdam (1903), whose interior is one of the city's great works of Art Nouveau; and the Brooklyn Academy of Music (1909). The larger brownstone at No. 109 was, from 1856 to 1904, the home of Dr. James Hyslop, one of the beloved physicians of his day. At No. 119, where Samuel Tilden's formal garden with its box hedges and shady lawns once were, is George B. Post's addition to the National Arts Club; and at No. 116 is a house that once had a brownstone front like its neighbors to the east and was the home, from 1875 to 1891, of Howard Crosby, the noted orator and spokesman of the temperance movement, who was also chancellor of New York University and pastor of the Fourth Avenue Presbyterian Church.

No. 80 Irving Place, at the northeast corner of

Nineteenth Street is a brick house built in 1853–54 for William Samuel Johnson after he had sold No. 20 Gramercy Park to Horace Brooks, and next to it, at No. 127 East Nineteenth Street, is his carriage house, built at the same time. The carriage house next to that, at No. 129, is slightly later, dating to 1861. Across the street is the 1846–47 house of Lincoln Kirstein, who, in 1933, with George Balanchine, established the School of American Ballet. At No. 132 is Albert and Frederick Sterner's early-twentieth-century studio building, built without kitchens, because Theda Bara, Mrs. Patrick Campbell, Cecilia Beaux, and the others who lived there were never expected to eat in. Other actresses who have lived on the block include Ethel Barrymore, Dorothy and Lillian Gish, and Helen Hayes. Various other persons of the neighborhood have presumably found "immortality" in the *New Yorker* cartoons of Helen Hokinson, who also lived here.

Farther down on the south side, beyond the Anglo-Italianate 1852–53 houses at Nos. 136 through 142, are the block's first two houses, Nos. 144 and 146, built in 1838–39 by George A. Furst, Samuel B. Ruggles's contractor. Presumably, they stood alone on the block until Nos. 137 through 145 were built across the street in 1842–43. The 1845 house at No. 135 was completely redesigned by Frederick Sterner in the 1920's for Joseph B. Thomas, and given its Tudor facade at that time. The giraffes over the front doors at Nos. 147 and 149 were designed by Robert Chanler, who lived there, and are plucking fruit from trees exactly as Chanler's other giraffes did in Stanford White's Gramercy Park music room.

George W. Bellows, who had come to New York from Ohio in 1904 to study with Robert Henri, bought No. 146 in 1910, and its third floor was his studio until his untimely death in 1925 at the age of forty-two. Henri, whose studio at the end of his life was at No. 10 Gramercy Park (its huge north light is still intact), was the legendary teacher whose advice—to paint life, not pictures,—had inspired the beginnings of the Ash Can School of American realist painting. Bellows's large, uncompromising paintings, expressing his revolt against academic painting, were, ironically, later accepted by the academy, and he became recognized as *the* American painter of his day. He was one of the organizers of the famous Armory Show of February-March 1913, at which the academy scoffed; in fact, he was in charge of the hanging of the paintings, which included some of his own. The 69th Regiment Armory, where the show was held, had been built at Lexington Avenue and Twenty-fifth Street only eight years before, in 1905, by Hunt and Hunt, the firm of Richard Morris Hunt's two sons, Joseph Howland and Richard Howland Hunt.

Plate 210 *Gramercy Park, as painted by George Bellows. The artist's daughter Anne is seen playing in the foreground.*

Plate 211 *Gramercy Park, as painted by Ludwig Bemelmans.*

In recent years, the effort to save the architectural heritage of Gramercy Park has been strengthened by the establishment of a historic district that includes the west and south sides of the Park, Calvary Church, and No. 34 Gramercy Park, as well as much of Nineteenth and Eighteenth streets and Irving Place. Unprotected buildings such as the New York Bank for Savings, built by Cyrus Eidlitz (1853–1921) at Park Avenue South and Twenty-second Street in 1894, must depend on the assistance of enlightened community effort. In the case of the bank, the wrecker's ball was stopped minutes before it was to swing. However, the magnificent Napoleon Le Brun interior court and grand staircase of the Metropolitan Life Insurance Company were not so lucky and were demolished in 1958.

Of the recent work of distinguished younger architects around the Park, two examples might be cited. One is the clean, white 1977–78 interior transformation of an apartment at No. 1 Lexington Avenue by Richard Meier, who used flying beams and fascias to redefine the space, and translucent glass walls to allow natural light into the center of the apartment. The other is the memorial garden to the east of the Brotherhood Synagogue, designed by James Stewart Polshek, the architect who accomplished the sensitive renovation of the old Friends Meeting House in 1975.

Hidden in an apartment at No. 155 East Twenty-second Street is a virtually unknown treasure. Sometime in the early 1950's, Le Corbusier was visiting New York and came for tea with a young friend who was living in the apartment at that time. She was about to have it repainted, planning on making it all white, but Le Corbusier said that, in his opinion, it should be painted in colors. He began suggesting which colors should go where. These were not merely idle suggestions, for the next day, an artist friend of the great architect arrived, bringing with him a complete color scheme that Le Corbusier had worked out from memory. He had even brought paint chips, and was ready to supervise the work. And so the walls and ceilings of the old apartment were painted in Le Corbusier's colors: sand, red, gray. Later, the apartment was repainted and the carefully worked-out color scheme covered up. It is there today, however, under layers of later paint, its colors waiting to be rediscovered.

The Trustees of Gramercy Park have, over the years, dealt with larger and lesser issues, insuring that the Park be carefully maintained as the ornamental square it must be to fulfill the obligations of the Deed. They have seen to it that the birdhouses are kept in good repair, that the gardeners keep the cast-

Plate 212

Plate 213

Plate 214

iron urns planted, that when it was thought advisable for the Park's guard to carry a pistol in 1912, a permit was secured, and that the Ruggles memorial fountain, with its Edmond Quinn plaque of the founder, was erected in 1919. When the newel posts of the north gate had settled so that they were in danger of falling over in 1921, they arranged to have the pavement taken up and a new foundation laid. Concerning Mrs. Sedgwick's little girl, who had been struck on the head with a bag of marbles by eight-year-old James Parton, they saw to it that James would not be allowed into the Park unless accompanied by some person who would have charge of him.

In 1921, they directed the J. W. Fiske Iron Works to execute four gate lamps designed by Charles I. Berg because, in those days, too, automobiles were running into the gates in the dark. When Mrs. George Bellows asked that bicycles be forbidden in the Park, her request was honored. In 1925, ten thousand English bluebells were "set out in appropriate places," and since "the deposit of coal products from factories and other coal burners and fumes from automobiles are constant foes to nearly all plants, and there are but a few trees and not many flowers and shrubs that can endure it," the planting of all but a few trees was abandoned in 1925 and the Park confined to "ornamental shrubs and flowers which would be least affected by the smoke-laden air: hollyhocks, foxgloves, chrysanthemums, and certain varieties of lilies." In addition, "the conscious depredations of dogs," which only reinforced the "unconscious hostility of the atmosphere" were dealt with, for "though they have no peculiar aversion to flowers and small shrubs, it is their nature to scratch them out or dig them up." It was admitted, however, that cats "elude all efforts to keep them out."

"When little boys hauled bicycles, sleds or other vehicles to the top of the flagstaff," in 1928, "and tied them there, the Park attendant was instructed to get them down, and when fights broke out between the boys, or bitter quarrels between the girls, he was to pacify them." When Mr. Henry Bruere presented a "very handsome carved marble wellhead," in November 1932, it was acknowledged and placed in the northeast quadrant of the Park.[8] The Trustees have seen to such things as these year in and year out, as well as to the more major concerns of taxation and legality, because it is their mandate to maintain their elegant little Park in its every detail.

Meanwhile, life goes on around the Park. Although Third Avenue has changed dramatically since 1956, when the El was finally removed, some places on the avenue have not lost a shred of their vitality.

Plate 215

Plate 212 *Bank for Savings, southwest corner of Fourth Avenue and Twenty-second Street, c. 1895.*
Plate 213 *Northeast corner of Lexington Avenue and Twenty-second Street, c. 1929.*
Plate 214 *No. 1 Lexington Avenue; apartment; redesigned by Richard Meier, 1978.*
Plate 215 *Gramercy Park, northeast quadrant; wellhead with bacchanalian scenes. (reproduction of an antique original).*

Plate 216 *Calvary Church vacation school children, leaving on an outing, 1911.*
Plate 217 *Northwest corner of Third Avenue and Twenty-first Street; the original Gramercy Park Florist's shop, c. 1954. The westernmost of the three identical houses at the left was No. 147 East Twenty-first Street, on the original lot No. 39 of Gramercy Park, demolished in 1955.*

Plate 216

Plate 217

Gramercy Park would not be the same without the Gramercy Park Flower Shop, a business at the corner of Twenty-first Street that has been run by the Sakas family since 1904. Though the original building (Plate 217) was torn down when No. 39 Gramercy Park was erected in 1956/7, unfazed, they engaged the same space in the new building. It was, of course, from them that Ben Sonnenberg ordered rare white anemones because Greta Garbo was coming to dinner.

Then, too, how could one live without Warshaw's? For over half a century—fifty-six years, in fact—not only hardware but advice on all things practical has been delivered by this family-run business with an air of great resourcefulness and humor. Warshaw's is a neighborhood institution and, of course, it was to the Warshaw family that Ben Sonnenberg turned to keep his house well lit. Among other neighborhood establishments that have been in business for over half a century is the Gramercy Bake Shop, founded in 1932; Tiffany's Coffee Shop preserves the old Gramercy Park Sweet Shop; Pete's Tavern is thriving; and Tuesday's continues the tradition of Scheffel Hall.

In 1912, the Gramercy Park Association was formed "to preserve and maintain the residential character of the neighborhood . . . and to promote the interest and comfort of the property owners and residents of the neighborhood." Part of the impetus to form the association was the need to mobilize residents concerning the very real threat at that time, that the Park might be cut in half by the city. Immediately, a subcommittee was formed on "Irving Place Extension," whose "duty" was "to keep informed as to any action on the part of the City looking forward to completion of the extension and to report thereon."

That first year, the Association had the Park benches painted dark green "as tending to greatly improve the appearance of the Park." They had been bright red. In 1913, it actively encouraged the Fifth Avenue Coach Company to include Gramercy Park in one of its new ten-cent routes. Its memorandum noted that the five-cent lines had become so crowded that

> the luxury of a seat . . . [was] now unobtainable during many hours of the day. . . . [And argued that]

Plate 218 *Gramercy Park, looking northwest from No. 24.*

Plate 219

Plate 220

> the establishment of a ten cent bus line will provide for the class of passengers who are willing and able to pay the extra price for the additional safety, comfort and convenience which such a line can alone afford.[9]

Gramercy Park had become "insulated by surrounding business and manufacture" and needed "direct, convenient and comfortable means of transit to other parts of the City." This effort failed, and when bus routes did eventually circle the Park, the Association found itself lobbying from the other side of the issue in the 1930's in an attempt to restrict their use to weekday and Saturday daylight hours lest the roar of the buses destroy the peace forever. In 1939, the Association president reported that he recently had been

on a southbound Lexington Avenue bus which, instead of pursuing its way . . . to the Park, turned at 23rd Street and went down Fourth Avenue. A passenger . . . who had expected to be delivered to Irving Place protested. The driver replied that [he] was not allowed to go south of 23rd Street after eight o'clock. The passenger insisted that it still lacked one minute of eight, to which the driver responded, "Well, you see the people of Gramercy are so on the lookout that we hear from them if we drive around the Park after hours, and the time is so close that I do not dare take a chance of a reprimand."[10]

Over the years, members of the Association (now called the Gramercy Neighborhood Associates) have planted trees, painted benches, encouraged and held competitions for flower boxes, replaced flagstone

Plate 219 *No. 251–255 Fourth Avenue, 1909, when first built.*
Plate 220 *No. 250 Fourth Avenue, under construction in 1911.*
Plate 221 *Gramercy Park North, looking west from Gramercy Park East, 1925. Gramercy Park Hotel under construction.*

Plate 221

Plate 222 *Christmas in Gramercy Park, 1966.*

Plate 223 *John Falter, cover of the* Saturday Evening Post.

Plate 224 *Charles Guth, custodian of Gramercy Park since 1958. The position carries a tradition of longevity; James A. (Teck) Hannan held it from 1901 to 1951.*

Plate 225 *Gramercy Park, as depicted by Saul Steinberg,* © *1983,* The New Yorker Magazine, *Inc.*

sidewalks, arranged for the beautiful Christmas tree to be erected each year, and sponsored Christmas carols around it. They have also carefully labeled all the different kinds of trees around the Park, and they judiciously monitor the services of the various city agencies that maintain the surrounding streets. Since 1947, each year, the Associates have presented the Gramercy Park Flower Show, now held at the National Arts Club. A juried exhibition that always attracts great numbers of entrants in many different categories, this is a spectacular affair and is the oldest annual flower show in New York. The Associates also sponsor an annual *Clean and Green* day in the spring, which has become one of the most active neighborhood events in the city. Baltic ivy, English ivy, five kinds of juniper, geraniums, and impatiens of various colors—dozens of different kinds of hardy plants are supplied for sale; people who live near the Park come out to plant gardens around the street trees, paint curbs yellow, prune bushes, water, spring clean, and get to know their neighbors.

All of this would have to please Samuel B. Ruggles, for he founded the Park to be an intimate, neighborly place, forever green, in a city he feared would possess far too few such places. His Park, one hundred and fifty-three years later, continues to be what he intended, and no less rare. It is still, in fact, one of the most special places in New York. The hero of Sinclair Lewis's *Main Street,* when describing the best New York had to offer, said, simply, "I went to symphonies twice a week. I saw Irving, Duse, Terry, and Bernhardt. I walked in Gramercy Park."

Notes

[1] Unpublished minutes of the meetings of the Gramercy Lot Owners, January 20 and 27, 1902.

[2] Ibid.

[3] John B. Pine, *The Story of Gramercy Park, 1831–1921* (New York: Knickerbocker Press, 1921), pp. 19–20.

[4] Minutes of the Trustees of Gramercy Park, June 4, 1923.

[5] Alistair Cooke, "The House of Sonnenberg," *The Benjamin Sonnenberg Collection* (New York: Sotheby Parke Bernet Inc., 1979)

[6] Roger Rosenblatt, *The Washingtonian,* December, 1978.

[7] *Alcoholics Anonymous Comes of Age, A Brief History of Alcoholics Anonymous* (New York: Alcoholics Anonymous World Services, Inc., 1957)

[8] Minutes of the Trustees of Gramercy Park, *passim.*

[9] Memorandum of the Gramercy Park Association, Before a Special Committee of the Board of Estimate and Appointment, New York, 1914.

[10] Report of the Retiring President, Parker McCollester, to the Members of the Gramercy Park Association, New York, February 5, 1939, p. 10.

Plate 226 Gramercy Park North, looking east from Lexington Avenue, c. 1905.
Plate 227 Gramercy Park North, looking east toward Lexington Avenue, c. 1905.
Plate 228 Gramercy Park North, looking west from Gramercy Park East, c. 1905.

Plate 226

Plate 227

Plate 228

Appendix A: The Original Deed of Gramercy Park, 1831

This Indenture, made the *Seventeenth* day of December in the year of our Lord one thousand eight hundred and thirty one. **Between** SAMUEL B. RUGGLES, of the City and State of New York, Counsellor at Law, and MARY R. RUGGLES, his wife, parties of the first part,—and CHARLES AUGUSTUS DAVIS, of the said City, Merchant, THOMAS L. WELLS, of the said City, Counsellor at Law, ROBERT D. WEEKS, of the said City, Gentleman, THOMAS R. MERCEIN, of the said City, Gentleman, and PHILO T. RUGGLES, of the said City, Counsellor at Law, parties of the second part:—**Whereas** the said SAMUEL B. RUGGLES is seised in fee of forty-two certain lots of land lying in the (now) twelfth ward of the said City of New York, in the block between the Third and Fourth Avenues, Twentieth Street and Twenty-first Street, and together forming a parallelogram containing five hundred and twenty feet in length from southeast to north-west, and one hundred and eighty four feet in breadth from Twentieth Street to Twenty first Street, and herein after more particularly described: **And whereas** the said SAMUEL B. RUGGLES proposes to devote and appropriate the said forty two lots of land to the formation and establishment of an ornamental private Square or Park, with carriage ways and foot walks at the south-eastern and north-western ends thereof, for the use, benefit and enjoyment of the owners and occupants of sixty-six surrounding lots of land belonging to the said Samuel B. Ruggles, and with a view to enhance the value thereof; which proposed Square and surrounding lots are laid down on the Map hereto annexed, made by Edwin Smith, City Surveyor, dated December 1st, 1831, and entitled "*Map of the Park laid out by S. B. Ruggles in the City of New York, with sixty six surrounding Lots.*" which Map is to be taken as part of these presents:—**And whereas** the said SAMUEL B. RUGGLES being about to sell and convey to various persons the lots so surrounding the said Square, desires to assure to those persons and their respective heirs and assigns owning such lots the use, privilege and enjoyment of the said Square, upon the terms and conditions, and subject to the duties, regulations and restrictions herein after referred to and contained: NOW THEREFORE THIS INDENTURE WITNESSETH, that the said SAMUEL B. RUGGLES and MARY R. RUGGLES his wife, parties hereto of the first part, to effectuate the objects above mentioned, and in consideration of the sum of Ten Dollars to them paid by the said parties hereto of the second part, the receipt whereof is hereby acknowledged, **Have** granted, bargained, sold and conveyed, and by these presents DO grant, bargain, sell and convey unto the said parties of the second part and to their heirs and assigns, in joint tenancy, **All** those certain forty two lots of land lying and being in the now Twelfth Ward of the City of New York, being part of the Gramercy farm of the Honorable James Duane deceased; the said lots forming a parallelogram and (taken together) being bounded as follows:—**Beginning** at a point in the north-easterly line of Twentieth street distant two hundred feet south-easterly from the south-easterly line of the Fourth Avenue, thence running north-easterly parallel with the said Fourth Avenue one hundred and eighty-four feet to the south-westerly line of Twenty-first street, thence running along the same south-easterly five hundred and twenty feet to a point thereon distant two hundred feet north westerly from the north-westerly line of the Third Avenue, thence running south-westerly parallel with the said Third Avenue one hundred and eighty-four feet to the said north-easterly line of Twentieth street, and thence running along the same north-westerly five hundred and twenty feet to the place of beginning: **Together** with all and every the rights, members, hereditaments and appurtenances thereunto belonging: *And also* all the estate, right, title, interest, dower, right of dower, possession, property, claim and demand of the parties of the first part, in and to all and singular the above granted and described premises, with the appurtenances. **To have and to hold** the same, and every part thereof unto the said parties of the second part, their heirs and assigns to their proper use and behoof forever as joint-tenants and not as tenants in common. **Upon trust** nevertheless, for the uses, intents and purposes herein after expressed and declared of and concerning the same, that is to say: upon trust and to the end and intent that they the said parties of the second part do and shall by the first day of May in the year one thousand eight hundred and thirty-three, surround and enclose by means of an iron fence with stone coping and ornamental gates a portion of the said parallelogram of land, to be in length from southeast to north-west not less than four hundred nor more than four hundred and twenty feet, as an ornamental Park or Square, and that by the first day of January in the year one thousand eight hundred and thirty-four, they do and shall lay out within such Park or Square ornamental grounds and walks, and plant and place therein trees, shrubbery and appropriate decorations, the first cost of all which including the said fence shall not exceed twelve thousand dollars,—and that they do and shall preserve, maintain and keep the said Park or Square and the said grounds, plantations and decorations in proper order and preservation, the annual cost of which in any one year after the first day of January in the year one thousand eight hundred and thirty-four, (including any new plantations and decorations) shall not exceed six hundred dollars:—**And** upon this further trust that they the said parties of the second part do and shall from time to time pay, satisfy and discharge all such taxes, charges and assessments as may at any time hereafter be lawfully levied or imposed upon the said Park or Square and carriage ways and foot walks, or any part thereof:—and further, that they the said parties of the second part do and shall from time to time and at all times hereafter permit, suffer and allow the owner and owners of any and every of the said sixty six lots surrounding the said Park, (that is to say, the sixty lots of land severally numbered on the said Map progressively from 1. (one) to 60. (sixty) inclusive, and the six lots of land severally designated on the same Map, by the letters A. B. C. D. E. and F.) and to the families of such owners and also to the respective tenants under such owner or owners, and their families, to have free ingress and egress to and from such Park or Square, to frequent, use and enjoy the same as a place of common resort and recreation under and subject always to such rules and regulations as the owners of two thirds in number of the said lots numbered from 1. (one) to 60. (sixty) shall from time to time make, establish and prescribe,—provided that in making and prescribing such rules and regulations the said owners (whether one or more) shall respectively be entitled to one vote in respect to each lot owned by them and no more, and provided also that in respect to each of the said lots not more than one family be permitted so to frequent, use and enjoy the said Park ;—and upon this further trust that when and as often as three of the parties hereto of the second part shall have died, or removed from the city of New York, or shall have resigned the trusts hereby committed to them, the surviving acting Trustees shall by apt conveyances cause the title and estate of and in the said Park or Square to be vested in themselves and three other Trustees (to be nominated by the owners of the major part in number of the said sixty lots numbered from 1. to 60.) to be thereafter had and holden by them and such new Trustees in joint-tenancy upon the like trusts as are herein expressed and contained, and that such new Trustees and their successors in the said trust shall, from time to time and at all times forever hereafter whenever the number of acting Trustees living in the City of New York shall be reduced to two, proceed in like manner to vest the said title and estate in five Trustees in the manner above specified,—and in case of any neglect or failure on the part of the major part of the said owners so to nominate new Trustees, that the two surviving acting Trustees do forthwith apply to the Court of Chancery to complete and fill up their number by the appointment of suitable persons for that purpose.

And the said Samuel B. Ruggles for himself and his heirs and assigns doth hereby declare, covenant and grant to and with the parties hereto of the second part, their heirs and assigns, that each of the said surrounding lots numbered progressively from 1. (one) to 60. (sixty) inclusive shall forever hereafter stand and remain bound and chargeable unto the said parties of the second part, and the survivors and survivor of them, and to such new Trustees as shall succeed them in the execution of the said trusts, for the payment of one full sixtieth part or portion of all such sum and sums of money as the said Trustees shall or may lawfully pay or expend from time to time under and by virtue of the powers and trusts herein and hereby granted, delegated and declared, and that in default of such payment it shall and may be lawful for the said parties hereto of the second part and the survivors and survivor of them and for such new trustees for the time being to institute and prosecute any legal proceedings at law or in equity, against the owner or owners of the lots so making default, to compel such payment with costs of suit, and moreover that each and every of the said lots, in respect to which any such default may be made, shall at all times on occasion of any such default be liable to sale under the order and decree of the Court of Chancery, upon the application of the Trustees for the time being to be made for that purpose, to the end that out of the avails and proceeds thereof, the amount chargeable on such lot may be raised and paid with costs of suit.

And the said Samuel B. Ruggles, for himself his heirs and assigns, doth hereby further declare, covenant, grant and agree to and with the said parties hereto of the second part, and the survivors and survivor of them, and with such new Trustees as may be substituted as aforesaid, that neither he, nor his heirs or assigns, shall or will at any time hereafter, erect within forty feet of the front of any or either of the said lots numbered and designated progressively from 1. (one) to 60. (sixty) and from A. to F. inclusive, any other buildings save brick or stone dwelling houses of at least three stories in height—and further that neither he nor his heirs or assigns shall or will at any time hereafter, erect or permit upon any part of any or either of the said sixty-six lots any livery stable, slaughter house, smith shop, forge, furnace, steam engine, brass foundry, nail or other iron factory, or any manufactory of gunpowder, glue, varnish, vitriol, ink or turpentine, or for the tanning, dressing or preparing skins, hides or leather, or any brewery, distillery, public museum, theatre, circus, place for the exhibition of animals, or any other trade or business dangerous or offensive to the neighbouring inhabitants :—and this covenant the said Samuel B. Ruggles for himself his heirs and assigns doth hereby impose upon and attach to each and every of the said sixty-six lots of land, as a specific lien and incumbrance thereon, and doth further more covenant, grant, and agree that whenever he, his heirs or assigns owning any of said lots shall infringe or attempt to infringe this covenant, it shall and may be lawful not only for any other person or persons who may at that time own any other or others of the said sixty-six lots of land, but also for the parties hereto of the second part, and the survivors and survivor of them and their successors in the trust for the time being, as Trustees in behalf and for the benefit of all the other owners of the said other lots, to institute and prosecute any proceedings at law or in equity against the person or persons violating or attempting to violate this covenant to prevent him or them from so doing, it being understood that the said covenant is to be taken as attached to and running with the said lots of land respectively, and that the same is not to be enforced personally against the said Samuel B. Ruggles or his heirs or assigns, unless he or they being the owner or owners of such lots, shall personally violate such covenant. **And** for the purpose of attaching all the covenants herein contained to the said sixty-six lots of land respectively, it is hereby declared that all conveyances which the said Samuel B. Ruggles or his heirs shall hereafter make of any or either of the said sixty-six lots shall be taken to be expressly subject to all and singular the covenants, charges, duties, regulations and restrictions in respect to the said sixty-six lots respectively which are created, declared, granted or contained in and by these presents.

And in order that the limits of the said *sixty-six lots of land may be the more distinctly defined and* understood, it is hereby declared that they are bounded and contain as follows, to wit :-The seven lots numbered 1. 2. 3 .4. 5. 6. and 7. are situate on the north-westerly side of the said Square, and taken together contain one hundred and eighty-four feet front thereupon, each of said seven lots having one equal seventh part thereof, and extending back north-westerly one hundred and ten feet to a line parallel with the Fourth Avenue and distant ninety feet south-easterly there from :—The fifteen lots numbered and designated 8. 9. 10. 11. 12. 13. 14. 15. 16. 17. 18. 19. D. E. and F. are situated on the south-westerly side of Twentieth street, each containing twenty six feet and eight inches in breadth front and rear, and extending back south-westerly half the distance from Twentieth to Nineteenth street, the north-westerly line of lot numbered 8. being parallel with the Fourth Avenue, and distant one hundred feet south-easterly from the south-easterly side thereof, and the south-easterly line of lot designated F. being distant five hundred feet south-easterly from the said south-easterly side of the Fourth Avenue:—The twelve lots numbered 20. 21. 22. 23. 24. 25. 26. 27. 28. 29. 30. and 31. are also situated on the said south-westerly side of Twentieth street; each of said lots 20. 21. 22. 23. 24. 25. 26. 27. 28. and 29. containing twenty-seven feet in breadth front and rear, and said lots 30. and 31. each containing twenty-five feet in breadth in front and rear, and all extending back south-westerly, half the distance from Twentieth to Nineteenth street, the north-westerly line of lot numbered 20. being parallel with the Third Avenue, and distant four hundred and twenty feet, and the south-easterly line of lot number 31. being distant one hundred feet north-westerly from the north-westerly line of the Third Avenue :—The seven lots numbered 32. 33. 34. 35. 36. 37. and 38. are situated on the south-easterly side of the said Square and taken together contain one hundred and eighty-four feet front thereupon, each of said seven lots having one equal seventh part thereof and extending back south-easterly to a line parallel with the Third Avenue, and distant Seventy-five feet north-westerly from the north-westerly line thereof:—The twelve lots numbered, 39. 40. 41. 42. 43. 44. 45. 46. 47. 48. 49. and 50. are situated on the north-easterly side of Twenty-first street, the said lots numbered 39. and 40 each containing twenty-five feet in breadth front and rear, and the said lots numbered, 41. 42. 43. 44. 45. 46. 47. 48. 49. and 50, each containing twenty-seven feet in breadth front and rear. and all extending back north-easterly half the distance from Twenty-first to Twenty second street, the south-easterly line of lot number 39, being distant one hundred feet. and the north-westerly line of lot number 50 being distant four hundred and twenty feet, north-westerly from the north-westerly line of the Third Avenue :—The ten lots numbered 51, 52, 53, 54, 55, 56, 57, 58, 59, and 60. are also situated on the north-easterly side of Twenty-first Street, each containing twenty-seven feet and six inches in breadth front and rear, and extending back half the distance from Twenty-first to Twenty-second Street; the south-easterly line of lot numbered 51, being distant four hundred and twenty-five feet, and the north-westerly line of lot number 60, one hundred and fifty feet south-easterly from the south-easterly line of the Fourth Avenue :—The three lots designated A. B. and C. are also situated on the said north-easterly side of Twenty-first street, each containing twenty-five feet in breadth front and rear, extending back half the distance from Twenty-first to Twenty-second street, and lying between the north-westerly line of lot number 50, and the south-easterly line of lot number 51.

And it is hereby understood and agreed that it shall and may be lawful for the said Samuel B. Ruggles his heirs or assigns, at any time hereafter in their discretion to lay out open streets in, through and over the said lots designated A. B. and C. and in, through and over the said lots designated D. E. and F. or to cede the same or any part thereof to the Corporation of the City of New York to be used as public streets.

And the said Charles Augustus Davis, Thomas L. Wells, Robert D. Weeks, Thomas R. Mercein, and Philo T. Ruggles, do hereby become parties to these presents of the second part and accept the powers and trusts hereby granted and declared,— on the condition nevertheless, that it shall and may be lawful for them or any or either of them, at any time hereafter to resign such powers and trusts by executing and delivering to their co-trustees for the time being apt and proper conveyances of all their estates, powers and interests in and over the lands and tenements hereby granted and conveyed to them as trustees as aforesaid.

In Witness Whereof the parties to these presents have hereunto interchangeably set their hands and seals, the day and year herein first above written.

Sealed and Delivered in the presence of
G. G. VanWagenen

Sam B. Ruggles

Mary R. Ruggles

Ch: Augs Davis

R D Weeks

Tho. R Mercein

Philo T. Ruggles

Thomas L. Wells

Recorded in the office of Register of the City and County of New York in Lib 150 of Mortgages page 145. the 20th day of Decr 1831 at 30 Min past 3 P.M.
Examd by Gilbert Coutant
Register

Recorded in the Office of Register of the City & County of New York in Lib 278 of Conveyances page 528 the 20th day of Decr 1831 at 30 min past 3 P.M.
Examd. by Gilbert Coutant
Register

Appendix B: "The Blue-eyed Lassie" by Robert Burns

This poem was inspired by Jane Renwick when she was a girl in Scotland and the poet visited her home.

. . .

I gat my death frae twa sweet e'en,
  Twa lovely e'en o'bonie blue.
'Twas not her golden ringlets bright,
  Her lips like roses, wat w' dew,
Her heaving bosom, lily-white,
  It was her e'en sae bonie blue.
    She talk'd, she smil'd, my heart she wyl'd,
  She charm'd my soul I wist na how.
    And ay the stound, the deady wound,
  Cam frae her e'en sae bonie blue.
  . . .

Appendix C: Calvary Church Spires

What follows is a general description of the spires for Calvary Church By the Carpenter, John Sniffin.

There will be two spires in front of the Church, each of which will be of the following form and construction. They will be carried up square from the top of the gables of the front and side aisle walls to a point 44 feet from the level of the top of the foundation. At this point there will be caps and open-work battlements; from this point to a point 81 or 82 feet above the top of the foundation, the towers will be carried up octagonally with buttresses and pinnacles, windows in each side and other ornaments with battlements at the top. At each of the four corners of the square, a large triangular pinnacle running first into a hexagonal pinnacle and then into a square with pannels [*sic*], finials and crockets will be raised.

From the top of each octagonal tower, an octagonal spire of open carved tracery will be carried up to a point 130 feet from the level of the top of the foundation. Above this a cross of from five to seven feet in height will be raised, making the whole height of the spire from the ground 137 feet. The whole of the work from the wall of the Church to the top will be of wood, painted and sanded to represent the stone of the Church. The spires will be framed down into the Church as far as the under side of the gallery floor, and will be firmly attached to the walls by bolts and anchors. The following is a more specific description of each spire.

Timber. An upright timber, 12 inches square, of white oak will be inserted in place of the first 9x9 inch pillar of the Church. Three uprights of white pine 8 inches square will be carried from the level of the gallery floor to the top of the square frame of the spire. These uprights will be firmly secured by iron anchors to the walls of the Church and will be framed into the floor timbers and beams of the galleries and other frames and well bolted and strapped to them. . . .

The eight uprights of the octagonal lanterns or towers will be 7x9 inches and will be carried down into the square towers to the second horizontal frame, to which they will be mortised and strongly strapped and bolted with iron. Between these uprights 32 sets of diagonal braces each composed of two 6x6 inch timbers, well mortised to the uprights and bolted together and to the uprights, will be framed in. The spire frame will run down into the octagonal lantern as far as the fifth horizontal frame. . . . Above the line of the top of the octagonal lantern, the spire will be finished as follows:

The eight corner posts will be 7x9 inches at the bottom and 5x6 inches at the top. They will be chamfered or splayed off at the outside angles to a mullion mould and a bead of 4 inches diameter of solid timber will be carried up each. The diagonal braces will be carved to the shape of a mullion mould, they will be 6 inches square at the lower part of the spire and 4 inches square at the upper part, diminishing gradually from bottom to top. All the foils in the mullions will be well carved and firmly attached to the diagonal braces, they will be of good design and approved of by the Architect before used. All the pannels above the octagonal lantern will have foils introduced into them; up each side of the main corner posts, an upright whose section shall be 2 inches by from 6 to 4 inches, carved to the shape of a mullion mould, with proper foils attached to them, will be carried. There will be 22 sets of diagonal braces between each of the eight corner posts of each spire, making 176 sets to each spire.

The cross on the top of the spires will be of solid timber and will be carried down into the spire at least 8 feet. The top of the spire will be hooped with three iron hoops of 3x1½ inch iron, the upper hoop to be at the top of the spire timbers and the second and third hoops to be 2½ feet and 5 feet respectively from that line.

All the timber and plank of every description above the line of the roof will be planed on all sides and well finished to receive the paint.

The outside of the square tower, and the outside and inside of the octagonal lantern, will be planked with 1¼ inch cypress plank planed on both sides—tongued and grooved on both sides and ends, laid vertically in pure white lead. All the pinnacles, window jambs with their pillars, window arches, hood moulds, crosses, battlements, gables and other ornaments to be of similar timber finished in a similar manner. The window jambs to be framed up of 3x4 inch white pine joist cased on all sides as above.

There will be a battlement carried all around the square section of the spires, of 3 thicknesses of 2 inch white pine plank, well nailed together and carved to shape with a heavy hood or label mould above and below it.

The four main corner pinnacles to be framed as follows:

Four upright timbers 8 inches square will be carried from the heads of the uprights of the square frames to the top of the pinnacles; on these the pinnacles will be ferred [*sic*] out, bracketted [*sic*] and finished, the outside of pinnacles to be 1¼ inch cypress plank laid as above described in pure white lead. The pannels in the faces of pinnacles to be sunk 5 inches and all the mouldings, crockets, finials, caps to be carved from solid white pine. These pinnacles are 34 feet high.

There will be eight buttresses to each octagonal lantern with caps, labels etc. to each, bracketted out from the corner posts and planked on the outside with 11/4 inch cypress, worked and laid as above.

A label mould will be carried under the eight windows of the lanterns. Each window will have a jamb and arch, plain splayed with pillars of from four to five inches in diameter with appropriate caps and bases to them; from the head of the pillars and around each arch a label will be run.

Over each window in the octagonal lantern a gable will rise running through the top line; in each gable there will be carved a quatrefoil. The gables will be crowned with a label mould with neat crockets cut out of the solid.

The top of the lanterns will have a label cornice run around them uniting with the label of hoods or gables over windows. Over each gable there will be placed a cross or other ornament well carved from solid. The battlements of the lanterns will be of the same description and form as the battlements of the square towers.

There will be eight pinnacles to each lantern, each 10 feet high with caps, finials and other ornaments.

Above the top of the octagon the spire will be finished and carved as hereinbefore described. All the crosses, gables, hood moulds [*sic*], finials, pillars with their capitals and bases, crockets, finials, buttresscaps, battlements, and all other ornaments to be of best well-seasoned white pine. All the timber and plank of every description in the towers and spires, unless otherwise specified above, to be of good, sound, merchantable white pine free from all sap, black or rotten knots, sun cracks or any imperfections that might endanger its strength.

John Sniffin
April 26, 1846

Appendix D: Mason's Contract for Calvary Church

What follows is a description from the contract of Horace Butler, mason for Calvary Church, March 2, 1846.

All the Masonry . . . shall be of good durable Stone of large size, laid in courses and levelled off every eighteen inches and well bonded. The joints shall be slushed full to the face of the Walls and all the interior joints shall be filled with mortar and spaulls to render the wall perfectly solid. The walls of the church . . . [are] to be faced with Brown Stone from the Little Falls Quarry in the State of New Jersey laid in courses not exceeding 13 nor less than 10 inches in height and no course to be more than one inch higher than the course immediately preceding it. The face of the Stone to be dressed equal to that of Dr. Phillips' Church in the Fifth Avenue between Eleventh and Twelfth Streets. The corners of the buttresses to be carried up true, even, and plumb and to be clean and sharp when finished with an arris on the angles. [The word *arris* is an elegant architectural term referring to the edge formed at the joining of two planes.] All the Stones to be laid in their natural beds . . . the whole of the face of the Church to be pointed with a mixture of Thomastown lime and blacksmiths scales [the film of oxide that forms on heated, hammered, or rolled metal] and sand coloured to the color of the Stone with a joint of paint run through the centre of the joint similarly to Grace Church. . . . All the mortar . . . shall be composed of the best quality of hydraulic or ground lime and clean sharp sand which shall be thoroughly mixed and tempered and of such proportions as the Architect shall direct.

[Butler's description of the work he would do on the plaster vault of the church is equally detailed. It would be] of two coats, viz: A scratch coat and a brown coat stucco finished and well hand floated. All the ribs, jambs, pillars, labels and all the ornamental work to be gaged with plaster and run in the most true and even manner. The whole Church to be jointed off to represent Stones and to be coloured according to the directions of the Architect. The ribs to be run and finished similarly to those of Grace Church. Bosses will be formed at the intersections of all the ribs, to be of good design with handsome foliage and well relieved. [Dealers such as Basham at 408 Broadway supplied plaster casts for bosses and capitals in a great variety of styles (Plate 229)].

Plate 229 *Advertisement of Basham's Shop at 408 Broadway, c. 1850.*

Appendix E: The Sixty Gramercy Park Lots

Dates the original houses were completed, and their owners. Where a house has been replaced, the new building and its new address are noted.

West side:
1. 1850 Norman White
2. 1850 Thomas Napier
3. 1847 Elizabeth M. Armistead
4. 1847 Norman White
5. 1843 Norman White
6. 1843 Elizabeth M. Armistead }
7. 1847 Charles A. Davis } demolished, 1912; No. 7 Gramercy Park, 1913

South side:
8. 1856 All Souls Parsonage, demolished, 1931; No. 8 Gramercy Park, 1938
9. 1848 William Thompson
10. 1848 E. J. Moore
11. 1856 Oliver DeForest Grant
12. 1847 Charles Oakley
13. 1847 Elihu Townsend
14. 1844 Nicholas K. Anthony }
15. 1845 George and Charles Belden } redesigned, 1881–84; now National Arts Club
16. 1845 Valentine G. Hall, redesigned, 1888, as The Players
17. 1845 James W. Gerard, demolished, 1938; No. 17 Gramercy Park, 1938
18.–19. 1845 William H. Smith, demolished, 1926; Parkside Hotel, 1927

20. (86 Irving Pl.) 1845 William S. Johnson; now No. 19 Gramercy Park and No. 20, 1909
21. 1854 Henry Trowbridge, defaced, 1954
22. 1846 Silvanus Rapelje (Trustee for Mrs. Silas M. Stillwell)
23. 1847 William S. Johnson
24. 1847 Charles Moran }
25. 1850 Samuel Mitchill } demolished, 1908; No. 24 Gramercy Park, 1909
26. 1850 Morris Ketchum, demolished, 1902; Hotel Irving, 1903
27.–30. 1859 Friends Meeting House/Brotherhood Synagogue
31. 1852 Charles H. Harbach

East side:
32.–38. 1854
- 32.–34. Oscar Stebbins, Charles E. Quincy } demolished, 1882; James Campbell } No. 34 Gramercy Park, 1883; John D. Phyfe } The Gramercy Company
- 35.–36. Sanderson Hotel (block divided into nine lots) } demolished, 1904; No. 36 Gramercy Park, 1909
- 37. reconstructed, 1968; No. 37 Gramercy Park
- 38. demolished, 1909; No. 38 Gramercy Park, 1910

North side:
39. (147 E. 21) 1851 Thomas E. Davis, demolished, 1955; No. 39 Gramercy Park, 1957
40. (145 E. 21) 1854 Robert C. Voorhees, destroyed by fire, 1948; now No. 39A Gramercy Park
41. (143 E. 21) 1854 Charles A. Minton; now No. 40 Gramercy Park
42. (141 E. 21) 1854 Sallie P. Lott }
(139 E. 21) 1854 Eder V. Haughwout }
43. (137 E. 21) 1854 Edward A. Strong }
44. (135 E. 21) 1852 Eliza T. Snelling } demolished, 1928; No. 44 Gramercy Park, 1929
45. (133 E. 21) 1861 Eder V. Haughwout }
46. (131 E. 21) 1861 Eder V. Haughwout }
47. (129 E. 21) 1858 James F. Lynch } demolished, 1925; No. 45 Gramercy Park, 1926
48. (127 E. 21) 1858 James F. Lynch; altered and facade replaced, 1968
49. (125 E. 21) 1852 David Dudley Field } redesigned as No. 1 Lexington Avenue, 1901;
50. (123 E. 21) 1852 Cyrus West Field } demolished, 1909; present building, 1910

51. (121 E. 21) 1847 Alexander M. Lawrence; redesigned, 1900 }
52. (119 E. 21) 1847 J. M. Moore }
53. (117 E. 21) 1847 John Thomson } demolished, 1924; Gramercy Park Hotel, 1925
54. (115 E. 21) 1848 S. W. Moore }
55. (113 E. 21) 1849 George T. Strong }
56. (111 E. 21) Open } demolished, 1928; Gramercy Park Hotel Annex, 1929
57. (109 E. 21) 1849 George W. Strong }
58. (107 E. 21) 1849 Olivia Templeton }
59. (105 E. 21) 1849 Philip R. Kearny } demolished, 1927; No. 60 Gramercy Park, 1928
60. (103 E. 21) 1849 Calvary Church Rectory, demolished, 1927; No. 61 Gramercy Park, 1928

Index of Names

Plate 230 *Metropolitan Life Insurance Co., South Building, marble staircase, 1893, demolished, 1958.*